LEARNING A SECOND LANGUAGE

LEARNING A SECOND LANGUAGE

Seventy-ninth Yearbook of the
National Society for the Study of Education

PART II

By

THE YEARBOOK COMMITTEE
and
ASSOCIATED CONTRIBUTORS

Edited by

FRANK M. GRITTNER

Editor for the Society

KENNETH J. REHAGE

Distributed by THE UNIVERSITY OF CHICAGO PRESS • CHICAGO, ILLINOIS

The National Society for the Study of Education

Founded in 1901 as successor to the National Herbart Society, the National Society for the Study of Education has provided a means by which the results of serious study of educational issues could become a basis for informed discussion of those issues. The Society's two-volume yearbooks, now in their seventy-ninth year of publication, reflect the thoughtful attention given to a wide range of educational problems during those years. A recently inaugurated series on Contemporary Educational Issues includes substantial publications in paperback that supplement the yearbooks. Each year, the Society's publications contain contributions to the literature of education from more than a hundred scholars and practitioners who are doing significant work in their respective fields.

An elected Board of Directors selects the subjects with which volumes in the yearbook series are to deal, appropriates funds to meet necessary expenses in the preparation of a given volume, and appoints a committee to oversee the preparation of manuscripts for that volume. A special committee created by the Board performs similar functions for the Society's paperback series.

The Society's publications are distributed each year without charge to approximately 4,500 members in the United States, Canada, and elsewhere throughout the world. The Society welcomes as members all individuals who desire to receive its publications. For information about membership and current dues, see the back pages of this volume or write to the Secretary-Treasurer, 5835 Kimbark Avenue, Chicago, Illinois 60637.

The Seventy-ninth Yearbook includes the following two volumes:

Part I: *Toward Adolescence: The Middle School Years*
Part II: *Learning a Second Language*

A complete listing of the Society's previous publications, together with information as to how earlier publications still in print may be obtained, is found in the back pages of this volume.

Library of Congress Catalog Number: 79-91182
ISSN: 0077-5762

Published 1980 by
THE NATIONAL SOCIETY FOR THE STUDY OF EDUCATION

5835 Kimbark Avenue, Chicago, Illinois 60637
© 1980 by the National Society for the Study of Education

First Printing, 8,000 Copies

Printed in the United States of America

iv

Officers of the Society
1979-80

(Term of office expires March 1 of the year indicated.)

JEANNE CHALL

(1981)
Harvard University, Cambridge, Massachusetts

MARGARET J. EARLY

(1982)
Syracuse University, Syracuse, New York

JOHN I. GOODLAD

(1980)
University of California, Los Angeles, California

PHILIP W. JACKSON

(1982)
University of Chicago, Chicago, Illinois

A. HARRY PASSOW

(1981)
Teachers College, Columbia University, New York, New York

KENNETH J. REHAGE

(Ex-officio)
University of Chicago, Chicago, Illinois

RALPH W. TYLER

(1980)
*Director Emeritus, Center for Advanced Study in the Behavioral Sciences
Stanford, California*

Secretary-Treasurer

KENNETH J. REHAGE

5835 Kimbark Avenue, Chicago, Illinois 60637

v

The Society's Committee on Learning a Second Language

FRANK M. GRITTNER

(Chairman)
Supervisor, Second Language Education
Wisconsin Department of Public Instruction
Madison, Wisconsin

HELEN L. JORSTAD

Associate Professor of Languages and Cultures Education
University of Minnesota
Minneapolis, Minnesota

ROBERT C. LAFAYETTE

Associate Professor of Language Education
School of Education, Indiana University
Bloomington, Indiana

C. EDWARD SCEBOLD

Executive Director
American Council of Teachers of Foreign Language
New York, New York

HAROLD G. SHANE

University Professor of Education
Indiana University
Bloomington, Indiana

Associated Contributors

JAMES E. ALATIS

Dean, School of Languages and Linguistics
Georgetown University
Washington, D.C.

KENNETH D. CHASTAIN

Associate Professor of Spanish
University of Virginia
Charlottesville, Virginia

vii

ANTHONY GRADISNIK

Curriculum Specialist, Milwaukee Public Schools
Milwaukee, Wisconsin

GILBERT A. JARVIS

Professor of Foreign Language Education
The Ohio State University
Columbus, Ohio

CONSTANCE K. KNOP

Professor of French and Education
University of Wisconsin
Madison, Wisconsin

WILGA M. RIVERS

Professor of Romance Languages
Harvard University
Cambridge, Massachusetts

FRANK G. RYDER

Kenan Professor of German
University of Virginia
Charlottesville, Virginia

REBECCA M. VALETTE

Professor of Romance Languages
Boston College
Chestnut Hill, Massachusetts

Editor's Preface

In the fall of 1976, Harold G. Shane, then a member of the Board of Directors of the National Society for the Study of Education, appeared as a speaker at the annual meeting of the American Council on the Teaching of Foreign Languages. On that occasion, Dr. Shane and various members of the Executive Council of ACTFL discussed the possibility of having a yearbook of the National Society for the Study of Education that would deal with the topic of second-language learning. It was noted that in the long and illustrious history of the Society's yearbooks no single volume had ever been devoted exclusively to such topics as bilingualism, foreign language education, and the teaching of English to speakers of other languages. Agreement was quickly reached with regard to the need for and value of such a volume, particularly in view of the emerging trend toward what is called "global" or "international" education. The concept of a yearbook on second-language education was subsequently endorsed by the Board of Directors of the Society and the Executive Council of ACTFL.

The volume envisioned at that time was to be one that would summarize the major issues and trends relating to second-language teaching and learning in American schools and colleges. Further, the yearbook was to be written in such a manner that readers who were neither linguists nor language specialists could profit from its content. The authors and topics were chosen with these specifications in mind. It is my fervent hope that this yearbook meets these standards and that it will help the reader to a better understanding of the past, present, and future status of second-language learning in America.

FRANK M. GRITTNER
Madison, Wisconsin
January, 1980

Acknowledgements

The Society is extremely grateful to Frank M. Grittner, editor of this volume, and to his committee for planning and bringing to completion this yearbook on an exceedingly timely topic. We are also indebted to all those who have contributed chapters to the volume. It is the hope of all who have been involved in the development of this work that it will provide an appropriate stimulus for continued discussion of the issues related to the learning of second languages in our schools. The National Society for the Study of Education is indeed pleased to have this volume in its series of yearbooks.

KENNETH J. REHAGE
Secretary-Treasurer and
Editor for the Society

Table of Contents

CHAPTER I

Second-Language Study: Historical Background and Current Status

KENNETH D. CHASTAIN

Introduction

FACTORS INFLUENCING SECOND-LANGUAGE LEARNING

The purpose of this chapter is to familiarize the reader with some major factors that have influenced second-language study in the United States and to provide the bases for a fuller comprehension of subsequent chapters in this volume. The intent is not to prepare an in-depth collection of historical data, but to examine the principal frames in second-language study and to analyze their relationships to other elements of society. Primary attention is paid to the threads that appear throughout the different historical periods. Other less widely generalizable factors, both those supportive of and those detracting from second-language study, are discussed within the historical context in which their presence is most noticeable.

The first thread, readily visible throughout the history of second-language study, is that such study has never enjoyed the security of an assured position in the center of American educational priorities. Entry into the curriculum was made only with considerable effort, and continued existence, even in the fringes of those curricular offerings that are expendable in difficult times, has required equal persistence. Second-language enrollments seem to be especially susceptible to a variety of factors outside the classroom itself.

The second thread becomes visible as one seeks to determine the reasons for this lack of commitment to second-language study in the United States. Why are not more Americans more interested

in studying a second language? Various replies have been given
to this question, but the most fundamental answer is that Americans
are not so ethnically oriented nor language conscious as is the
case in many other cultures. Fishman describes the situation among
Americans as follows:

Just as there is hardly any ethnic foundation to American nationalism,
so there is no special language awareness in the use of English. . . .
Americans have no particular regard for English, no particular pride
in English as an exquisite instrument, no particular concern for its
purity, subtlety, or correctness. Even the fact that so few Americans
command any other language than English—if, indeed, they can be
said to command English itself—is largely a result of educational failure,
cultural provincialism, and the absence of pragmatic utility for bilingualism.[1]

The third thread appears in the last line of the previous quote,
that is, the "pragmatic utility of bilingualism." In general, Americans have been characterized by a pervading pragmatism; they
seem to require concrete benefits in return for any expenditure of
time and effort. An examination of the history of second-language
study reveals recurring efforts to associate language programs with
concrete, practical goals.

A fourth thread is that, given the circumstances in the schools
and in society, the overall vitality of second-language study depends on the extent to which it is supported and promoted by
individuals and groups outside the profession itself. The opposing
forces are too powerful and the resources of the profession too
limited to insure success without assistance.

These four threads provide the basic pattern within which
other factors can be discerned and understood. They are the con-
necting fibers with which other influences mingle and intertwine
during each of the historical periods upon which attention is
focused in this chapter.

MENTAL DISCIPLINE, ELITISM, AND CULTURAL PLURALISM

Many diverse influences have shaped the nature and scope of
second-language study in the United States. Tradition has played

1. Joshua Fishman, *Language Loyalty in the United States* (The Hague:
Mouton, 1966), p. 30.

an influential role by helping to determine which languages were studied, for how long, and at what level. The long-held connection between second-language study and mental discipline has affected the type of instruction and the type of students studying second languages. Social and economic factors have been major considerations in determining who would study a second language as well as what constituted the primary goals of the course. Associated with this factor is the popular image of second-language study as being only for the academic elite.

At one time, the need for speakers of a wide variety of languages led to increased enrollments in and funding for second-language study. The degree to which international understanding and international relations have been stressed has tended to change the numbers of students studying second languages. Also, the relations between the United States and other countries have led to positive or negative reactions among the nation's citizens with respect to language study. Areas with large numbers of immigrants have tended to be those with higher interest in second-language learning.

The number of students throughout the world who are studying English as a second language has influenced the extent to which Americans have felt a need for second-language skills. Government funds have been a major source of the support needed to hold meetings, hire staff, publish instructional materials, train instructors, and the like. Court decisions have at times controlled directions taken in second-language teaching, especially in recent years. Language requirements have always been a fundamental element in determining the number of students in second-language classes, not only in the United States but in most other countries as well. Finally, the concept of cultural pluralism is a critical component influencing the attitude toward and the enrollments in what are typically referred to in the United States as foreign-language classes.

The Colonial Period

Early colonists were forced by the exigencies of their situation to devote their time and energies mainly toward surviving in an unfamiliar and often harsh environment. Shelters had to be constructed, land cleared, food produced and gathered, clothes made and mended, and territory secured. Each day was filled with essential work, and everyone's assistance, including that of the children, was necessary in this struggle to survive. The luxury of classroom instruction would be delayed until the needed leisure time and finances were available.

The lack of schools among the first immigrants should not be interpreted as a lack of concern for education. From the time of their arrival, many families tutored their children in rare, stolen moments. After all, they were products of their European background in which the ideal of an educated person included literacy. Especially among the Puritans, knowing how to read was an essential skill for believers, who were expected to study the Scriptures daily and diligently. In fact, the first school legislation in the English-speaking world was passed in 1642, and was followed in 1647 by the "Old Deluder Satan Act." The fundamental objective of this Massachusetts act was to teach children to read in order that the "one chief project of that old deluder, Satan, to keep men from the knowledge of the Scriptures" might be nullified. The fact that this first measure was enacted only twenty-two years after the arrival of the *Mayflower* attests to the persistent dedication and the faithful religious devotion of these earliest settlers.

THE CLASSICAL TRADITION

The purpose of the first schools was to teach the four R's: reading, writing, arithmetic, and religion. Little need was felt for nor attention given to higher education among most of the populace. Those more well-to-do students who continued their education proceeded into Latin grammar schools, which were patterned after the schools in Europe. Thus, the classical tradition became as entrenched in the new world as in the old. Latin, Greek, and sometimes Hebrew, were the basic curriculum components for students preparing to become ministers, lawyers, or teachers. Above all, these future leaders were to be solidly grounded in classical languages in order that they might gain a thorough knowledge of the Scriptures.

With both tradition and purpose so completely on the side of the classics, the study of modern foreign language was normally not included in the curriculum of the early schools. The first recorded modern-language classes were given in German in 1702 in Germantown, Pennsylvania.[2] The earliest known French class was given in New York in 1703.[3] Provisions were made for the inclusion of Spanish in the curriculum of the first academy, founded in Philadelphia in 1749 with the assistance of Benjamin Franklin, although instruction was not given until 1766.[4]

IMMIGRANT LANGUAGES AND RELIGION

Even though modern foreign languages were rarely studied in the schools, they were learned. Some immigrant groups established classes to teach the language of the homeland. This practice and the organization of societies were the most common approaches to language maintenance during this period. These schools were associated with the church, and the primary purpose was to maintain the religious traditions and beliefs of the group. Private tutors were also available, and newspapers carried advertisements announcing their services. Individuals interested in learning a modern foreign language had the option of studying with a tutor or of teaching themselves, which many early colonial leaders did. Several prominent people in the colonies knew a second language, although normally their skills were limited to reading, and there was an active interest in French, German, and Spanish literature, with French being the most popular. It is said that Madison was the only "French scholar" at Princeton, but that he could neither understand the language nor speak it.[5]

As early as 1725, Cotton Mather supported the study of French as a way of achieving a better knowledge of English.[6] Franklin, Jefferson, and other leaders encouraged the study of modern for-

2. Klaus J. Bartel, "German and the Germans at the Time of the American Revolution," *Modern Language Journal* 60 (March 1976): 96.

3. George B. Watts, "The Teaching of French in the United States: A History," *French Review* 37 (October 1963, Part 2): 14.

4. Sturgis E. Leavitt, "The Teaching of Spanish in the United States," in *Reports of Surveys and Studies in the Teaching of Modern Foreign Languages* (New York: Modern Language Association, 1959-61), p. 310.

5. Paul M. Spurlin, "The Founding Fathers and the French Language," *Modern Language Journal* 60 (March 1976): 85.

6. Ibid., p. 86.

eign languages. These attitudes, however, were not shared by the general public, who looked with some considerable suspicion on the religion and the morals of most Europeans, especially those of the French.

The Revolutionary War to the Civil War

Following the Revolutionary War there was tremendous expansion in several areas. Politically, the ties with England had been severed, and a new government had to be conceived, agreed upon, accepted, and established. Territorially, the United States grew in fifty-one years from the original thirteen colonies into a giant nation that spanned the continent. Economically, the government, with the assistance of Alexander Hamilton, developed a sound monetary system. Government protection also encouraged the growth of American industry, and the industrial revolution began around the turn of the century. Commercially, the country, now free from the restrictive mercantile system that had prevailed under British rule, increased its trade with other countries. Nationally, the country began to develop a literature and heroes of its own. Religiously, the people were becoming more secular, in spite of the Great Awakening, and government began to assert more influence in the lives of the people, while the major role played by the church during colonial times began to recede. Numerically, the population increased rapidly and moved toward the west.

GROWTH OF HIGH SCHOOLS AND ACADEMIES

The educational system underwent an equally significant expansion. The academies, which were started prior to the Revolutionary War, gradually replaced the Latin grammar schools of the colonial era. The curriculum of the academies was much wider in scope than that of their predecessors. As life became more diversified, expectations placed upon the schools also increased and expanded. More emphasis was placed on providing a practical education, one that would train young people for jobs. As the number and the practicality of the offerings increased, so too did the numbers of students. Church control of the schools gradually gave way to political control as the high school, first established in Boston in 1821, began to compete with the popular academies.

RESISTANCE TO MODERN LANGUAGES

Modern foreign languages gained their first entry into the curriculum as a result of the move toward an expanded curriculum and more practical courses in the academies and in the high schools. There was no wholesale defection, however, from the classics to the study of modern foreign languages, and Latin and Greek dominated throughout the entire period. Modern foreign languages were usually offered as electives, and many educators refused to consider them as serious subjects. The president of Washington and Lee University, for example, opposed the substitution of French for Greek because it was not such a good "exercise of mental faculties."[7] Not until 1782 did Harvard permit the substitution of French for Hebrew, but there was no salaried French instructor at Harvard until 1787.[8] The Boston Public Latin School did not list French among its courses until 1852.[9]

Areas with large concentrations of immigrant groups, such as the French in Louisiana and parts of New England and the Germans in Pennsylvania and parts of the upper Midwest, were exceptions to the comparatively weak condition of modern foreign languages in the academies and high schools. In these areas, the family and church promoted native language study as a means of perpetuating their religion. German was not widely taught in public schools until large numbers of political immigrants began to arrive in 1848.[10] Outside the classroom, tutors were available to help adults learn a language, and many continued to learn languages through self-study.

The influences contributing to this state of affairs were many and varied. Obviously, the strong classical tradition had completed a successful transfer from the curriculum of the Latin grammar schools to that of the academies and the high schools. The fact that the study of modern language did not fit the image of being sufficiently rigorous to promote mental discipline was a negative

7. Watts, "The Teaching of French," p. 72.

8. Spurlin, "The Founding Fathers," p. 87.

9. Watts, "The Teaching of French," p. 36.

10. Edwin H. Zeydel, "The Teaching of German in the United States from Colonial Times to the Present," *German Quarterly* 37 (September 1964): 346.

factor. In order to meet the prerequisite of academic rigor, most instruction in modern foreign language was patterned after that of the classics. In some levels of society, French was held in particularly high esteem. However, the long-held distrust of French Catholicism and French morals persisted among American Protestants. Even Jefferson, a longtime friend and proponent of modern-language study, described his feelings as follows: "In France a young man's morals, health and fortune are more irresistibly endangered than in any country in the universe."[11] The net result of these attitudes, plus the negative reaction to the French Revolution and the XYZ affair, was the elimination of French from the curriculum for some time. A factor that came to counteract these unfavorable feelings was the positive image created by the French Huguenots, who emigrated in large numbers to the United States toward the end of the century.[12]

The Civil War to World War I

The building momentum of the rapid expansion prior to 1860 virtually exploded after the Civil War. Dreams could come true in America. The availability of jobs created by the nation's systems of production and distribution and of cheap land to the west were the basic components of this economic and geographic expansion. The attraction of riches lured people to the cities and to the west. The same attraction lured millions of immigrants into the country. The peak immigration years were from the 1840s to 1920. During that period, the number of immigrants per one thousand American citizens ranged from 5.3 to 10.4 per year.[13] As the population grew, so did the economy. Men like Rockefeller, Vanderbilt, and Carnegie used the mineral resources, the readily available labor supply, and the favorable economic conditions to help convert the country into an economic giant. In an astonishingly short time the United States became one of the world's major powers.

11. Spurlin, "The Founding Fathers," p. 86.

12. Ibid., p. 95.

13. *Statistical Abstract of the United States,* 1977 (Washington, D.C.: Bureau of the Census, U.S. Department of Commerce, 1978), p. 81.

The extent of growth and change in the nation's schools matched that of the country as a whole. During this period enrollments at all levels rose by leaps and bounds as public education replaced the basically private system of the academies. This shift to public education was in accord with the country's image as a land of opportunity, and it was supported by government assistance and court decisions. The Morrill Act of 1862 gave large tracts of federal land for the establishment and support of agricultural and technical colleges, and in 1874 the Michigan Supreme Court ruled in the *Kalamazoo* decision that taxes could be levied to support public education at the secondary level. As larger numbers and a greater variety of students entered the schools, the curriculum underwent an equally extensive expansion. As the nation's schools sought to educate everyone, the variety of courses and curricula needed to meet such a broad set of objectives led to the typical "comprehensive" school at the secondary level and to the current system of "electives" at the college and university level.

CURRICULAR EXPANSION AND LANGUAGE ENROLLMENTS

This curricular expansion was a boost for the teaching of modern foreign languages. Enrollment in modern foreign languages rose from 16.3 percent of the high school population in 1890 to 35.9 percent in 1915. German was by far the most popular. In that year, 24.4 percent of the students were studying German, 8.8 percent French, and 2.7 percent Spanish, which had an enrollment of only 0.7 percent in 1910 and numbers too small to report in 1905. At the same time, the classical tradition remained strong. Enrollments in Latin rose from 34.7 percent in 1890 to a high of 50.6 percent of the total high school student population in 1900. By 1915 the percentage had dropped to 37.3 percent, but the popularity of Latin still was higher than that of the combined total of all the modern foreign languages.[14]

IMMIGRATION AND INTERNATIONALISM

Much of the popularity of German can be attributed to the large number of German immigrants who had entered the country

14. William R. Parker, *The National Interest and Foreign Languages*, 3d ed., U.S. Department of State Publication 7324 (Washington, D.C.; U.S. Government Printing Office, 1961), p. 85.

during the middle of the nineteenth century. Modern foreign-language study was also popular because of the rather strong bilingual tradition in the United States during this peak period of immigration. As immigrant groups sought to maintain their language and culture, many non-English newspapers and periodicals were published, and the general public was aware of the number and influence of the immigrants, especially of the German immigrants. Also, many educators supported foreign-language programs on the basis of the belief that such study constituted beneficial training for the mind. Many educators considered second-language study, especially Latin, to be a part of basic education.

Other outside events also tended to encourage second-language study. The Michigan Supreme Court ruled in 1874 that taxes could be used to support secondary schools in which foreign languages were taught, and the Illinois court ruled in 1881 that, although the students were to be taught in English, the teaching of foreign languages could not be prohibited.[15] In 1875, Harvard initiated a trend that was to become a basic support for second-language study when it adopted the first foreign language requirement.[16]

Economically, the country was strong, and there were no international events to cause a wave of negative feeling toward second-language study. As a result of the Spanish-American War, the United States acquired territory in which the people spoke Spanish. Perhaps it was this stimulus toward an increased awareness of Spanish that accounted for the initial interest in Spanish shortly before World War I.

The rising importance of modern foreign languages was reflected in the founding of several important language organizations and journals such as the Modern Language Association of America in 1883, the *Modern Language Journal* in 1916, and the American Association of Teachers of Spanish and Portuguese and its journal, *Hispania,* in 1917.

15. Shirley Brice Heath, "Our Language Heritage: A Historical Perspective," in *The Language Connection: From the Classroom to the World,* ed. June Phillips (Skokie, Ill.: National Textbook Co., 1977), p. 30.

16. Zeydel, "The Teaching of German," p. 348.

World War I to 1952

ISOLATIONISM

The end of World War I found Americans anxious to return to the "normalcy" of the prewar period. The failure of the effort to end all wars had left them disillusioned with international alliances. The national mood favored the isolationist policies pursued after the war. Tariffs were raised to extremely high levels as the United States sought to disassociate itself from international economic and political entanglements. Meanwhile, the country enjoyed a prosperous decade. The sudden crash of the stock market in 1929 was followed by a depression that left millions out of work and millions more ruined financially. Although President Roosevelt managed to reestablish confidence and the security of the banks, the country did not recover fully from its economic woes until the advent of World War II. Governmental policies instituted to combat the disastrous plight of the economy, however, established the history-making precedent in the United States that the government is responsible for the social welfare of its citizens, a thesis that has resulted in a much larger governmental role in education. Isolationist sentiment remained strong as Japan marched into Manchuria in 1931, Italy into Ethiopia in 1935, Japan into China in 1937, and Germany into the Rhineland in 1936, Austria in 1938, and Czechoslovakia and Poland in 1939. It was not until the attack on Pearl Harbor in 1941, however, that Congress and the people were ready to enter the world conflict. The end of World War II and the beginning of the atomic age were inaugurated by a mushroom-shaped cloud at Hiroshima on August 6, 1945. The interests of the United States did not shrink to the boundaries of its own frontiers after this war. Instead, the country committed itself to assisting the recovery of the war-torn areas of the world. At the same time, the United States was gradually but definitely becoming embroiled in a continuing cold war with the nations of the Communist bloc.

Meanwhile, the growth of the nation's schools continued unabated. Enrollments rose steadily, except in those years affected by the lower birth rates of the early depression years. There were more students due to immigration and population growth. Also, the passage of child labor laws and compulsory school attendance laws brought increasing numbers of students from low-income families into the high schools. This change in the composition of the school population in turn led to an even greater variety of courses in the secondary school curriculum and to an effort to incorporate greater flexibility as the schools attempted to adapt to the needs of all their students. To some degree, the expanding curriculum reflected the vocational and progressive education movements of the 1930s. Such programs sought to provide experiences in the schools that would help the students adjust to life and to the vocational demands that would be made on them after graduation. The growing acceptance of the idea that the schools must pass on many of the skills and much of the knowledge formerly learned in the family and the home, as well as the goals of life-adjustment education, led to an altered view of the role of the school in society.

POST WORLD WAR I DECLINES IN ENROLLMENT IN FOREIGN LANGUAGE CLASSES

Perhaps the most disastrous impact on foreign language study had been the public reaction against all things foreign, especially German, at the outset of America's entry into World War I. Although it had been the most popular modern foreign language prior to the war, German almost disappeared from the curriculum. The percentage of high school students studying German fell from 24.4 percent in 1915 to .6 percent in 1922. French and Spanish benefited temporarily, but all languages continued to suffer from falling enrollments until the early 1950s. Enrollment in Latin dropped from 27.5 percent of the high school population in 1922 to 6.9 percent in 1954, in French from 15.5 percent to 5.6 percent, and in Spanish from 11.3 percent to 7.3 percent.[17]

Like the national economic depression of the 1930s, the depression in enrollments in second-language classes was very severe. In addition, the tradition of the classics was gradually being eroded, and the long-held belief in the value of foreign-language study as a mental discipline was apparently coming to an end. Other more

17. Parker, *The National Interest and Foreign Languages*, p. 86.

acceptable and more attractive benefits needed to be formulated, but none was forthcoming. After World War I, a few second-language instructors experimented briefly with a conversational approach called "the direct method" in response to complaints by returning soldiers that their high school language courses had not prepared them to use the language. But this oral-aural approach was soon rejected on the basis that an active command of the language was not possible within the time constraints present in the American educational system. The Coleman Report of 1929 accepted the prevailing two-year sequence as being inevitable and recommended that a reading objective was the only viable one within such a limited time period.[18] Most instructors tended to teach according to grammar-translation procedures carried over from the classics. This particular methodology is often cited as a contributing cause of declines in enrollment through the 1930s and 1940s. The negative effect on second languages extended well beyond the classroom. The existing bilingual presence in many parts of the country gradually disappeared during the years following World War I. Several factors have been suggested to explain this development. First, the rate of immigration slowed from a high of 10.4 per thousand between 1901 and 1910 to a low of .4 between 1931 and 1940. Second, large numbers of foreign-born already in the country "melted" into the American milieu. The publication of non-English dailies decreased by 57 percent between 1930 and 1960. The number of weeklies dropped 63 percent between 1930 and 1960. In 1910, 54 percent of the non-English dailies were published in German. This figure had dropped to 7 percent by 1960.[19]

All was not entirely bleak, however. Movements had begun in psychology and linguistics that would culminate in an emphasis on oral language skills and in a revitalization of procedures for teaching a second language. Behavioral psychologists were saying that learning results from the changing of behaviors, and descriptive linguists were stressing that language is primarily oral. Also, in response to a critical need for second-language speakers during

18. Zeydel, "The Teaching of German," p. 364.

19. Fishman, *Language Loyalty in the United States*, pp. 51-54.

World War II, the government had initiated the Army Specialized Training Program (ASTP) with the goal of producing bilingual graduates. The curriculum and instructional techniques of the ASTP were also based upon the new ideas of descriptive linguists and behavioral psychologists.

From 1952 to the Late 1960s

POST-SPUTNIK INTEREST IN FOREIGN LANGUAGES

The end of the doldrums, lethargy, and despair into which second-language study had settled was signaled by the establishment of the foreign-language section of the Modern Language Association of America and the appointment of William Riley Parker, an English professor, as its first head. Seed funds from the Rockefeller Foundation enabled Parker and other leaders to initiate the movement that later energized the profession. The single most influential publication in this successful drive for increased support for and recognition of second-language study was Parker's *The National Interest and Foreign Languages,* first published in 1954. Parker's forceful argument that the availability of second-language speakers during war time was a matter of "national interest" was a major factor in the passage of the National Defense Education Act of 1958, part of which was designed to stimulate and support second-language study.

More than $43 million were spent on improving second-language teaching between 1958 and 1960, including $13 million in matching funds to the states for the development of materials, institutes to retrain teachers in the recommended audiolingual method, and language laboratories plus other electronic equipment.[20] With the help of funding under the National Defense Education Act, the second-language profession blossomed into intense activity. Stimulated by favorable publicity and public reaction to the new oral methods of teaching second languages, enrollments began to rise for the first time since World War I. The number of students studying a modern foreign language climbed from 16.4 percent

20. Zeydel, "The Teaching of German," p. 377.

of all high school students in 1958[21] to 27.7 percent in 1968.[22] One unfortunate concomitant of the popularity of modern foreign languages was the continued decline in Latin enrollments, which reached a low of 2.9 percent in 1968. It is important to note that even in this era of relatively high popularity of modern foreign languages, high school enrollments in all other curricular areas (except art, agriculture, vocational and industrial eduation, and distributive education) were higher than enrollments in foreign language classes.[23] A similar trend occurred at the college level, where enrollments in foreign languages grew 60.3 percent between 1960 and 1965 and 10 percent between 1965 and 1968. These figures are somewhat deceptive, however, since the total student college population grew by 54.2 percent and 25.4 percent during these same two periods.[24]

FOREIGN LANGUAGES IN THE ELEMENTARY SCHOOLS

One movement in second-language study that was peculiar to this period, although a commonly accepted aspect of second-language study in most other countries, was the temporary popularity of offering second-language study in the elementary school. Many schools introduced a second language in the curriculum, normally in the third or fourth grade, only to drop it a few years later. The movement for the study of foreign language in elementary schools was the direct result of the theory that young children learn languages more easily and more quickly than do people over the age of twelve. The early start was also supposed to generate a greater interest in second-language learning so that enrollments would increase at the junior and senior high school levels. There were objections, however, that learning a second language required too much time and money, that few elementary school pupils obtained the expected mastery, that few elementary

21. Julia G. Kant, "Foreign Language Offerings and Enrollments in Public Secondary Schools, Fall 1968," *Foreign Language Annals* 3 (March 1970): 403.

22. *Digest of Educational Statistics, 1973* (Washington, D.C.: U.S. Government Printing Office, 1974), p. 41.

23. Ibid., pp. 41-42.

24. Scott E. Morrison, "Foreign Language Enrollments in U.S. Colleges and Universities, Fall 1974," *ADFL Bulletin* 10 (1978): 15.

teachers were qualified to teach a second language at that level, that bilingualism tended to interfere with learning the native language, that second-language study did not meet the needs or interests of all students, and that supportive research to indicate that children do learn a second language better than adults was not available.[25] Various research studies involving children with a FLES (foreign language in elementary school) background were not conclusive regarding the overall value of FLES programs.[26]

The influence of second languages outside the classroom continued to be significantly less than had been true in the latter part of the nineteenth century and the first part of the twentieth. However, the number of immigrants, having reached a low during depression years, began to rise again after the war. At the same time, the economic and political influence of the United States on the international scene reached the point at which English gradually assumed a position of dominance in international business and diplomacy. The result was that English became the most commonly studied second language in the world. Thus, larger and larger numbers of speakers of other languages were able to communicate with Americans in English. In spite of the use of English as the major international language, the ever-increasing contacts around the world motivated large numbers of American businessmen, politicians, and travelers to enroll in commercial second-language classes. Enrollments in these language schools began to increase at an unprecedented rate in the late 1950s and 1960s. One private language training school reported that demand from corporation personnel had increased ten times in ten years. The Inlingual School of Languages had expanded to a network of 130 branches within nine years of its formation.[27]

25. Richard A. Thompson and Janet M. Blackwell, "FLES: To Be or Not To Be," *Elementary English* 51 (April 1974): 541-42.

26. John G. Bordie, "When Should Instruction in a Second Language or Dialect Begin?" *Elementary English* 48 (May 1971): 551-58; Clare Burstall, "Primary French in the Balance," *Foreign Language Annals* 10 (May 1977): 245-52; John W. Oller, Jr. and Naoko Nagato, "The Long-term Effect of FLES: An Experiment," *Modern Language Journal* 58 (January 1974): 15-19.

27. Wynona H. Wilkins, "Corporate Competition for Foreign Language Customers: Is There an Answer?" *Foreign Language Annals* 9 (December 1976): 519, 521-22, 524.

Throughout this period the government was a major force in education and in second-language study. Millions of dollars were expended to protect the national interest during war time, and these dollars fostered a higher interest in second-language study in the United States. Other factors, however, played negative roles. As had been true since World War I, the process of Americanization among non-English speaking groups encouraged the learning of English. Too, large numbers of non-English speakers were enrolled in English classes around the world. Thus, as more people in the United States and abroad were learning English, the need of the people of the United States to learn a second language appeared to be decreasing.

Late 1960s to the Present

As the war in Vietnam persisted in spite of attempts to end American involvement, leaders, sympathizers, and interested observers alike became increasingly disillusioned by the unresponsiveness of the bureaucracy to public opinion. The result was twofold. First, those in the forefront of the protest movement turned to the same tactics of nonviolence that had been employed earlier and so successfully in the civil rights movement. Second, a general dissatisfaction with huge, impersonal institutions led to a rejection of conformity and an emphasis on individuality and a "do-your-own-thing" attitude. The stress on individual freedom culminated in demands for more active participation in the decision-making process and for a greater voice in determining those rules and regulations that affect the lives of each member of society. The outgrowth of this changing emphasis in society was the replacement of the traditional ideal of the American melting pot with that of a pluralistic societal structure. The focus moved from the collective cohesive elements of society to the varying and varied interests of minorities and individuals. An associated phenomenon was the tendency of some to reject traditional values and to drop out of traditional society.

CHANGING ATTITUDES OF STUDENTS TOWARD ACADEMIC SUBJECTS

Schools exist within society, and sooner or later the currents in society are reflected in what happens in the schools. This period was no exception. Students were less willing to follow rules and to complete assignments simply because they were told to do so. They were more independent and asked more questions. They wanted more freedom and a greater voice in their own governance. This desire for fewer restrictions and less conformity ranged from hair styles to dress codes to academic requirements. In essence, the same pluralism and stress on the individual that characterized society in general became characteristic of the schools also.

With regard to the foreign language curriculum, the schools responded by introducing more varied content and by attempting to individualize instruction. Stress was also placed on the emotions, attitudes, personality, and socialization of students as well as on the intellect. Mini-courses were incorporated into the foreign language curriculum as a way to maintain student interest, to provide relevant content, and to meet the wide range of student capabilities and needs. In short, the schools and their curricula became more diverse as the diversity of their clientele and of the demands being made on them increased. The entire period was filled with a tremendous number of innovations as the schools attempted to react to the varying demands being made by the public, the courts, and the government.

The general diversity that was characteristic of all schools during this period was even more pronounced in those schools in areas enrolling significant numbers of minority children. With regard to race, federal judges ordered that children be bused from one part of a school district to another in order to meet federal guidelines for integration. With regard to linguistic and cultural minorities, the Supreme Court, basing its decision on Title VI of the Civil Rights Act of 1964, ruled in *Lau* vs. *Nichols* (1974) that the schools must provide programs in bilingual education if they have significant numbers of non-English-speaking students. The principal federal statutes supporting bilingual education were Title VI of the Civil Rights Act of 1964, Titles I and III of the Elementary and Secondary Education Act of 1965, and the Bilingual Education Act. The major source of revenue for bilingual/bicultural education was Title VII of the Elementary and Secondary Education Amendment of 1967 and 1974.[28]

28. H. N. Geffert et al., *The Current Status of U.S. Bilingual Education Legislation* (Arlington, Va.: Center for Applied Linguistics, 1975), pp. 2-3.

In spite of all the time, effort, energy, and funds expended, the latter part of the period was marked by falling achievement scores, drug abuse, problems of discipline and integration, and a growing suspicion among taxpayers that results had not matched the amount of money being put into the schools. Public resistance to increased taxes for schools increased, and public pressure for more rigid discipline and higher academic achievement grew. Some states passed laws requiring minimum competencies, that is, minimum scores on tests in reading and mathematics, for gradua-tion, and a "back to the basics" movement seemed to be accelerating. Another factor that was to have a far-reaching effect on the schools was the fact that for the first time in the history of education in the United States, except for the years of depression, overall en-rollments were falling. After the children born during the "baby boom" years following World War II passed through the schools, many classrooms were left empty, and other children were not on the way to refill them. The number of children under five in 1960 was 20.3 million, but the number had dropped to 16.7 million by 1973.[29] Colleges and universities that had struggled since World War II to keep pace with ever-rising enrollments began to lose enrollment or to prepare for a "steady state" in which facilities, faculty, and numbers of students were not in a constant state of expansion.

ENROLLMENTS IN LANGUAGE CLASSES IN THE 1970S

The years including and following the student unrest of the late 1960s were not favorable to second-language study in the United States. As university students began to challenge traditions, one of the first to come into question was the idea of college re-quirements. In many institutions, requirements for a second lan-guage were eliminated or cut back. Frequently this affected enroll-ments in high school language classes in that many college-bound high school students who would previously have taken second-language classes now began to enroll in other courses. The number of colleges requiring second-language study for entrance dropped from 33.6 percent in 1966 to 18.6 percent in 1975, and the number

29. *Statistical Abstract of the United States, 1974* (Washington, D.C.: U.S. Government Printing Office, 1975), p. 114.

requiring second-language study for graduation dropped from 88.9 percent in 1966 to 54 percent in 1975.[30] Consequently, college and university modern language enrollments fell .5 percent between 1968 and 1970, 9.7 percent between 1970 and 1972, 6.9 percent between 1972 and 1974, and 1.5 percent between 1974 and 1977. This disastrous decline occurred while the total student population was rising 14.3 percent, 4.4 percent, 9.2 percent, and 10.2 percent respectively during these same periods. Ancient Greek, Italian, and Spanish were the only languages to gain students from 1974 to 1977. In that period Spanish was by far the most popular second language, with approximately 46 percent of the enrollment in university modern foreign-language classes. Between 1968 and 1977, higher education enrollments plummeted 36.6 percent in French, 37.4 percent in German, and 31.7 percent in Russian, while enrollment in Italian rose 9.8 percent and in Spanish 3.2 percent.[31] At the secondary level, the percent of total student population studying a second language dropped from a high of 31.5 percent in 1965 to 23.3 percent in 1974. The percentage of students taking a modern foreign language reached a peak of 27.7 percent in 1968 before falling to 22.1 percent in 1974. With some exceptions (for example, in Italian), the actual number of students in all language classes decreased from 1970 to 1974.[32]

FOREIGN LANGUAGES FOR ALL STUDENTS

High school language teachers responded to this discouraging trend by adopting a variety of curricular alternatives designed to counteract the negative forces at work in society and in schools. In order to overcome an elitist image, second-language educators urged the importance of second-language study for everyone in the public schools, not just the academically talented college preparatory students. In order to counter the feeling that languages were not relevant, teachers incorporated exercises and activities involving

30. "Survey of Foreign Language Entrance and Degree Requirements," *ADFL Bulletin* 6 (1975): 3.

31. Morrison, "Foreign Language Enrollments," pp. 15-18.

32. W. Vance Grant and C. George Lind, *Digest of Education Statistics, 1977-78* (Washington, D.C.: National Center for Education Statistics, U.S. Government Printing Office, 1978), p. 49.

values and group dynamics, and they took steps to stress the value
of a knowledge of a second language as an adjunct to career
plans. Trying to make second-language study more practical, they
developed specialized courses, especially at the college level, designed to teach language for specific purposes—such as Spanish
for nurses, policemen, and so forth. In order to help the students
relate more readily to second-language speakers and to realize goals
of intercultural understanding, they included more cultural materials in their classes. In order to refute the oft-heard remark
that a speaker had studied a second language but could not say
anything in the language, they designed courses and activities that
contained more stress on communication in the second language.
In order to encourage larger numbers of students to study second
languages and to do so in a variety of frameworks, they developed
individualized second-language courses, mini-courses that can be
taken in one semester or less, and exploratory courses to be offered
in the junior high school or in lower grades. In order to help
erase the boundaries that often separate second-language courses
from other parts of the curriculum, they devised interdisciplinary
courses taught in the second language but focusing on subject
matter in other disciplines.

THE BILINGUAL MOVEMENT

The bilingualism that had prevailed during most of the nineteenth century and the early part of the twentieth as a result of
the large numbers of immigrants settling in close proximity to
each other underwent a sharp decline during and after World War
I. Beginning with the 1960s, this trend was reversed, and current
social leaders and planners envisioned a multilingual/multicultural
society in which linguistic skills and cultural traditions would be
actively pursued and maintained. In part, this switch has come
about as a result of the turn to individualism and cultural pluralism
in the United States, and in part, it reflects the international attention being given to individual rights and humanistic concerns. The
recently established bilingual/bicultural programs in all areas with
non-English-speaking students, mandated by the courts in 1974
and subsequently funded by the federal government, represent
efforts to incorporate this vision into the nation's schools. Too,

these classes represent a recognition of the diversity within the ethnic and linguistic makeup of the people living in the United States. For example, Heath estimates that there are between 15.2 and 28.7 million people living in the United States who either were born abroad or who normally speak a language other than English. Of this number, 3.6 to 8.1 million are between the ages of four and eighteen.[33]

The Spanish-speaking population grew between 1950 and 1960 by 37 percent in Texas, by 88 percent in California, by 51 percent in Arizona, and by 31 percent in Colorado.[34] This increase represented larger numbers of non-English speakers than was the case with other immigrant groups. There appeared to be a stronger tendency to maintain native language skills among Spanish-speaking people than among any other of the language groups.[35] In any case, Spanish had become the most common non-English language in the United States by the 1970s.

Fishman and Lovas distinguish four different types of bilingual programs that may be adopted: (a) a *transitional* bilingual program designed to assist the students in making the switch to the second language; (b) a *monoliterate* bilingual program that teaches oral skills in both languages, but the students are not taught to read in their native language; (c) a *partial* bilingual program that contains training in both oral and written skills in both languages, while reading in the mother tongue is limited to material related directly to the student's cultural heritage; (d) a *full* bilingual program that includes all skills and subject matter in both languages.[36] Title VII of the Elementary and Secondary Education Act was passed to help non-English-speaking students "achieve competence in the English language."[37]

The desirability of establishing bilingual/bicultural programs

33. Heath, "Our Language Heritage," p. 46.

34. Fishman, *Language Loyalty in the United States,* p. 290.

35. Ibid., p. 363.

36. John F. Kunkle, "The 'L' Connection: The Interdependence of Second-Language Programs," in *The Language Connection,* ed. Phillips, pp. 215-16.

37. Malcolm N. Danoff, *Evaluation of Impact of ESEA Title VII Spanish/English Bilingual Education Program* (Washington, D.C.: U.S. Office of Education, 1978), p. 1.

is not universally and wholeheartedly accepted. Many Americans, aware of the Quebecois movement in Canada, fear that English might be supplanted in some areas and that separatist political movements could be the result.[38] This attitude is reflected in a New York *Times* editorial that warned "against the potential of creating political splinter groups among linguistic minorities." Too, there is concern among teachers of English as a second language and teachers of other foreign languages that their fields will suffer as the major amounts of funds, publicity, and favor are bestowed on bilingual/bicultural programs.[39] Even among minority groups of non-English speakers there is no unanimity of opinion. Many parents feel that such programs may actually hinder their child's progress in acquiring English skills and in moving into the mainstream of the American economy.

Nor have the benefits of bilingual education been firmly supported by research. Engler states that the question of how best to handle students who do not speak the language of the school has been an educational, sociological, psychological, and political issue for the last fifty years. The two major questions center around whether a child will learn to read more rapidly in the second language if he learns to read first in his native language and whether he will learn more in other subjects if he studies them first in his mother tongue. For many, the issue was definitely settled at a UNESCO conference in the early 1950s when "the assembled experts established as *axiomatic* that the best medium for teaching is the mother tongue of the pupil."[40] The various empirical studies of the 1970s, however, revealed no clear-cut, consistent conclusions. Overall, the evidence suggests the plausibility of the following generalizations: (a) the teaching of reading without prior oral training does not appear to be successful; (b) participation in bilingual programs apparently does not retard native language development, (c) bilingual children have an initial disadvantage and a slower learning rate; (d) the training of the teacher

38. Heath, "Our Language Heritage," p. 24.

39. Kunkle, "The 'L' Connection," p. 212.

40. Patricia L. Engler, "Language Medium in Early School Years for Minority Language Groups," *Review of Educational Research* 45 (Spring 1975): 283.

and his ethnicity probably are factors, but this suspicion has not been proven; (e) to be effective the program should include oral training in the beginning; (f) achievement depends upon a large number of variables, many of which lie outside the classroom itself; (g) the extent to which the Hawthorne effect has influenced results is unknown; (h) a transfer from one language to another without instruction has been observed.[41]

A recent study by American Institutes for Research (AIR), published in 1978, indicated the following conclusions: (a) achievement scores in English reading and mathematics of participants in the Title VII programs were not "substantially different" from nonparticipants; (b) the percentile rank of the average participating Hispanic student remained approximately the same during one year of the program; (c) participation in the program had no overall impact on achievement in English language arts or mathematics; (d) the scores of all students in all grades revealed that Title VII students were worse in English than nonparticipating students, and there was no difference between the two groups in mathematics; (e) students in Title VII programs did not develop a more positive attitude toward school; (f) there was an increase in the students' ability to read Spanish.[42] These and other findings of the AIR study have been strongly criticized.

As a result of increased contact among linguistic groups and emphasis on language maintenance as a human right, second-language study has assumed much greater national and international importance than in the past. This significance can be clearly seen in subsection (d) of the Helsinki Agreement "Foreign Languages and Civilizations," which committed signers to promote the study of second languages and second-language cultures and civilizations.[43] Current enrollment figures and educational expenditures in the United States are inconsistent with the articles of this agreement, and America's commitment to second-language study has been

41. Ibid., p. 309.

42. Danoff, *Evaluation of Impact of ESEA Title VII Spanish/English Bilingual Education Program*, pp. 14, 18-19.

43. *New Contexts, New Teachers, New Publics*, ed. Warren C. Born (Montpelier, Vt., Northeast Conference on the Teaching of Foreign Languages, 1978), pp. 13-14.

criticized. In response, President Carter appointed the President's Commission on Foreign Language and International Studies in 1978, to recommend ways and means of improving the status of second-language study in this country.[44] The Modern Language Association, in cooperation with the American Council on the Teaching of Foreign Languages, has also established a national task force to address the same problems.

Conclusion

From the point of view of potential public benefits, knowledge-able professional concerns, recognized national needs, and obvious international realities the present popularity of second-language study in the United States is undesirably low. Lacking the impetus provided by requirements and any indwelling motivation to learn a second language for its own sake, students have defected to other disciplines in large numbers.

The four threads mentioned at the beginning of this essay continue to be operative and influential. However, these overall patterns can be changed, and selected indications are encouraging. Here and there productive programs grow and thrive in spite of the opposing forces outside the classroom. These programs serve as verifying examples of existing possibilities. Too, others besides second-language educators are beginning to realize the seriousness of the situation, and they seem disposed to offer their assistance. These individuals provide hope that second-language educators may soon be joined in their efforts to reverse the decline in second-language study.

The task before the profession is not an easy one, but interesting and worthwhile classroom experiences and cooperation with those who share the concern for second-language knowledge and skills can alter the present picture.

44. "Executive Order 12054," *Federal Register* 43 (1978), no. 80.

CHAPTER II

The Value of Second-Language Learning

GILBERT A. JARVIS

Introduction

The context for American education is rapidly changing. Of particular importance to the teaching of a second language is an essential change in the role of education within society. Many educators have historically seen themselves as struggling to identify and then to provide the kind of education that would lead to the maximum possible benefit for each individual learner. As an educational goal, development to one's maximum potential was unquestioned. We all sought more and better education for all young people, and we labored with the support of most citizens to provide it. Within a few short years, however, the message coming from much of the citizenry has changed dramatically. Instead of asking for an education that is maximally beneficial for each individual, many citizens began to ask for the minimal education necessary to function without becoming a burden to the rest of society. In many ways the goal seems to have become the least education that "we can get by with." In the face of rising costs, dissatisfaction with students' performance, and concepts such as cost-benefit analysis or overeducation, many persons found it easy to reduce the purposes of education to literacy and computational skills.

Concurrent with the development of interest in minimal education, the consequences of earlier questioning of educational requirements began to have their effect. During the first half of the 1970s, many colleges and universities reduced or even eliminated their language requirements for graduation. Without the protective umbrella of the college requirement, language teachers in secondary schools confronted for the first time many questions of value. A history of being viewed as an "enrichment" area could not immediately be reconciled with a concept of "basics." They struggled with broad questions of collective benefit for society and with practical problems like the individual student's inquiry, "Why should I take your German course?"

One of the results of this turmoil has been a growing realization by language teachers that their subject matter should not be viewed merely as an enrichment area but rather as an area of learning that has become fundamental in the late twentieth century. This learning can be viewed in terms of several different areas of human functioning, or it can be subsumed under one general principle. In terms of areas of value, traditional categories such as cognitive learning, social interaction, and benefits in the workaday world of occupational skills are appropriate and descriptive. In terms of a broad statement that subsumes all three areas of value, language seems particularly related to the way in which one views one's life experience. A fundamental difference exists between the ways educated and uneducated persons see their lives. A person who has not benefited from education lives in a remarkably limited context. Such a person is extraordinarily time bound, space bound, and appearance bound, perceiving all experiences in terms of the here and now. In the extreme, life is a matter of a few city blocks or miles, a few associates or family members, and simple explanations of the phenomena that impinge on their environment. ("The wind blew up a storm, and I caught cold from being wet.") There is very little sense of participation or membership in a world, nation, or even community. There is little awareness of explanatory ideas; the worlds of theory, interpretation, analysis, and synthesis do not exist. Curiosity is conspicuously absent. Educated persons, on the other hand, have freedom to perceive and interpret their life experiences without these constraints. Their views are broad, so that phenomena can be perceived as complex and interrelated within a large context.

When considered in the abstract, this distinction may be little more than interesting. When it is embodied in a thinking, feeling, hoping human being, however, it must be poignantly felt by any sensitive person who has observed human behavior and who cares about the impact of education. It is not realistic to claim that second-language study makes all the difference between an educated and an uneducated person. It does appear reasonable, however, to view language study as having a particular affinity with this distinction. The most descriptive term for the effects of the study of language is "broadening," for such study results in a broadening of opportunities in careers and in leisure activities, of intellectual or thinking potential, and of one's ability to interact with other human beings, particularly in light of the world that seems to be evolving in the late twentieth century.

Language Study and an Interdependent World

THE END OF NATIONAL SELF-SUFFICIENCY

Language teachers have long emphasized the value of a knowledge of language that can be used in travel and in careers. For years, however, it seemed that few persons believed them. Then, rather suddenly, the cumulative effects of an evolving world reached a level where consciousness of the world's interdependence was unavoidable. The flight across the Atlantic no longer required fifteen or more hours but could be made in three and a half hours. Air fares dropped significantly in the late 1970s. From the mid-1950s to the late 1970s the number of overseas phone calls increased—not two-, three-, or even ten-fold, but sixty-seven-fold. The "world of business" took on a new literal meaning. We discovered that many of the most mundane resources had to be imported. Nearly 100,000 tons of rock salt for use on icy roads, for example, is now imported annually from Tunisia, Spain, Chile, and the Bahamas.[1] Probably the most visible and significant resource for which we are dependent on other nations is oil. During the 1970s it became vividly clear—for the first time to many Americans—that the people who heat our homes, power our automobiles, and keep our factories operating do not speak English. Whereas it had been easy to overlook millions starving in various parts of the world, it was impossible to ignore long waits at the gasoline pumps and tripled prices within a few short years. Al-

1. Mike Hendricks, "More Foreign Salt on U.S. Roads," Columbus (Ohio) *Dispatch*, 3 April 1978, p. A-11.

though many Americans would probably have difficulty in finding Iran on a map, they became quickly aware of the relationship between political turmoil in that country and the operation of their neighborhood service stations.

In hundreds of ways the status of the United States changed from one of self-sufficiency and independence to one of inter-dependence. We were clearly as dependent upon the rest of the world as the rest of the world was upon us. Just as dramatic as the fact of interdependence was the increase in awareness of global interrelatedness and mutual need among the peoples of the world. The magnitude of this change is evident in Clark's analysis of our insular history:

> Ours is the largest national system; we know this massive complex is the system most widely acclaimed since the second quarter of this century; we are geographically separated from the other major national models; we have many unique features; and we are busy and have more pressing things to do in Montana as well as in New York than to ask how the Austrians and Swedes do it.[2]

APPLICATIONS OF FOREIGN LANGUAGES IN BUSINESS

It would be erroneous to view the change solely in a negative light. It is a promising new era for much of American business. In community after community, foreign language teachers report they are being asked to help local companies by translating letters, invoices, advertising, and orders. In trade journal after trade journal, articles appear that deal with the new potential for inter-national business (and usually with difficulties in communication). As one typical example (in an occupation that traditionally has little affinity with second-language study), Cooper described spon-sorship by the Ohio Farm Bureau of a trade mission to the Far East to "find out what the people in Japan, Taiwan, Korea, and Hong Kong need that Ohio farmers have to sell" and "to see if the products we're sending them now are satisfactory."[3] He em-phasized the need to select mission members who were knowledge-

2. Burton R. Clark, "The Insulated Americans: Five Lessons from Abroad," *Change* 10 (November 1978): 24.

3. Ivan Cooper, "Developing Agricultural Markets in the Far East," *Buckeye Farm News* 56 (April 1978): 12.

able about their industry and products, who could handle the stress of travel, and who were able to communicate well. Recognizing that this type of scenario is being repeated daily in state after state and in industry after industry, one can readily see how the effectiveness of those who have had no formal study of other languages and cultures contrasts with that of persons who have studied another language, perhaps even for only a year in high school. It is routine in the business world to do research on relatively trivial matters such as a client's or associate's preferences for brands of liquor. In that context it is little short of preposterous for us to be collectively ignorant of cultural differences and to be unable, for the most part, even to greet and engage in small talk in the language of those with whom we do business.

Many believe that the situation is not merely one of a business advantage accruing from looking abroad. William F. Spengler, president and chief operating officer of international operations for Owens-Illinois, Inc., sees the situation as one of necessity. He observes that the United States has requirements for energy, materials, and certain technology that cannot be met from within. Other nations, too, are bound in a "similar web" of need and mutual economic cooperation. "Business people, through the multinational enterprise, long ago learned and accepted how essential international cooperation is and how to achieve it." [4] In a sense, then, the business world has found a means of international cooperation that is still lacking in the political arena.

POLITICAL NEED FOR FOREIGN LANGUAGES

The need for cooperation is indeed apparent in the political area. The problems arising from shortages of energy, the pollution of air and water, the danger of nuclear holocaust, and the complexity of economic interrelationships are all global. They will not be solved single-handedly by any nation. Thus in a world where 2,800 different languages are spoken, the importance of communication cannot be exaggerated. Moreover, the importance of second-language education is intensified by the evolving posture of much

4. Quoted in "Multinationals Cooperate," *OSU on Campus*, 30 March 1978, p. 9.

of the world regarding language use. After generations of assuming that the world would come to us, humbly asking to be heard (in our language), we must adjust to a world of greater linguistic parity. Ours is but of one of the major languages of the world and not the first language of 95 percent of the world population.

Our need is not simply for more speakers of all languages. That need is great and provides definite career advantages for persons who add second-language competence to their other job skills. Our problem is a collective disinclination toward language study. It is the cumulative effect of years of educational experience in which second-language study was marginal in the total curriculum. Because of the small numbers of Americans who studied even the "popular" foreign languages, we have few experienced language learners. That lack is an immediate problem because experience in learning one foreign language is beneficial in subsequent learning of other languages. Thus, time invested in learning French or Spanish in 1980 will not only yield skill in a widely used language but will also make the learner more skilled at learning Chinese, Arabic, or another language of particular importance in the late 1980s, 1990s, or 2020s.

It is very easy to argue that collectively we need a nation—indeed, a world—of people who can understand and respond in many languages. It is also clear that there are opportunities for jobs for the person with second-language skills. There is not an imperative need for everyone to develop native-like proficiency, unless one is entering a language profession such as translating or language teaching. Rather, any amount of proficiency expands one's value as an employee or as a self-employed person. In any profession, opportunities to utilize language will continue to increase for the foreseeable future. We shall all be abroad more, and more persons from other countries will be in our midst. As columnist Sylvia Porter has argued:

> With a language skill added to your other skills, you might double your chances of getting the job you want. There are openings for an auto mechanic who also speaks Arabic, an electronic radio expert who knows Japanese, a chef (even a woman chef) who understands French. It even could be a foreign language would be more useful to you during the next ten years than a college diploma. . . . You should weigh

the judgment of one executive: "A person who speaks two languages is worth two people." Language is, in fact, your hidden job insurance.[5]

Language Study and Intellectual Development

FOREIGN LANGUAGES AND CRITICAL THINKING

"To be a good thinker," "to be able to think critically and analytically" are educational goals in nearly all schools. Yet it is also true that courses rarely deal specifically with critical thinking or other intellectual skills. The skills that are referred to are a composite of many micro-level skills. Perhaps the closest we can come to describing these skills is in the verbs we use to describe the various operations the brain can do (for example, analyze, discriminate, identify, categorize, induce, infer, reconstruct). These operations fill our waking hours. As an example of the kinds of decisions we make that involve myriad subtle intellectual skills, a narrative of a few moments during the preparation of a manuscript shows the complexity of thought about even small matters that are involved in a writer's decisions:

I noticed that my yellow pad was getting very messy—words crossed out, erased, rewritten. I found myself doing an instant analysis of whether or not my secretary might still be able to read it. How much of what I had written might be illegible to her? Was the content of the type that she could reconstruct? Would she likely take the risk of reconstructing it, or would she ask me about each word? Or would she become irritated with me? What are the relative benefits and costs of these consequences? How pressed am I for time? Should I take the time to rewrite and at the same time gain one more polishing of the wording?

Such an analysis could continue—not through an extended period of time, for it happens within a few moments. It represents the type of micro-level "thinking" skills we all utilize continually. A very close analysis also reveals striking similarities to an entirely different domain of behavior. This particular example reflects a parallel with the behavior of a language learner while reading a paragraph in which guesses must be made about new words, a whole must be constructed out of parts, and the relative risks of being wrong in various ways must be considered. Such parallels

5. Sylvia Porter, "Foreign Language Is Job Insurance for Future," Field Newspaper Syndicate, 1978.

(and many more could be described) give face validity to the hypothesis that language study benefits such skills. The case for such benefits rests, however, on more than mere face validity.

FOREIGN LANGUAGE AND MENTAL DISCIPLINE

Claims about intellectual benefits of language study are not new. Over many decades, many students of language have been told that the study of another language, especially Latin, was good for mental discipline. Similarly, the intuitions of many successful second-language learners cannot be ignored. They nearly unanimously believe that language study benefited their intellectual development.

These beliefs have their modern roots in the theories of faculty psychology of the nineteenth century. According to these theories, the brain was a muscle to be exercised. Just as lifting barbells or bricks developed the muscles used in lifting, so also did mental gymnastics strengthen and exercise the mental muscles. During recent decades many language teachers as well as others dismissed this notion as an enrollment ploy of desperate Latin teachers; clearly we had learned that the brain was not a muscle. In light of today's knowledge, however, it may well be that these early intuitions were correct but that they simply had the wrong explanation for the phenomena.

IMPROVED COGNITIVE FUNCTIONING AND FOREIGN LANGUAGE STUDY

Current support and evidence comes from both cognitive learning theory and empirical research. One characteristic of most modern conceptualizations of learning is that they postulate learning as a pluralistic phenomenon. They also assign a major role to the learner. No single mechanism (for example, stimulus-response association) can account for all human behavior, nor can a full understanding of all the conditions surrounding the learning. Thus, in conceptualizations like those of Gagné,[6] Bloom,[7] Guilford,[8] or

6. Robert M. Gagné, *The Conditions of Learning*, 2d ed. (New York: Holt, Rinehart and Winston, 1970).

7. Benjamin S. Bloom et al., *Taxonomy of Educational Objectives, Handbook I: The Cognitive Domain* (New York: David McKay Co., 1956).

8. J. P. Guilford, "Three Faces of Intellect," *American Psychologist* 14 (August 1959): 469-79.

Ausubel,[9] learning is viewed as having multiple forms, levels, or varieties and as involving active participation of the learner. When these conceptualizations are applied to second-language tasks, one characteristic is immediately apparent: second-language learning is particularly rich or intense in the various types of learning or kinds of cognitive functioning. An analysis of a task in second-language learning (for example, reading a new sentence or paragraph), as compared with tasks in most other subjects, consistently indicates that more of the various types of learning are involved in the second-language task and that they appear to be virtually simultaneous rather than serial. Such analysis indicates, in other words, that a given amount of time spent in learning a language provides considerable experience in doing all of the various operations that the brain can do—perhaps more than occurs in most other human activities.

This richness or intensity of practice must be linked to another fundamental and well-established principle of learning. We learn what we practice, what we do, what we experience. Forty years ago, Bode wrote that every normal act of the mind leaves as an enduring result an increased power to act again in like manner. The power and tendency of the mind to observe are increased by observing, to imagine by imagining, to judge by judging, and to reason by reasoning.[10] Given this principle, it is entirely plausible to argue that language study provides especially abundant and relevant practice in all these mental skills. It should also be noted that such mental skills are largely beyond the range of today's capacity for measurement and research.

There is a growing body of research in support of this hypothesis, albeit indirect and sometimes flawed by weaknesses of design. Research in the United States on the question is unfortunately restricted by the fact that second-language study is universally an elective area, in one way or another. Students choose to study a language or choose a field that requires language study.

9. David P. Ausubel, Joseph D. Novak, and Helen Hanesian, *Educational Psychology: A Cognitive View,* 2d ed. (New York: Holt, Rinehart and Winston, 1978).

10. Boyd H. Bode, *How We Learn* (Boston: D. C. Heath, 1940), pp. 88-89.

Thus, one cannot claim that language students and nonlanguage students belong to the same population. It is entirely possible that the two groups of students may be inherently different in pertinent ways, since those favorably predisposed toward language study may already have better skills or greater potential for developing them. Without the possibility of random assignment to language study, research designs permitting causal inferences are precluded. An informal meta-analysis across the various studies nevertheless supports the hypothesis and provides clues to some of the kinds of benefits that may result.

Typical studies include that of Skelton, who found a significant relationship among college students between second-language study and superior academic performance.[11] He concluded that the study of a second language contributed to such performance by improving one's control of subject matter in fields where language was the vehicle of instruction. Although intelligence was controlled by the design, a causal relationship still cannot unequivocally be inferred.

Masciantonio has summarized evidence supporting benefits from the study of Latin.[12] His summary includes what are well described as program evaluations in Philadelphia; Indianapolis; Washington, D.C.; Easthampton, Massachusetts; Erie County, Pennsylvania; Alexandria, Virginia; Los Angeles; and Worcester, Massachusetts. In general, students of a second language in the elementary schools and, in some instances, in junior and senior high schools outperformed other students significantly on measures of English vocabulary, word knowledge, reading, and comprehension. Attitudes tended to be positive, and even self-concepts may have benefited.

The relationship between language study and higher verbal scores on the *Scholastic Aptitude Test* has been widely recognized.[13] Likewise, in other parts of the world similar findings sup-

11. Robert B. Skelton, "High School Foreign Language Study and Freshman Performance," *School and Society* 85 (June 8, 1957): 203-5.

12. Rudolph Masciantonio, "Tangible Benefits of the Study of Latin: A Review of Research," *Foreign Language Annals* 10 (September 1977): 375-82.

13. Merrill Sheils, "Why SAT Scores Decline," *Newsweek* 90 (September 5, 1977): 82-83.

port the benefit of language study in developing various verbal skills. In Australia, for example, Boyd concluded that transfer from second-language study contributed to improved performance in English vocabulary.[14] The study examined development between year seven and year ten in two Sydney high schools.

It should not be surprising that second-language study seems to benefit language-related abilities. In many ways studying a second language provides an opportunity to study language—not just a language but language in the abstract. One can step back and see it as a phenomenon or entity outside one's self. This perspective is usually impossible with one's native language, which is inseparably intertwined with one's own thought processes. Salience is clearly an important variable in learning and may account for benefits while learning the new language but before achieving genuine bilingualism.

An extensive analysis of the skills inherent and observable during language behavior could lead to a much more extensive list than is appropriate here. The list might include items such as learning that words which are virtual synonyms sometimes cannot be used interchangeably. Insights into the power of language to evoke tears, cause joy, or lead to wars are very apparent when one studies language from what is initially a great distance. Willingness to hypothesize about meaning—to guess the meaning of an unknown word—is a crucial skill in reading or listening behavior. Learning a new language provides an enormous amount of practice in this skill. Such a skill involves, furthermore, many important related skills, such as using all available information, tolerating ambiguity, and judging when to remain tentative and when to assign definite meaning to the new word. A list of such skills is less important here than the recognition of their pervasiveness in all daily human activity.

FLEXIBILITY, CREATIVITY, AND FOREIGN LANGUAGE STUDY

Various research efforts have also identified mental dexterity, flexibility, or creativity as other outcomes of language learning. Modern evidence dates back to 1962 in Canada, when Peal and

14. Rachel Boyd, "Influences of Foreign Language Study on English," *Babel* 13 (April 1977): 19-22.

Lambert concluded that the bilingual's "experience with two languages systems seems to have left him with a mental flexibility, . . . a more diversified set of mental abilities in the sense that the patterns of abilities developed by the bilinguals were more heterogeneous."[15] They found that the monolingual, in contrast, appeared to have a more unitary structure of intelligence that must be used for all types of intellectual tasks.

Cummins and Gulutsan recently replicated the Peal and Lambert study in a western Canadian setting.[16] Among their findings was a significantly higher level of verbal originality or divergent thinking for the second-language students. Carringer similarly found bilingual students superior to monolingual students on the verbal flexibility, verbal originality, figural fluency, and figural originality scales of the *Torrance Tests of Creative Thinking*.[17] During a five-year evaluation of an immersion program in Canada, Swain and Barik found that when a nonverbal battery of the *Canadian Cognitive Abilities Test* was used as a measure of intelligence in grade four, there was a significant difference favoring the immersion language students.[18] The subtests of this instrument are described as emphasizing a flexibility in manipulating relationships expressed in figure symbols or patterns.

In the United States, Landry detected greater creativity, as measured by tests of figural fluency and flexibility, among sixth-grade students who had studied a second language when compared to similar students without the language-learning experience.[19]

The outcomes of these studies (and several similar studies),

15. E. Peal and W. E. Lambert, "The Relations of Bilingualism to Intelligence," *Psychological Monographs* 76 (Whole no. 546, 1962).

16. James Cummins and Metro Gulutsan, "Some Effects of Bilingualism on Cognitive Functioning," in *Bilingualism, Biculturalism, and Education,* ed. Stephen T. Carey (Edmonton, Alberta: University of Alberta Press, 1974).

17. Dennis C. Carringer, "Creative Thinking Abilities of Mexican Youth: The Relationship of Bilingualism," *Journal of Cross-Cultural Psychology* 5 (December 1974): 492-504.

18. Merrill Swain and Henri C. Barik, *Five Years of Primary French Immersion* (Toronto: Ontario Institute for Studies in Education, 1976).

19. Richard G. Landry, "The Enhancement of Figural Creativity through Second Language Learning at the Elementary School Level," *Foreign Language Annals* 7 (October 1973): 111-15.

although variously described by labels like "cognitive flexibility," "mental dexterity," "creativity," and "intellectual agility," all seem to be a particular ability to see alternatives and options. In a way, one is better able to overcome the "blinders" of previous experience. One sees a fuller context of possibilities.

Such skills are not surprising when one analyzes the nature of language learning. It is difficult to set aside what is most familiar—one's way of thinking and communicating—and adopt a totally unfamiliar way of coding all one's environment and one's own thought creations. Flexibility is developed of necessity. In learning a language such as Arabic, for example, it is initially very difficult even to envision how a language could function without a verb "to be." As a novel perspective on the matter, it is entirely plausible to imagine an advertisement in a magazine like *Psychology Today* for a training program in intellectual flexibility. The advertisement might depict a psychologist showing a picture of a dog to a learner while saying, "This is no longer a dog; it's a *chien*," or "Here is the preposition *de*; it can have meanings like 'of,' 'from,' 'in,' 'toward,' or 'with.' Decide which is appropriate here."

The extent to which such abilities transfer is not clear. It may be that transfer extends through all one's potential to deal with the unfamiliar. Thus, even when confronting rapid technological or social change, which frequently produces "future shock," problems may be alleviated by experience in dealing with an unfamiliar language.

The evidence supporting intellectual benefits from language study comes from multiple sources and perspectives. Indeed, in that lies its persuasiveness. Any single argument is limited, and one can find fault with virtually any individual research study. We are dealing with subtle but important changes in the brain—not a very observable or accessible place. Value judgments are, moreover, inevitable. The collective effect of the evidence, however, is more impressive, as is the fact that the growing evidence is all consistent with the Whorfian hypothesis that language structures one's view of reality. Thus, many educators would today argue: study a second language; expand your potential by doubling your view of the world.

FOREIGN LANGUAGES AND "BACK TO THE BASICS"

The benefits to a society of any expansion of intellectual potential, even if we someday learn the expansion is relatively small, are cumulative. Moreover, such abilities take on even more importance in an era where one frequently hears a cry for "back to basics." Goodlad has convincingly presented a likely scenario for an excessive emphasis on basics:

My guess is that those relatively low-level cognitive processes most easily measured and most emphasized in the current back-to-basics movement will show some improvement in test scores during coming years. But my further guess is that those more complex intellectual processes not easily measured will decline at an equal or greater rate.

And I am convinced that continuation along the impoverished curricular and pedagogical lines implied by "back to basics" would lead ultimately to educational bankruptcy in our schools, acceleration in alienation and dropout rates, and in grades having even less relevance to life than they do now.[20]

Few would want to see the "pendulum model" predict the educational unrest that would result from Goodlad's scenario, particularly when subjects like languages have so much to offer.

Language Study and a Pluralistic Society

DISCARDING THE MELTING POT MODEL

The relationships among people have changed dramatically in our nation and in the entire world during the past decade. This change has a direct pertinence to language study. Pluralism is now recognized as an essential characteristic of today's world. Nationally, we have abandoned a melting-pot model, simply because it did not work, in favor of a culturally pluralistic concept of our society. Ethnic identity has become one prominent way, among several others, in which we see ourselves as diverse. Increasingly, we seem to be more accurately described as a mosaic of cultures, subcultures, interest groups, and differences among individuals. The news each day presents a panorama of varied groups asserting themselves.

20. John I. Goodlad, "Can Our Schools Get Better?" *Phi Delta Kappan* 60 (January 1979): 344.

A pluralistic society that is to flourish and maximize the quality of life for its members requires certain perceptions on the part of the members. It requires not only awareness of differences but also a valuing of diversity in people. Pluralism is the antithesis of an assimilation model, such as the melting pot that preceded it and that still has a legacy of conflicting attitudes. A pluralistic view recognizes that there are multiple ways to be a worthwhile human being and that not one of these multiple ways should exact a penalty of second-class citizenship. It is, in a sense, a recognition of "selfness." This recognition requires awareness that everyone has an identity, uniqueness, and value; moreover, it requires a subsequent value system that permits "me to be me and you to be you" and, at the same time, values a sense of community. In light of these needs and in light of 200 years of valuing the basic core that we all share more highly than the differences that make us unique, the role of education in optimizing a pluralistic society becomes all the more important.

UNDERSTANDING HUMAN DIVERSITY THROUGH LANGUAGE STUDY

Second-language learning has a unique affinity with these needs. To an educated person who sees others from a broad perspective, recognition that people differ dramatically is a very elementary observation. For a young person, however, it is a profound and significant bit of learning. No one is born with knowledge about sameness and differences among people. It is nevertheless an insight that can influence every interaction each of us has every single day of our lives. To some extent we learn about these differences in an incidental way as we mature and interact with others. At the same time, it must be argued that learning which is so crucial to the effective and harmonious functioning of society cannot be left to an incidental basis.

Second-language learning is pertinent in two ways. First, it is a long-established educational principle to present or model a concept or principle in its most vivid form or manifestation. Thus, the discovery of differences is best made in its most vivid context—differences from one culture to another. For most language students, the discovery that other people carry different realities in their heads is an extraordinary bit of learning. They have had only monocultural experiences; they have not seen the other side of where they live. Once tuned in to these differences, a person is more likely to perceive differences on any level or in any dimension (age, region, ethnic group, attitudes, occupation, values, and the like).

A second dimension of learning about people is sometimes overlooked, even by second-language teachers. Practicing the new language in a classroom can be a means to discovering and clarifying what one really is and how this is similar to and different from other students in the class. Our insights into our own unique natures are clearly increased when we make comparisons and contrasts between ourselves and others. By expressing what we think or feel about any topic or idea whatsoever and by hearing others express what they think or feel—all with the new language forms that are being learned—we inevitably learn what we are and what others are. Each of us is a product or composite of our experiences. As human beings, we have the ability to symbolize these experiences in words—words of our native language or, as we learn them, words of a new language. All that is necessary to cause this sharing to occur is the classroom use or practice of the new language in a meaningful way. Fortunately, techniques and materials for this type of practice are now available to instructors.

It should be acknowledged that in the past most language classes were not characterized by meaningful practice of the language where students send and receive messages. One could have observed classes in which students made statements in the foreign language such as "I don't like blue jeans," but one never knew whether the students did or did not like blue jeans. Usually, the student was only making the sounds of the words because the drill or exercise required the making of them. Sometimes the exercise looked very much like communication, but it was only a question-answer drill where each student was to answer the question negatively. It was only a semblance of communication, and there was no learning about people.

It is true that whether or not a person likes blue jeans is not especially important in the totality of life. But a like or a dislike is one particle that contributes to the make-up of a unique personality. When repeated with literally thousands of ideas, attitudes, perceptions, beliefs, and observations, a learner inevitably comes to understand better the self called "me" and how it is both like and unlike other "selfs." This is a very special value for the language classroom, which is uniquely free to deal with any content. Instead of being limited to geometric theorems, American history, or invertebrates, the content is as broad as people, life, the universe. In order to practice new vocabulary and structures the content can be anything.

Thus, second-language study is particularly suited to enhancing insights into the nature of humankind. It provides an expansion of one's perspective from a view that "everyone is nearly like me" to an understanding that "no one is quite like me." This fundamental insight will certainly become even more important in the newly interdependent world. Our contacts will expand, and our understanding and acceptance of diversity must likewise expand. Second-language learning has direct pertinence and value.

Conclusion

During the past 200 years, second-language study has not been accorded high priority in the United States. Such study was, in a word, "foreign." Likewise, the national milieu was not conducive to the study of other languages and cultures. As the country entered its third century, however, contact with other nations increased and our own heterogeneity was recognized. One might even envision neighborhoods someday populated by persons from other cultures (or who have lived in another culture) in a way that is analogous to today's neighborhoods being populated by persons brought up in other states. Concomitant with these changes is a growing concern with the quality of education that we are providing. The public, the media, and educators have all begun to question why Johnny has not seemed to be able to do much of anything. Of particular concern is the ability of young people in verbal areas.

These forces are neither trivial nor transitory fads. They are powerful and they each have a direct affinity with second-language study. Collectively they form a compelling rationale for the study of a second language by every young person. They do not argue for particular languages. There is a need for persons to know any of the nearly 3,000 languages of the world. Most of the benefits are not language-specific; they would accrue regardless of the language studied. It would seem that diversity in interests, supply and demand, and simple preferences and interests are adequate determiners of language choice. What seems much more important is the creation of a milieu where all or most persons will include some study of a language in their total educational experience. How much language study? Probably, the best answer is *any amount*. In any dimension of benefit, there seems to be a direct relation between the amount of benefit and the length of study. Nevertheless, a student who learns only to greet or count or read signs in another language has benefited compared to the student who has had no second-language experience. Many fundamental insights into the nature of language and the communication process occur in the beginning stages of language learning. No young person should be deprived of them.

The three areas of benefit accruing from language study are not all-inclusive. Some would argue that languages should be studied because, like Mt. Everest, they are there. Others would argue that such learning is responsive to basic human drives like curiosity. Still others would focus upon a particular activity like travel as a principal rationale for language study. All such reasons are compelling for certain persons, but not necessarily for everyone. The reasons emphasized in this chapter are relevant to anyone. They lead to an expansion of the context of one's own life —an expansion that is geographical, intellectual, and emotional. Second-language students come to see themselves as part of humanity—not an abstract humanity but one of interdependent people who must understand an increasingly complex world and who must care about one another in a way that has never before been realized. The citizens of the twenty-first century—our students—need language learning.

CHAPTER III

Psychology and Linguistics as Bases for Language Pedagogy

WILGA M. RIVERS

Introduction

THE "MIRACLE" OF LANGUAGE ACQUISITION

Parents and teachers alike are struck by the ease with which small children acquire language—the language or languages of their parents, their grandparents, or their playmates. They compare this with the often painfully slow and discouraging acquisition of a second or third language by teenagers and adults and wonder how one can replicate natural language learning in school situations. They want to see school learners using the language with some spontaneity and confidence and this also is seen as a desirable goal by the learners themselves. But how to achieve this goal in a reasonable amount of time, before discouragement sets in, has been, and continues to be, a major preoccupation of language teachers who care about motivation and the students' satisfaction in learning.

LINGUISTICS OR PSYCHOLOGY?

The obvious disciplines to which to turn for help in achieving this goal are linguistics and psychology, the sciences that investigate respectively the content and the process of language learning. In other words, we ask, "What is language?" so that we may see how best to present language material to facilitate student learning; or we ask, "How do individuals acquire a language so that they can use it effectively in life situations?" and then try to apply answers developed by behavioral research in psychology to language learning in and out of the classroom. The importance of both of these questions, and the many unresolved issues which linguists and psycholinguists face, have, rightly or wrongly, kept language pedagogy, as an applied field, in a ferment for nearly half a century, to go back no further. Linguistics is an ancient preoccupation of scholars and a relatively young science, as is psychology. Modern psychology and modern linguistics have both burst into full vigor since the latter part of the nineteenth century. They have thus shared in that evolving spirit of the times which can be seen through history to influence scientists in various disciplines at approximately the same period, as new findings radically modify previously unquestioned theoretical models. We will now trace the influence of the switches and changes in theoretical orientations in linguistics and psychology on the teaching of second languages in the United States.

Language Use As Patterned Oral Behavior

In the 1920s and 1930s, most behavioral psychologists were committed to a nonintrospective study of human behavior which concentrated on what could be objectively observed, described, and measured, without resort to the presumption of inner motives or innate mechanisms as determinants. Since much of overt human behavior takes the form of actions repeated in similar circumstances (that is, in response to similar stimuli), learning theorists of this period focused on habits and tried to determine how they are acquired. They observed and measured events which co-occur when habits are formed (stimuli and responses) and they manipulated the consequences of responses to study the effect these had on repeated occurrence. They tried to find out why habits sometimes disappeared. Extending Thorndike's work on reward and punishment (his law of effect, elaborated at the turn of the century), reinforcement theorists maintained that an action was most likely to recur when pleasurable consequences followed immediately upon its appearance, and that the continuation of this sequence of stimulus-response-reward increased the probability of specific actions recurring in response to particular stimuli, thus establishing a habit pattern.

Language behavior was regarded by reinforcement theorists as being the same in kind as other forms of behavior and, therefore, subject to the same laws of learning. In this paradigm, language acquisition was described as follows. As an infant is babbling, it utters a sound which resembles the appropriate word for some person or object nearby. This utterance is rewarded or reinforced, with approving noises and smiles from the person attending to the child and, as a consequence, the probability of the emission of the same groups of sounds in a similar situation is increased. With repeated reinforcement a habit is established and the child continues to name the person or object in the same way. Inappropriate responses disappear through lack of reinforcement. As more combinations of sounds are reinforced and as the use of these is generalized to similar stimuli, the child learns to combine verbal responses in more and more complex ways. Oral responses are gradually refined through differential reinforcement in actual communication situations.

During the years when the reinforcement theorists were elaborating this model of learning, structural linguists were taking specimens of language as emitted (often for little-known languages, such as the American Indian languages) and endeavoring to describe the regularities of their phonological and grammatical patterning, without having to resort to the nuances of meaning particular speakers intended to convey. They were thus able to bypass what seemed to them the murky quagmire of semantics in their descriptions of linguistic behavior. Following the lead of the cultural anthropologists of the period, the structuralists viewed language use as a set of habits acquired within the social group in which the child was growing up. The set of arbitrary vocal symbols which constituted the language of the group was clearly encountered in spoken form first and this was the form acquired by the child. Since in many cultures written language is nonexistent, the spoken language was regarded by the structuralists as of primary importance.

A number of these structural linguists were language teachers in universities. During World War II, others became interested in language teaching when the American defense authorities called on the linguists to help develop as rapidly as possible a large pool of interpreters for different languages, many of them not generally taught in regular academic institutions.

Not surprisingly, linguists trained to describe and analyze recurring surface forms of language, without necessarily having recourse to meaning as the key to use, found compatible a psychological approach to habit formation which similarly did not require presumptions of unobservable mental processes at work. The methods the structural linguists as language teachers developed for language learning similarly emphasized overt patterned behavior of responses to stimuli. This combination of habit-formation techniques became known as the audiolingual approach. Because of its success in the army training programs, the techniques of the audiolingual approach gradually became the predominant methodology in teaching English to foreign students who were flocking into the universities. Soon it spread to foreign-language classrooms in colleges and high schools. It retained the emphasis on spoken language of the structuralists and on teaching the language as it is spoken in everyday circumstances by native speakers.

THE AUDIOLINGUAL APPROACH

The hallmark of audiolingual teaching, then, is emphasis on presentation of the language in its spoken form first. Only after practice in the aural-oral mode (first listening, then producing utterances) are students presented with a graphic representation of what they have been learning.

Initial language study usually takes the form of the memorization of dialogues, which are composed of useful situational utterances that can be varied to meet a number of conversational needs within the foreign culture. Students learn to give responses to the stimuli of the dialogue sentences, at first in the exact form memorized, then with variations. Grammar is learned through drilling in substitution, expansion, or conversion of elements in the language patterns. These drills often concentrate on points of contrast between the structure of the native language and that of the foreign language, as being areas of probable interference from well-established first-language habits. Explanation, which usually comes after the initial practice, is kept to the minimum required for comprehension of the working of particular structures. In this pattern or structure drilling, quickfire response with immediate confirmation of the correct form is the focus.

Reading is introduced systematically, beginning with the reading of what has been learned orally, with careful attention to sound-symbol correspondences. Texts move through various levels of reading difficulty until the student can read all kinds of materials. Writing acts as a supportive exercise to oral learning in the early stages. Translation does not figure prominently in learning activities, except that native-language stimuli are used occasionally to elicit responses in the foreign language during structure drill. A few written exercises may involve translation when this is the most direct way to elicit complex responses, such as idiomatic expressions which it is preferable not to analyze.

The objective of the audiolingual approach is to provide students, as soon as possible, with useful building blocks of language material which they can use in communication and from which they can generalize by analogy to parallel forms and functions. These useful expressions and structures are to be learned to a level of automatic production through saturation practice. Choral response is frequently elicited in class to provide every student with many opportunities to produce acceptable responses in a situation where confirmation of the right response is immediately available. Practice in the language laboratory, or with recorded cassettes, also gives students ample opportunity to practice structures in a stimulus-response format, with immediate confirmation by the recorded model of the correct response. Both the learning materials and the classroom situation are structured in such a way that the student need rarely make mistakes and, in this way, correct habits are presumed to be formed. To ensure transfer to real-life conversational situations, all language material is presented with authentic native accents and intonation at a speed of utterance which is normal for speakers of that language. The ultimate aim is for students to achieve near-native mastery of the language and this presumes a long sequence of study, even though quite spectacular results in language use within structured bounds can be observed very early in the learning process.[1]

1. For a more detailed account of audiolingual techniques, see Wilga M. Rivers, *Teaching Foreign-Language Skills* (Chicago: University of Chicago Press, 1968), chap. 2.

MODIFYING THE AUDIOLINGUAL APPROACH

In the early 1960s, criticisms were leveled against the audio-lingual approach.[2] These focused on the overemphasis on tedious mechanistic processes to which the student is not expected to make any spontaneous, personal contribution. Critics questioned whether real learning can take place when students are giving automatic responses in drill, without understanding the crucial element they are practicing or its relationship to other features of the language system. It was found that students who could use with facility language material in the exact form in which it had been practiced in dialogues or drills were at a loss to adapt this material for the expression of a multitude of personal meanings in communication with others. The value of learning by trial and error began to be reemphasized. Structured situations in which students would rarely make errors were found to provide insufficient preparation for spontaneous expression which requires flexibility, alertness, and audacity in extending what one has learned to new contexts. Teachers began to realize that if students were to communicate, they needed practice in communicating personal messages, not just formulas presented by the teacher or the textbook writer. Finally, individual differences in students received fresh consideration. It began to be recognized, once again, that some students learn efficiently through oral materials, whereas others need the support of a visual representation; some students feel traumatized when they are expected to produce rapid foreign-language responses, while others feel stimulated.

As a result of these criticisms, modifications were made to prevalent audiolingual practices. More explanation was provided before or during practice. More attention was paid to the creation in the classroom of situations as close to real-life language interaction as possible, and new materials attempted to present the culture in which the language is embedded in a more authentic way. Above all, teachers felt the need to relax the tension of early language learning. They sought to introduce more variety of activity, more friendliness and humor, within an atmosphere in which the stu-

2. For an early evaluation and critique, see Wilga M. Rivers, *The Psychologist and the Foreign-Language Teacher* (Chicago: University of Chicago Press, 1964).

dents felt at ease with the teacher and with each other, in what could otherwise be an ego-threatening situation.

The Mentalistic Trend

The tide in linguistics and in psychology soon turned definitively. Linguistic theorists declared themselves to be frankly "mentalistic" and cognitive psychology became active in studying processes of the mind. Perception, memory, thinking, how meaning is encoded and expressed, and information processing became areas of major concern. Languages were no longer regarded by the linguists as distinct sets of arbitrary vocal symbols, nor as systems of habits acquired through conditioning by the psychologists. Transformational-generative linguistic theory pointed out that apparent similarity of surface forms of a language may camouflage important differences in meaning, and that drilling of such surface features, indiscriminately selected, can lead to error when the student begins to extend by analogy the use of structures that have been practiced in a mechanical, unthinking fashion.

Chomsky hypothesized that language was not acquired by children through a form of conditioning dependent on reinforcement or reward. He maintained that human beings come into the world with innate language-learning abilities in the form of a language acquisition device that proceeds by hypothesis testing. Children make hypotheses about the form of the grammar of the language they are learning and compare this with their innate knowledge of possible grammars based on the principles of universal grammar. In this way, the individual's competence, or internalized knowledge of the grammar of the language, is built up and this competence makes language use, or performance, possible. Language use is thus rule-governed behavior that enables speakers to create new utterances which conform to the rules they have internalized.[3]

The terms "rule-governed behavior," "creative language use,"

3. See Noam Chomsky, *Aspects of the Theory of Syntax* (Cambridge, Mass.: MIT Press, 1965), pp. 25-26, and idem, "Linguistic Theory," in *Language Teaching: Broader Contexts*, ed. Robert G. Mead, Jr., in *Reports of the Working Committees* (Middlebury, Vt.: Northeast Conference on the Teaching of Foreign Languages, 1966), pp. 43-49.

and "hypothesis testing" soon replaced "building in habits" and "saturation practice" as the catchwords of language teaching.

RULE-GOVERNED BEHAVIOR

The words "rule-governed" applied to language use appealed to those teachers who had worried about the fact that rules of grammar were not systematically presented, explained, and learned in the inductive procedures of the audiolingual approach. They proposed a return to explaining grammar rules first, thus involving students' reasoning processes in language learning, in contrast to what some called the "mindless" drilling in audiolingual classes. This emphasis on explanations of grammatical functioning was a major feature of what came to be known as cognitive-code learning.

Chastain claimed as the "one basic tenet of the cognitive approach" that "students [should] never be expected to meet new structures prior to the explanation of those forms." "The term 'cognition'," he continued, "implies proceeding from mental understanding and awareness to practice; from studying a structure to seeing it used in context."[4] Chastain's deductive order of learning was the following: step 1, comprehension of new grammatical concepts which are presented deductively; step 2, practice in selection of linguistic forms to fit the context in exercises; step 3, the study of reading and listening materials, with some opportunity provided for students to produce messages intended to communicate their thoughts to another person.[5] This approach put language analysis before language use and instruction by the teacher before the student practices forms. That a deductive instructional approach of this type is more "cognitive" than the inductive, discovery approach to grammar of audiolingual methodology cannot be sustained on the basis of any psychological evidence, since induction requires just as much cognitive processing as deduction. Furthermore, the "rules" to which Chomsky had been referring were not pedagogical explanations of language functioning but rules "of great abstractness and intricacy" inherent in the structure

4. Kenneth Chastain, *The Development of Modern-Language Skills: Theory to Practice* (Philadelphia: Center for Curriculum Development, 1971), p. 48.

5. Kenneth Chastain, *Developing Second-Language Skills: Theory to Practice,* 2d ed. (Chicago: Rand McNally, 1976), pp. 156-57.

of a language, which according to Chomsky there is no reason to suppose can be brought to conscious awareness.[6] However, the spirit of the times was such that these facts were usually ignored in the rush to be in the vanguard.

In 1971, Carroll, who had first advanced the term "cognitive-code learning" in an article in 1965,[7] deplored the growing tendency to oppose "rule-governed behavior" and "habits" as incompatible concepts in language learning. He defined a "habit" as "any learned disposition to perceive, behave, or perform in a certain manner under specified circumstances." He further maintained that "to the extent that an individual's language behavior conforms to the habits of the speech community of which he is a member, we can say that his behavior is 'rule-governed'." To Carroll, a rule is an abstraction, but a habit is what has actually been learned; in other words, "the notion of 'habit' is much more fundamental, psychologically, than the notion of 'rule'." [8] This article was heeded by those who had ears to hear, but overlooked or not discovered by others.

CREATIVE LANGUAGE USE

Chomsky drew attention to the fact that most sentences one utters have never been heard before in that particular form. They have been created by the speakers in conformity with the grammar they have internalized (the individual's "competence," in Chomsky's terms). Miller supported this viewpoint graphically, as follows:

If you interrupt a speaker at some randomly chosen instant, there will be, on the average, about ten words that form grammatical and meaningful continuations. . . . A simple English sentence can easily run to a

6. Noam Chomsky, *Topics in the Theory of Generative Grammar* (The Hague: Mouton, 1966), p. 10. For a more detailed discussion of Chomsky's viewpoint, see Wilga M. Rivers, *Speaking in Many Tongues*, 2d ed. (Rowley, Mass.: Newbury House, 1976), chap. 1, "Rules, Patterns, and Creativity," pp. 9-20.

7. John B. Carroll, "The Contributions of Psychological Theory and Educational Research to the Teaching of Foreign Languages," *Modern Language Journal* 49 (May 1965): 273-81.

8. John B. Carroll, "Current Issues in Psycholinguistics and Second Language Teaching," *TESOL Quarterly* 5 (June 1971): 103-4.

length of twenty words, so elementary arithmetic tells us that there must be at least 10^{20} such sentences that a person who knows English must know how to deal with. Compare this productive potential with the 10^4 or 10^5 individual words we know—the reproductive component of our theory—and the discrepancy is dramatically illustrated. Putting it differently, it would take 100,000,000,000 centuries (one thousand times the estimated age of the earth) to utter all the admissible twenty-word sentences of English. Thus, the probability that you might have heard any particular twenty-word sentence before is negligible. Unless it is a cliché, every sentence must come to you as a novel combination of morphemes. Yet you can interpret it at once if you know the English language.[9]

Affirmations such as these caused teachers to take another look at the popular technique of requiring students to memorize long dialogue sentences and practice using them in the precise form memorized. This viewpoint added support to the reemphasis on teaching students to understand the operations of the grammatical system, so that they could use it effectively to generate new utterances. It also reinforced the trend toward encouraging students from the beginning stages to experiment creatively with the small amount of language they had acquired, thus learning to form new combinations to meet new circumstances. Teachers began to provide many more opportunities for spontaneous discussion and for impromptu activities that simulated actual situations in which the students might find themselves in the foreign culture. Writers of materials looked carefully at their dialogues and concentrated on producing much shorter exchanges, containing useful building blocks of language that students could adapt to express their meaning in their own way.

HYPOTHESIS TESTING

The theory of an innate language acquisition device that proceeds by hypothesis testing had considerable influence for a while on studies of the acquisition of a first language by children. This led researchers interested in the acquisition of second and third languages to investigate whether a later language was acquired in

9. George A. Miller, "The Psycholinguists," in *The Psychology of Communication: Seven Essays* (New York: Basic Books, 1967), pp. 79-80.

the same fashion as the first language, drawing in some way on the same innate language acquisition faculty.

A number of early studies in second-language acquisition tried to find a parallelism between the order of acquisition of a limited number of grammatical morphemes of English by first-language learners (L_1) and second-language learners (L_2).[10] This they felt would demonstrate that the L_1 and L_2 learners were following a similar developmental path and using comparable strategies in language acquisition. The order of acquisition of these morphemes was found to be significantly different for L_1 and L_2 learners, although the same morphemes did seem to be among the first acquired by both groups of learners. The acquisition order of morphemes reported for L_2 was considered by some to be an artifact of the measuring instrument.[11] Others found that the order of acquisition reported for L_1 correlated highly with some features of the language the children were hearing from their mothers (Motherese).[12] L_2 researchers then became interested in the speech L_2 learners were hearing. This reintroduced the question of the role of imitation and environmental factors versus that of innate developmental strategies in L_2 acquisition.

Research on second-language acquisition is still in its early stages and, to date, efforts have concentrated for the most part on the acquisition of a second language by young children (and some adults) in informal settings or bilingual classes.[13] Some studies of older learners in formal instructional settings are being conducted

10. The particular morphemes involved in these studies are listed in Nathalie Bailey, Carolyn Madden, and Stephen D. Krashen, "Is There a 'Natural Sequence' in Adult Second Language Learning?" *Language Learning* 24 (December 1974): 236.

11. John H. Porter, "A Cross-Sectional Study of Morpheme Acquisition in First Languages Learners," *Language Learning* 27 (June 1977): 59.

12. Elissa L. Newport, Henry Gleitman, and Lila R. Gleitman, "Mother, I'd Rather Do It Myself: Some Effects and Non-effects of Maternal Speech Style," in *Talking to Children: Language Input and Acquisition*, ed. Catherine E. Snow and Charles A. Ferguson (Cambridge: Cambridge University Press, 1977), pp. 109-149.

13. For a useful summary and assessment of developments in this area, see Kenji Hakuta and Herlinda Cancino, "Trends in Second-Language Acquisition Research," *Harvard Educational Review* 47 (August 1977): 294-316.

and these should provide more useful insights for the foreign-language classroom teacher.[14]

Researchers on first-language acquisition with a strong interest in syntax observed that young children seemed to pass through a series of interim grammars, of increasing degrees of complexity, as they tested hypotheses about the form of the language they were learning. These interim grammars were described and studied synchronically as discrete syntactic systems. This approach interested those concerned with the acquisition of second or foreign languages and the term "interlanguage" came into use to describe the kind of language a particular second-language learner was using at a given time,[15] that is, the learner's version of the new language, which deviated in certain ways from that of a native speaker. This interlanguage was considered to be the product of hypotheses the second-language learner was testing about the form of the grammar of the new language. Lack of comprehension on the part of the hearer, or inability to draw coherent meaning from a text, would lead the learner to reject one hypothesis and develop another, thus modifying the interim grammar which had produced the aberrant utterance or interpretation. Controversy raged as to the degree of interference, or negative transfer, from the first language which could be detected in the student's interlanguage and the degree to which deviations from authentic second-language forms represented developmental errors of a universal character (that is, deviant forms similar to those observable in children learning the same language as a first language or in other children from different language backgrounds learning this particular language as a second language).

Some L_2 researchers discounted the notion of interference, or negative transfer, from first-language use rather vehemently, because they saw it as support for a habit-formation view of language acquisition. (Positive transfer is more difficult to distinguish from

14. See, for instance, Jacquelyn Schachter, A. F. Tyson, and F. J. Diffley, "Learner Intuitions of Grammaticality," *Language Learning* 26 (June 1976): 67-76, and Herbert W. Seliger, "Does Practice Make Perfect? A Study of Interaction Patterns and L_2 Competence," *Language Learning* 27 (December 1977): 263-78.

15. Larry Selinker, "Interlanguage," *International Review of Applied Linguistics in Language Teaching* 10 (August 1972): 209-31.

new learning.) Later longitudinal L_2 acquisition studies, however, brought to light instances of what looked very like negative transfer of L_1 features, or at least of L_1 concepts, in L_2 use, although the nature and degree of such transfer is still under investigation. It has been suggested that what has been observed represents hypothesis testing, in the sense that L_2 learners are testing the hypothesis that L_2 structure $= L_1$ structure. It may also represent the natural process of falling back on what one knows and adapting it, when faced with a situation for which one does not have the L_2 linguistic means.

Whatever the final issue of this controversy, foreign-language classroom teachers were rather bemused and bewildered to be told that negative transfer from L_1 was practically nonexistent, since they had regularly observed instances of something which looked very like it in the speech and writing of their L_2 learners.

The hypothesis-testing and interlanguage theories slowly began to affect classroom practice. Teachers who had been trained to structure classroom situations so that students would not make errors, or hear errors from others, were now urged to accept errors in second-language production as indicators of progress through interim grammars and as guides to the incorrect hypotheses their students had formed. Others pointed out that a study of the errors made by individual students would reveal to the teacher the strategies these students were employing in trying to learn the language. Attention was also drawn to the problem of fossilized forms, that is, incorrect forms which remain in the speech and writing of student learners despite the fact that they have been taught, and appear to understand, the rules. Since, in testing hypotheses, a serious disconfirmation causes one to seek another hypothesis that fits the facts and to adjust one's operation accordingly, this well-documented existence of fossilized forms which persist, often for years, in the speech of well-informed second-language speakers has to be taken into consideration as an awkward fact by supporters of the hypothesis-testing approach.

NATURAL LANGUAGE LEARNING

The convergence of the emphases just discussed has led to the emergence of a new-old approach to the learning of another language. Called "natural language learning,"[16] it recalls efforts in the middle of the nineteenth century to simulate in the classroom an environment that will approximate the context in which children learn their first language, as they create utterances to express their own thoughts.

In its latest form, this methodology does not overlook the need that adolescent or adult learners feel for the security of structured learning. Students study the grammar of the language out of class (as programmed or individualized preparation based on the textbook or language laboratory practice), so that class time can be devoted to communicative interaction from a basis of linguistic knowledge. This means skill-getting out of class and skill-using in group activities in class. The proponents of "natural language learning" maintain that, in this way, the innate capacities to acquire a language that all individuals possess will be tapped; students will have ample opportunities to test their hypotheses about the nature of the new language; their interim grammars will be accepted and tolerated while they are refining their hypotheses through individual study, and they will get much practice in creating new utterances in actual communication.

Meaning in Social Contexts

The field of sociolinguistics, or sociology of language, had been growing rapidly during the 1960s and 1970s. This branch of linguistics concerns itself particularly with language as it is used for communication within the social group. It employs the concepts and research techniques of sociology and social psychology, as well as linguistics. It brings to light interesting information about language in organized communicative interaction within a community, about domains of language use, speech varieties within a community, the language behavior of ethnic groups, bilingualism and multilingualism, and language planning at a national level. Clearly, these are subjects of great concern to the language teacher.

16. For a description of this approach to natural language learning, see Tracy D. Terrell, "A Natural Approach to Second Language Acquisition and Learning," *Modern Language Journal* 61 (November 1977): 325-37.

COMMUNICATIVE COMPETENCE

Hymes elaborated a concept of "communicative competence," which soon began to affect the foreign-language teaching community. To Hymes, the most novel and important aspect of sociolinguistic research was to establish the "rules, patterns, purposes, and consequences of language use, and to account for their interrelations." According to Hymes, the child learning the first language acquires, along with a system of grammar, "a system of its use, regarding persons, places, purposes, other modes of communication, . . . patterns of the sequential use of language in conversation, address, standard routines."[17] In other words, "communicative competence" represents "what a speaker needs to know to communicate effectively in culturally significant settings."[18]

Although the term "communicative competence" was batted around as though it meant "creative language use," Hymes's concepts soon began to have considerable effect. Writers of materials and classroom teachers realized that students needed to know more than how to express ideas in correct grammatical patterns (or in incorrect patterns, as they struggled to express ideas and concepts for which they did not yet have the linguistic means). Students needed also to know the culturally acceptable ways of interacting orally with others—appropriate levels of language to use in different situations; conversational gambits; what gestures and other body language were appropriate; when one might intervene in conversation and when one should wait for others; what questions and comments might be made and which would offend. They also needed to understand the message content of stress and intonation.

As the study of the culture in which the second language is embedded became a preeminent preoccupation in foreign-language teaching, these matters began to receive more emphasis. Teachers and students alike realized that, if this type of cultural competence was to be acquired, they needed opportunities to interact with

17. Dell Hymes, *Foundations in Sociolinguistics: An Ethnographic Approach* (Philadelphia: University of Pennsylvania Press, 1974), p. 75.

18. John J. Gumperz and Dell Hymes, *Directions in Sociolinguistics: The Ethnography of Communication* (New York: Holt, Rinehart and Winston, 1972), p. vii., and Dell Hymes, "The Ethnography of Speaking," in *Readings in the Sociology of Language,* ed. Joshua A. Fishman (The Hague: Mouton, 1968), pp. 99-138.

native speakers in natural settings. Teachers, therefore, encouraged participation in such activities as exchange programs and study abroad, ethnic festivals, and language camps, where communicative interaction might take place in authentic social contexts. Where it was appropriate, students were encouraged to mingle with the local community of speakers of the language they were learning, and help them when they could. Teaching aides and paraprofessionals were also recruited from the local community in some cases to add authenticity to the classroom experience.

SEMANTICS AND PRAGMATICS

Meanwhile, the theoretical linguists had been exploring new areas. The case grammar of Fillmore,[19] the generative semantics of John R. Ross, George Lakoff, and James D. McCawley,[20] and the meaning-structure grammar of Chafe[21] all declared semantics to be basic to any theoretical model of language. With the emphasis on semantics, pragmatics rose in importance, since meaning was seen to be dependent to a large degree on the situations in which speech acts occurred. Pragmatics had been particularly stressed by the functionalists whose interests lay in the study of language in use. The purposes language serves in normal interaction were seen by the functionalists to be basic to the determination of syntactic functions.[22]

These approaches influenced work on first-language acquisition. Researchers like R. W. Brown and I. M. Schlesinger found the early utterances of young children to be more readily explicable in semantic terms, such as agent, action, instrument, patient, ex-

19. Charles J. Fillmore, "The Case for Case," in *Universals in Linguistic Theory*, ed. Emmon Bach and Robert T. Harms (New York: Holt, Rinehart and Winston, 1968), pp. 1-88.

20. See George Lakoff, "On Generative Semantics," in *Semantics: An Interdisciplinary Reader in Philosophy, Linguistics, and Psychology* (Cambridge: Cambridge University Press, 1971), pp. 232-96.

21. Wallace L. Chafe, *Meaning and the Structure of Language* (Chicago: University of Chicago Press, 1970).

22. For a fuller discussion of these developments, see Wilga M. Rivers, "Language and Cognition: Directions and Implications," in *Language in American Life*, ed. E. Michael Gerli, James E. Alatis, and Richard I. Brod (Washington, D.C.: Georgetown University Press, 1978), pp. 32-44.

periencer, or what Brown called "semantic roles." Others preferred to emphasize functions. Bruner found that "use is a powerful determinant of rule structures," [23] and Halliday analyzed his
child's initial utterances in terms of distinct functions (instrumental,
regulatory, interactional, personal, heuristic, imaginative, representa-
tional, and ritual).[24]

Language teachers found the functional approach of more
value for application than some of the more abstract linguistic
models of the preceding decade.[25] There was a growing emphasis
on designing classroom activities, so that the language use elicited
would reflect normal purposes of language in interactional contexts. Teachers began to recognize the artificiality of many language exercises and adapt them so that they reflected more authentic
uses of language.[26]

There were proposals to reconstruct the language syllabus so
that learning communicative conventions would become as important as learning grammatical conventions. Wilkins proposed a
"notional syllabus" that is "organized in terms of the purposes for
which people are learning language and the kinds of language
performance that are necessary to meet those purposes." [27] A
notional syllabus implies a careful analysis of particular communicative situations in order to identify what students should most
usefully be able to communicate in those situations. Only then can

23. Jerome S. Bruner, "From Communication to Language—A Psychological
Perspective," *Cognition* 3, no. 3 (1974-75): 283.

24. Michael A. K. Halliday, *Learning How to Mean: Explorations in the
Development of Language* (London: Edward Arnold, 1975; New York:
Elsevier-North Holland, 1977).

25. For an application of Halliday's functions to language teaching, see
Wilga M. Rivers, "The Natural and the Normal in Language Teaching:
Where's the Difference?" in *Personalizing Foreign Language Instruction:
Learning Styles and Teaching Options*, ed. Renate A. Schulz (Skokie, Ill.:
National Textbook Co., 1977), pp. 101-8.

26. See Rivers, *Speaking in Many Tongues*, chap. 2, "Talking off the Tops
of Their Heads" and idem, *A Practical Guide to the Teaching of French*
(New York: Oxford University Press, 1975). See also companion volumes for
the Teaching of German, Spanish, and English as a second or foreign language
(1975-78).

27. David A. Wilkins, *Notional Syllabuses* (Oxford: Oxford University
Press, 1976), p. 13.

one decide the most appropriate forms to be learned by the students. "In short, the linguistic content is planned according to the semantic demands of the learner." [28]

A notional syllabus would deal with such categories as time, quantity, space, relational meaning, judgment and evaluation, suasion, argument, rational enquiry and exposition, personal emotions, and emotional relations, rather than such traditional grammatical areas as definite and indefinite articles, moods, tenses, relative and interrogative pronouns. For the learning sequence, Wilkins proposed a cyclical, rather than linear, presentation of concepts and functions, so that as they advance students will be learning to express the same semantic notions with more finesse and nuance. Role playing becomes an important activity in this type of learning.

Elaboration of a notional syllabus has been undertaken by the language specialists of the Council of Europe, particularly to meet the needs of adults within the European Economic Community. A threshold level, or basic course, has been developed which sets out in specific detail exactly what students with minimum requirements should know in order to communicate in particular situations.[29] Work is proceeding in adapting this approach to the needs of the schools and to teaching adults by television.

In 1978, New York State issued a curriculum guide, *Modern Languages for Everyone*, which aimed at meeting the needs of students who wished to learn a language with particular purposes in mind. This curriculum proposed a basic course which would be followed by a series of options: a four-skill sequence, a listening-speaking sequence, a reading-writing sequence, and special-interest courses (like "French for Travelers," "German for Auto Mechanics," "Music and Dance in Hebrew," "Spanish for Community Service"). This curriculum culminated nearly a decade of

28. Ibid., p. 19.

29. See Council for Cultural Cooperation, *Systems Development in Adult Language Learning* (Strasbourg: Council of Europe, 1973), which contains contributions by: J. L. M. Trim, René Richterich, J. A. Van Ek, and David A. Wilkins; J. A. Van Ek, *The Threshold Level in a European Unit/Credit System for Modern Language Learning for Adults* (Strasbourg: Council of Europe, 1975); and René Richterich and Jean-Louis Chancerel, *Identifying the Needs of Adults Learning a Foreign Language* (Strasbourg: Council of Europe, 1977).

experimentation in the schools with diversified options, mini-courses, and the like.[30]

Language and Cognition

Early in the 1970s, some cognitive psychologists who were interested in language acquisition, production, and comprehension began to find the abstract theoretical models of transformational-generative linguists too constricting in their research.[31] From trying to show experimentally that models proposed by the linguists had psychological reality, they returned to developing their own models from their research findings and testing these empirically. Others devoted their energies to the promising and burgeoning areas of perception and computer simulation of cognitive processing. It seemed to many that what might be innate was not so much a specific capacity to acquire languages as general cognitive and perceptual processes which were basic to other areas of human learning as well. Thus, it became easier to align psychological studies of language acquisition and use with the findings of Piaget on the stages of cognitive development from infancy to maturity.

Just as much new information was becoming available on perceptual processes, sections of the language teaching profession were turning their attention to listening and reading. Postovsky advocated an initial period of listening to a new language, with writing as a supporting activity, before students would attempt to produce anything orally. He considered this a more efficient approach than practicing structures and memorizing sentences of the language. In his experiments, students were not expected to begin to produce sentences themselves for some time, unless they felt like doing so.[32] Whether teachers accepted this view or not, they began to pay much more attention to developing the listening skill as a most important area of language learning. It was realized

30. For mini-courses, see Frank M. Grittner, *Teaching Foreign Languages,* 2d ed. (New York: Harper and Row, 1977), pp. 197-201, 279-83.

31. As one example, see Dan I. Slobin, *Psycholinguistics* (Glenview, Ill.: Scott, Foresman and Co., 1971), p. 24.

32. Valerian Postovsky, "Why Not Start Speaking Later?" in *Viewpoints on English as a Second Language,* ed. Marina Burt, Heidi Dulay, and Mary Finocchiaro (New York: Regents Publishing Co., 1977), pp. 17-26.

that for developing ability to understand native speakers, students needed much practice in listening to authentic materials recorded in natural situations, rather than to artificial materials concocted for school purposes.[33] Reading again achieved prominence as an important area of language learning and much attention was paid to new information on the reading process as "a psycholinguistic guessing game."[34]

Research into cognitive processes is an area which teachers will watch with interest as they look for guidance in improving the teaching and learning of languages. As teachers of second or foreign languages, we are interested in how human beings perceive messages, in speech or writing, and how they process and interpret them. We are interested in the way new information is transformed by receivers as they relate it to information already stored; how what they receive is recoded and organized for storage, not as atomic items but within complex semantic networks; how recoded information moves from short-term to long-term storage, and how it is retrieved. We are interested in forgetting, which is intricately involved with the concept of memory as an active process, not as a repository of inert items. This leads us to what will be remembered. Here we are at one of the interfaces between cognitive and dynamic psychology, because what we process from what we perceive is related to individual motivation and meaningfulness. We can learn much also from studies of concept development, particularly cross-cultural conceptualization, and for the teaching of another culture we need to understand the formation and retention of stereotypes and how these may be adapted and changed.

The Affective Element

Sensitive teachers have always recognized the determining role that the affective component plays in interpersonal communication. Students who do not feel at ease with their teacher and their fellow

33. See Rivers, *A Practical Guide to the Teaching of French,* chap. 3, "Listening" and parallel volumes for German, Spanish, and English as a second or foreign language.

34. Kenneth S. Goodman, "Reading: A Psycholinguistic Guessing Game," *Journal of the Reading Specialist* 6 (May 1967): 126-35, and *Psycholinguistics and Reading,* ed. Frank Smith (New York: Holt, Rinehart and Winston, 1973).

students are reluctant to attempt to express themselves in another language—an experience which involves not only stripping oneself of the protective devices that refined use of a well-known language provides, but also returning to a much less mature level of expression which can make the adolescent or adult learner feel both foolish and vulnerable. Once language learning becomes more than the study of rules and paradigms, and their exemplification and demonstration in reading and writing, and moves toward real communication of ideas, emotions, and aspirations, dynamic and personality psychology have a contribution to make. For these reasons, affect-based approaches to learning began to have an impact on foreign-language teaching in the 1970s, in particular humanistic psychology, as elaborated by Maslow, Rogers, and Brown.[35]

Maslow maintained that the individual has a hierarchy of needs to be satisfied: at base level, there are physiological needs to be filled; then, in ascending order, needs for security, belongingness, esteem for self and for others, and finally self-realization, which cannot be achieved while the lower-level needs remain unsatisfied. These needs of the individual lead to complex interrelationships within a group, the individuals of which are in need of support and fulfillment at different levels of the hierarchy at any one time. Since any genuine communication requires that one feel at ease in the situation, these interrelationships among students and between teacher and student affect the success of the communicative interaction, even apart from differing levels of language control. Affective factors also determine what is meaningful and relevant for the students at any particular stage. Brown's confluent education emphasizes the importance of working with both feelings and intellect at the same time in both individual and group learning.

In practice, the humanistic approach has resulted in the inclusion in language-learning materials of vocabulary and activities for expressing one's feelings, for sharing one's values and viewpoints with others, and for developing a better understanding of their feelings and needs. A foreign-language class is a particularly suitable

35. See Abraham H. Maslow, *Motivation and Personality*, 2d ed. (New York: Harper and Row, 1970); Carl R. Rogers, *Freedom to Learn* (Columbus, Ohio: Charles Merrill, 1969); and George Isaac Brown, *Human Teaching for Human Learning: An Introduction to Confluent Education* (New York: Viking Press, 1971).

environment for meeting affective needs, because much of the activity can take the form of role-playing, simulation games, and small-group discussions. Masks and puppets help the more inhibited to express themselves with less risk. The expressive arts (impromptu drama, music, and song) allow for free flow of imagination and self-expression. Yet all of these activities require the student to seek the most appropriate forms in the foreign language to express nuances of meaning.

With this reemphasis on individual worth and difference, foreign-language teachers became conscious of the fact that individual students have preferred modalities of learning: some learn best through the ear, some through the eye. They also learn at different rates and employ quite different strategies for understanding and retaining the material to be learned. With this new understanding, teachers were no longer satisfied with a monolithic "what is good for one is good for all" approach. The 1970s saw a flowering of experimentation with individualized learning programs, diversified content, and courses of differing lengths and intensity.

What of the Future?

The many new directions opened up by research in linguistics and psychology have provided teachers with many ideas for program development and teaching approaches. By their very diversity, they have liberated teachers to plan and adapt their programs with due attention to the objectives of their students and the needs of the area in which they are teaching. Teachers now feel free to develop the style of teaching with which they themselves feel most at ease, for it is only by feeling at ease themselves that they can set their students at ease in the potentially anxiety-creating environment of the active second-language class. They will continue to learn more about language from the linguists and about language-learning processes from the psychologists, but it is only the classroom teacher who is experiencing daily the interaction of these two who can finally decide the most appropriate approach to teaching and course content in the local situation. Foreign-language teachers of the future must make their own decisions as informed professionals, if study of another language is to provide the mind-expanding, humanistic experience, the insight into other ways of thinking and behaving, and the career skills which are its potential contributions to general education in our schools.

CHAPTER IV

Differentiation of Language Instruction

ROBERT C. LAFAYETTE

Introduction

An examination of the professional literature of the 1970s on the teaching of foreign language reveals a heavy concentration in the area of instruction. Because of the present-day lack of a dominating approach in second-language teaching, this literature focuses mainly on discrete segments of language teaching, especially communication and culture, rather than on global approaches such as the direct method or the audiolingual approach. When the literature does deal with those global approaches, it tends to compare and contrast several of them rather than focusing on a specific one. For example, Westphal describes the grammar-translation approach, the direct method, the audiolingual approach, media-based approaches, cognitive code learning, individualized instruction, the communicative approach, and humanistic approaches.[1] Diller provides detailed discussions of the mimicry-memorization and pattern drill method, the Gouin series method, and the direct methods of Berlitz and de Sauzé.[2] Stevick describes less widely known methods such as the silent way, community language learning, and the St. Cloud method.[3]

Individuals practicing each of these various methods could be identified, but they would constitute the exceptions and would

1. Patricia B. Westphal, "Teaching and Learning: A Key to Success," in *Building on Experience-Building for Success*, ACTFL Foreign Language Education Series, vol. 10, ed. June K. Phillips (Skokie, Ill.: National Textbook Co., 1979), pp. 119-56.

2. Karl C. Diller, *The Language Teaching Controversy* (Rowley, Mass.: Newbury House Publishers, 1978).

3. Earl W. Stevick, *Memory, Meaning, and Method* (Rowley, Mass.: Newbury House Publishers, 1976).

not represent the mass of second-language teachers today. Although many teachers probably have not heard of several of these methods, many are familiar with the strategies and techniques related to some of the them. They tend to use those strategies and techniques because they have found them effective in the classroom. During the 1960s, for example, many audiolingual classrooms were infused with various grammar-translation techniques. Similarly, the current emphasis on cognitive learning in the language classroom is often accompanied by audiolingual activities judged to be indispensable by some teachers. Thus, language instruction is based not so much on the dominance of a particular method in vogue but rather on the teacher's selection of specific instructional activities. Therein lies the basis for the differentiation of language instruction.

In 1961, Carroll postulated five variables that contribute to the learning of a second language.[4] The model included three variables relating to students (general intelligence, aptitude, and motivation) and two instructional variables (adequacy of presentation and opportunity for learning). In order to discuss differentiation of language instruction, I shall pay special attention to the first instructional variable, adequacy of presentation or quality of instruction. Since research has not established the supremacy of one specific method, it is obvious that success in language learning is not so much dependent on how, but rather on how well language is taught. It follows that the teacher's role is all-important, as well as the teacher's ability to select and implement those teaching strategies that will lead to students' success.

Although quality of instruction is synonomous with the teacher's effectiveness, the latter is often highly dependent upon a variety of school-related circumstances over which the teacher has little control, such as the sequencing and scheduling of second-language courses, enrollment patterns in these courses, the teacher's work load, and the teacher's preparation. In advocating innovation and change in language teaching, the profession has paid little attention to these factors and their sometimes overbearing impact on the teacher's effectiveness. Yet it is often these very factors that

4. John B. Carroll, "A Model of School Learning," *Teachers College Record* 64 (May 1963): 723-33.

will determine the degree to which teachers attempt to differentiate instruction. Thus it is necessary to discuss such topics as individualized instruction and small-group instruction in the light of a typical teacher in a typical school, considering existing constraints as well as potential avenues for limited change. Although there is merit in featuring successful innovative programs, the purpose here is to discuss the reality of today's second-language instruction and to explore realistic channels for improvement.

The Typical Instructional Program

There is a danger in attempting to generalize on the implementation of second-language instruction in contemporary American schools. At opposite ends of the continuum are exemplary programs often described in the professional literature and unsuccessful programs best left undescribed. These, however, constitute the exceptions. Between the two poles one finds the mass of second-language instruction in this country. Considering the constraints brought to bear upon the average program, it is surprising that so many succeed as well as they do. The data used in this chapter to describe the typical instructional program and the status of language instruction pertain chiefly to the state of Indiana.

THE STANDARD SEQUENCE

There are two common second-language sequences in today's schools: the four-year high school sequence (grades nine through twelve) and the six-year combined junior/senior high school sequence (grades seven through twelve). During the 1950s and 1960s, numerous school districts maintained second-language programs in the elementary schools, usually beginning in grade three, but all but a very limited number of those programs have disappeared. Today, most second-language instruction at the elementary school level falls in the category of bilingual education or "language switch" programs.

The four-year sequence. Although the minimum course offerings in any Indiana high school, as well as in secondary schools accredited by the North Central Association of Colleges and Secondary Schools, mandate only two units (five classes per week for one year) of one second language, the common pattern today is to offer at least a four-year sequence in one language. This sequence usually consists of four levels (I-IV), each of which is equivalent to one of the four years of high school. The first two levels normally emphasize basic grammar and vocabulary, with a heavy focus on the oral skills of listening and speaking. In the great majority of schools the adopted texts define the scope and sequence of each level. Levels III and IV include continuous reinforcement of basic grammar and vocabulary, an introduction to more complex grammatical structures, an increase in time devoted to reading and writing, and, in many instances, an introduction to selected literary works. Teachers view the content of these two levels as being a great deal more flexible and often make use of a variety of readings, grammar review, and other supplementary materials instead of adopting a specific third- or fourth-level textbook. It is at these two levels that one finds the highest degree of variety in both curricular content and instructional processes.

The six-year sequence. In many schools, second-language instruction is begun in grade seven and extends through grade twelve. This pattern adds one level of instruction (V) to the sequence, since the content of Level I described above is covered in grades seven and eight. School districts that offer a six-year sequence usually also offer a four-year sequence, thus permitting the student the choice of beginning a second language in either grade seven or nine. Some districts, however, still restrict enrollment in grade seven to the more capable students.

A recent development in junior high and middle schools has been the introduction of exploratory courses, which have been defined as courses "designed to allow students to explore some area of foreign language study for the purpose of acquainting them with the phenomenon of language itself, of determining their interest and potential in future foreign language study, or of meeting some special student need."[5] In some cases, these courses are offered in grade six, thus extending the sequence by one year,

5. Beverly Enwall et al., "Exploratory Foreign Language Programs" (Working draft of a position paper prepared for the annual meeting of the National Council of State Supervisors of Foreign Languages, ACTFL Convention, Washington, D.C., November 1975) mimeographed, p. 1.

while in others they constitute the curriculum of the first year in the six-year sequence in grades seven through twelve.

ENROLLMENT PATTERNS IN THE STANDARD SEQUENCE

Selected data on enrollment patterns for the state of Indiana are presented here because they include information not normally found in national surveys, such as attrition rates and percentages of full- and part-time teachers. All of the information presented here is based on data for grades nine through twelve in Indiana public secondary schools.

During the school year 1958-59, 17.6 percent of the students in public secondary schools (grades nine through twelve) were enrolled in second-language courses. A peak was reached in 1968-69, when 30.2 percent of the population was enrolled. By 1977-78, the figure had fallen to 22.2 percent. This information, however, tells only a very small part of the story. Many more serious implications are derived from the 1977-78 enrollment patterns presented in table 1 and the figures on attrition shown in table 2.

TABLE 1

PERCENT OF LANGUAGE ENROLLMENTS BY LANGUAGE
AND BY LEVEL IN INDIANA (GRADES 9-12), 1977-78

LANGUAGE	LEVEL I	LEVEL II	LEVELS III-VI
French	52	31	17
German	49	33	18
Latin	58	33	9
Spanish	56	30	14
All Languages	55	32	13

Source: Office of the Coordinator for School Foreign Languages, Indiana University, Lorraine A. Strasheim, Coordinator.

TABLE 2

PERCENT OF ATTRITION BETWEEN LEVELS I AND II
IN INDIANA HIGH SCHOOLS (GRADES 9-12)
IN SELECTED YEARS, BY LANGUAGE

LANGUAGE	1968-69	1973-74	1977-78
French	25	32	35
German	35	35	36
Latin	43	52	48
Spanish	34	42	53

Source: Office of the Coordinator for School Foreign Languages, Indiana University, Lorraine A. Strasheim, Coordinator.

A brief examination of the data in table 1 reveals an extremely bottom-heavy population in second-language courses. More than half of the entire population is enrolled in Level I while Levels I and II account for 87 percent of the total. The remaining 13 percent is spread out among however many advanced levels of instruction exist. The Department of Public Instruction in Indiana formerly provided a breakdown of enrollments for Levels III and IV, but they no longer do so because the enrollments are so small. Moreover, in 1978, a year in which there were statewide adoptions of textbooks for second-language classes, the list of texts for Level IV was eliminated, since too few publishers could afford to bid their texts because of the small number of students.

Equally alarming are the attrition rates between Levels I and II shown in table 2. Many teachers assume that the most serious exodus of students occurs after two years of instruction. That indeed is true in terms of percentages, but in actual numbers of students the greatest loss always occurs after one year of language study.

IMPLICATIONS OF ENROLLMENT PATTERNS

When coupled with present-day budget constraints, the second-language enrollment patterns seriously affect the instructional program through the imposition of extremely heavy work loads for teachers and the use of large numbers of instructors who teach second-language courses part-time.

Teacher work loads. Unless a high school has a total population of more than 2000 in Indiana, it is likely that all language teachers except teachers of Spanish will have a minimum of four different preparations per day. The French, German, and/or Latin staffs will each be limited to one individual responsible for teaching all courses offered in each language. If administrators abide by a minimum enrollment of fifteen students in each class, it is also likely that these teachers will have to teach a multilevel class where more than one level of instruction (usually levels III and IV) are combined and taught during the same period. Table 3 shows the teaching schedule for a school in a comprehensive urban school corporation. Table 4 shows sample schedules for schools in school corporations that are of medium or small size.

TABLE 3

Sample teaching Schedule in a Comprehensive Urban School Corporation

Teacher A	Teacher B	Teacher C	Teacher D
Spanish III (31)	Study Hall	German I (29)	Study Hall
Spanish III (29)	French II (24)	Advanced German	Latin III/IV
Spanish IV (28)	French I (33)	Composition (8)	combined (8)
Spanish V (15)	French II (24)	German Short Story (11)	Study Hall
Corridor Duty	French I (36)	German II (17)	Exploratory Latin (13)
Spanish IIX (15)	French IIX (18)	German III (21)	Latin II (12)
Spanish III (22)	Study Hall	German IIX (11)	Latin I (27)
		German III (16)	Spanish I (25)

Note: The corporation operates nine forty-minute periods daily. Teacher contracts call for seven assignments (class or duty) plus one lunch period and one preparation period. The numbers in parentheses indicate enrollment, while an "X" indicates an accelerated class. This table indicates only the nature of the seven assignments.

TABLE 4

SAMPLE TEACHING SCHEDULES IN MEDIUM TO SMALL SCHOOL CORPORATIONS

TEACHER A (GRADES 5-8)	TEACHER B (GRADES 6-12)	TEACHER C (GRADES 9-12)	TEACHER D (GRADES 9-12)
Beginning French (regular)	Sixth-grade spelling	First-year German	Study Hall
Beginning French (regular)	Eighth-grade language arts	Second- and third-year German	Third- and fourth-year Spanish
Beginning French (regular)	Eighth-grade French	English Composition	First-year Spanish
Beginning French (enriched)	Freshman English	World Literature	Second-year Spanish
Beginning French (enriched)	First-year French	Language Arts Variety Pak	First-, second-, and third-year French
Advanced French (enriched)	Second-year French		
Advanced French (enriched)			
Introduction to French (enriched)			

Note: These schedules emanate from different school corporations. They were selected from responses to a survey conducted by the Office of the Coordinator for School Foreign Languages, Indiana University.

Part-time teachers. In addition to coping with multiple daily preparations including multilevel classes, more than half of Indiana's second-language teachers also teach in a second academic area. In 1976-77, only 43 percent of Indiana's language teachers taught full-time in one language. The percent of full-time teachers by language was as follows: French, 38 percent; German, 48 percent; Latin, 16 percent; and Spanish, 54 percent. The situation is complicated by the fact that we do not know whether the nearly 60 percent part-time language teachers are language teachers with a minor in another academic area or majors in a nonlanguage area with a language minor. Of the 848 part-time language teachers in 1976-77, approximately half (420) also taught English and one-third (268) taught yet another second language.

Multiple daily preparations as well as teaching in more than one subject-matter area are commonplace not only in Indiana but in many other states as well. In fact, only in the New England and Mid-eastern states, where language enrollments constitute more than 30 percent of the school population, might the situation be somewhat different.

A TYPICAL SECOND-LANGUAGE PROGRAM

Based on information available from Indiana, it is possible to describe a typical second-language program serving a total of 440 students in a hypothetical high school in that state (grades nine through twelve) enrolling a total of 2,000 students, as shown in table 5. In examining this model, it should be noted that Indiana enrolls 22 percent of its total secondary school population in second-language courses, while the comparable national figure is 19 percent.

TABLE 5

A TYPICAL SECOND-LANGUAGE PROGRAM

LANGUAGE	ENROLLMENT	ENROLLMENT BY LEVEL			TEACHERS NEEDED
		I	II	III-IV	
French	110	57	34	19	1 full-time
German	70	34	23	13	1 part-time
Latin	31	18	10	3	1 part-time
Spanish	229	128	69	32	2 full-time
Total	440	217	136	67	

Based on average class size of second-language classes for the state of Indiana, the French teacher in the program shown in table 5 would have two sections each of Levels I and II plus a combined multilevel section of Levels III and IV. The German teacher would have a similar load, less one section of Level II, and would thus have to teach at least one class in another subject. The Latin teacher would be assigned one section of Level I plus a multilevel section possibly including Levels II, III, and IV, in addition to at least three other classes in a different field. Only the two Spanish teachers could arrange their schedules to have no more than three preparations, often the maximum negotiated in teacher contracts. There would be five sections of Level I, three of Level II, and one each of III and IV. If there were no accelerated sections of Levels I or II, these two teachers could arrange their schedules so that each would have three preparations and no multilevel classes.

It is significant that, even in a high school with such a large student population, teacher work loads are very heavy. In Indiana, a state with 371 high schools, only twenty-six of them have an enrollment of 2000 or more. One hundred schools have enrollments between 1000 and 2000, and 245 have a student body of less than 1000. Thus the sample teacher schedules presented earlier represent the norm rather than the exception. In fact, it is somewhat mind-boggling to imagine the schedules of teachers in schools with 1000 or fewer students.

PROJECTED OUTCOMES OF THE STANDARD INSTRUCTIONAL PROGRAM

When one considers all of the above interrelated factors—student enrollment patterns, teacher work loads, part-time teachers —several consequences come to mind. First, in a great majority of schools the chances are that the same teacher will be responsible for teaching all available courses in a particular language, so that the student wishing to take four years of a language had best be enamored with that individual. Four years with even an outstanding teacher might eventually become burdensome, let alone that same amount of time spent with a somewhat less enthusiastic one. Although no specific information appears in the professional literature, it seems reasonable to hypothesize that a significant cause of attrition is the student's desire not to continue studying with the same individual.

A second consequence could very well be a drop in the quality of instruction due to the large number of part-time teachers, many of whom are teaching second languages as a minor field. This would be true especially in the area of oral language, where even majors experience difficulty in achieving a high degree of proficiency. The phenomenon is also aggravated by the fact that so many teachers today already have acquired a professional or life certificate and need not further their education in order to continue teaching. It is estimated conservatively that at least 70 percent of all teachers in Indiana fall in that category. Loew states that the percentage of permanently certified second-language teachers in New York state rose from 60.6 in 1972-73 to 83.8 in 1976-77.[6]

Strasheim claims that the continued increase in multiple daily preparations, in the number of multilevel classes, and in the number of part-time second-language teachers will have the following effects on language instruction:

1. The quality of the student product will decline, especially in the skills, for the teacher will concentrate more and more on the types of grammatical exercises that do not demand a great deal of preparation. Teachers will become excessively "textbook bound."

2. Teachers' participation in professional meetings, study, and travel experiences, and the like will decline as teachers either go to refresher courses in the other disciplines they teach or use any free time for rest and family.

3. There will undoubtedly be a decline in the number of courses offered at the advanced levels of foreign language study as the teachers' time is more urgently needed in the second discipline they teach. Since enrollments in these levels tend to be small there will be a tendency for schools to drop them. The proliferation of "combined classes," the offering of two, sometimes three, levels in a single class period is testimony to the erosion of upper levels. It is unrealistic to expect teachers pressured by

6. Helene Z. Loew, "Modifying the Program and Providing for Change," in *Building on Experience-Building for Success,* ed. Phillips, p. 273.

this type of work load to innovate; to adapt lengthy materials, making many choices; or to individualize instruction for the many levels in one class while simultaneously preparing for three or four other classes daily.[7]

It is obvious that the reality of the situation militates against a high degree of differentiation in instructional processes. Most ironic, however, is the fact that these very processes are probably indispensable for the success of multilevel classes.

Attempts to Meet Individual Needs

It is abundantly clear that whole-class instruction based on a standardized textbook constitutes the primary mode of instruction in second-language learning. This in and of itself is not necessarily a bad omen, since there is virtually no conclusive research pointing to the superiority of a specific method or mode of instruction for language learning. There have been, however, significant attempts to devise language instruction that will meet the needs of individual students. These activities can be classified into two broad interrelated categories: individualized instruction and small-group learning.

INDIVIDUALIZED INSTRUCTION

Although the concept of individualized instruction dates back to the early years of the twentieth century with the implementation of the Winnetka and Dalton Plans, it experienced a long period of inactivity until its reincarnation in the late 1960s and early 1970s. Among the many subject-matter areas involved in the movement, second language was one of the most active. The professional literature on the latter is replete with articles on the topic. *Foreign Language Annals*, the official organ of the American Council on the Teaching of Foreign Languages, included a special feature on individualized instruction in every issue for a period of three years. There are several books of edited readings. Other volumes provide very practical suggestions for implementing individualized instruction in second-language classes, not only for

7. Lorraine A. Strasheim, *Foreign Language Teachers in Indiana*, report issued by the Office of the Coordinator for School Foreign Languages (Bloomington, Ind.: Indiana University, 1977), mimeographed, p. 8.

teachers especially interested in this mode of instruction but for other teachers as well.[8]

Although individualized instructional programs in colleges and universities included work with computer-assisted instruction and programmed instruction, most of the programs in the schools were of the continuous progress variety, making heavy use of homemade learning activity packets. During the early 1970s, these packets often consisted of study guides to standard texts, since individualized texts were not available at that time. In their source-book of innovative second-language programs, Love and Honig describe nine different programs committed to individualization, seven of which make use of learning activity packets to facilitate self-paced instruction.[9] In addition to the few programs dedicated totally to individualizing instruction, there are many others that have adapted a variety of features of individualized instructional programs that are basically teacher-centered. Joiner[10] and Phillips[11] present a myriad of ideas that the teacher could use to help meet individual needs of students, including the efficient use of short-range objectives, learning activity packages for enrichment pur-poses, minicourses for travelers, affective learning activities, sug-gestions for learning centers, and many others.

Unfortunately the interest in individualized instruction has not been accompanied by definitive research efforts. At the school level, research has been limited to a handful of studies. Grittner

8. See, for example, Renee S. Disick, *Individualizing Language Instruction: Strategies and Methods* (New York: Harcourt Brace Jovanovich, 1975); Frank M. Grittner and Fred H. LaLeike, *Individualized Foreign Language Instruction* (Skokie, Ill.: National Textbook Co., 1973); Gerald E. Logan, *Individualized Foreign Language Learning: An Organic Process* (Rowley, Mass.: Newbury House Publishers, 1973); and Florence Steiner, *Performing with Objectives* (Rowley, Mass.: Newbury House Publishers, 1975).

9. F. William D. Love and Lucille J. Honig, *Options and Perspective* (New York: Modern Language Association, 1973).

10. Elizabeth G. Joiner, "Tailoring Language Instruction to Student Needs," in *The Challenge of Communication*, ACTFL Foreign Language Education Series, vol. 6, ed. Gilbert A. Jarvis (Skokie, Ill.: National Textbook Co., 1974), pp. 151-84.

11. June K. Phillips, "Individualization and Personalization," in *Responding to New Realities*, ACTFL Foreign Language Education Series, vol. 5, ed. Gilbert A. Jarvis (Skokie, Ill.: National Textbook Co., 1974), pp. 219-61.

conducted an extensive evaluation of the first two years of the West Bend (Wisconsin) continuous progress program.[12] He found that the dropout rate declined from 24 percent to 14 percent between Levels I and II and from 65 percent to 38 percent between Levels II and III when compared with figures from previous years. Using the Form A of the *Pimsleur Proficiency Test* to measure achievement in reading and listening comprehension at the end of the first year, Grittner found the mean percentile scores to be at or near the fiftieth percentile in both skills. At the end of the second year, the stanine distribution of listening scores was slightly lower than those of the norm group while the distribution of reading scores fell considerably below. Grittner attributes the latter result to the fact that many of the students who remained in the program would have been eliminated from a traditional sequence.

Papalia and Zampogna conducted two experimental studies in French classes at Clarence (New York) High School. The first sought to compare the results in achievement as well as the social climate of an individualized French III class with the results in a traditionally taught class at a similar level. Results on all four skills tested by the *MLA Cooperative Tests* were significantly higher for the experimental group and the *Learning Environment Inventory* showed that students in the individualized class felt more challenged and satisfied by their work and cared more about one another.[13] In the second study, the individualized class once again achieved significantly higher scores on all four skills measured by the same test. In addition, 63 percent of the Level III experimental group enrolled for French IV as opposed to 35 percent of the control group.[14]

Unfortunately the research in individualized second-language learning in the schools is much too sparse to generate any firm con-

12. Frank M. Grittner, *Individualized Foreign Language Program,* End-of-project Report (Madison, Wis.: Wisconsin Department of Public Instruction, 1972).

13. Anthony Papalia and Joseph Zampogna, "An Experiment in Individualized Instruction through Small-group Interaction," *Foreign Language Annals* 5 (March 1972): 302-6.

14. Anthony Papalia and Joseph Zampogna, "An Experimental Study on Teachers' Classroom Behaviors and Their Effect on FL Attrition," *Modern Language Journal* 56 (November 1972): 421-24.

clusions. The only conclusion that can be reached from reading the voluminous descriptive literature on the topic is that the movement has had a peripheral impact on traditional classroom instruction.

SMALL-GROUP INSTRUCTION

Probably the most significant outgrowth of individualized instruction has been the steadily increasing use of small-group learning in second-language classes. Although commonly associated with individualized instruction, small-group work is increasing steadily in teacher-centered classrooms. Two other factors contribute to this phenomenon: affective learning and the emphasis on meaningful communication. It is necessary to keep in mind that our students are social creatures brought up in a highly interactive social environment. Furthermore, language is itself the essence of this interaction. To limit the process of learning a second language either to totally individualized study in isolation or to the traditional large-group classroom environment with twenty-five or more students is to contradict both our understanding of communication and the social process.

Small-group instruction provides individuals an opportunity to develop knowledge and skills in cooperation with other students; it permits students to teach each other; it helps satisfy the student's desire to interact and communicate with others; and, most important, it permits the development of meaningful communication in the second-language classroom. Baker provides a completely developed rationale for small-group work as well as operational procedures and sample small-group activities. He suggests the following guidelines to maximize the possibility that small-group learning will constitute productive learning:

1. Students should clearly understand the purpose of a group activity and how the activity ties in with what they are learning.
2. Each group should have appropriate materials with which to work. These should contain explicit instructions for use and be organized in such a way that they can be handed to groups without lengthy and complicated explanations.
3. Students should clearly understand the outcome or product

of each activity. Performance objectives are especially helpful in this connection.[15]

It is suggested that second-language teachers select small-group activities that primarily emphasize communication. Communication is a fundamental goal in the vast majority of second-language classrooms and the teacher must see that students not only utter grammatically correct sentences but also make use of creative and spontaneous language as well. Students must be able to engage in meaningful exchange of information.

Bonin and Birckbichler suggest the use of conversation and interview cards to promote communication.[16] The cards include a set of closed as well as open questions so that they may be used at different levels of sophistication. The student's task is to interview a classmate and gather the necessary information. An extension of this activity would be to ask the student to relay the information to a third party. Zelson describes numerous role-playing activities designed to stimulate communication among two or more individuals. He claims that the most stimulating kind of role-playing activity is a situation involving conflict or a problem of some sort. He offers the following example:

You would like X to come to your house for supper on a particular night, but he does not seem to be interested. You may change days or times, but your acquaintance continues to decline. Try to influence the reluctant recipient of your invitation, while he continues to make excuses very diplomatically.[17]

An excellent collection of practical small-group activities designed to promote communication is also found in the 1976 Report of

15. Reid E. Baker, "Small-group Learning," in *An Integrative Approach to Foreign Language Teaching: Choosing among the Options*, ACTFL Foreign Language Education Series, vol. 8, ed. Gilbert A. Jarvis (Skokie, Ill.: National Textbook Co., 1976), p. 57.

16. Thérèse M. Bonin and Diane W. Birckbichler, "Real Communication through Interview and Conversation Cards," *Modern Language Journal* 59 (January 1975): 22-25.

17. Sidney N. J. Zelson, "A Relevant Curriculum: Linguistic Competence Plus Communicative Competence Equal Proficiency," in *Teaching for Communication in the Foreign Language Classroom*, ed. Renate A. Schulz (Skokie, Ill.: National Textbook Co., 1976), pp. 18-32.

the Central States Conference on the Teaching of Foreign Languages.[18]

Gunderson provides a highly classroom-oriented guide to all facets of small-group instruction.[19] She includes recommendations for the scheduling and organization of activities, suggests small-group responsibilities, appropriate materials, and learning activities, and gives advice on grading procedures. For the teacher who fears the potential problems of control in small-group instruction, Boylan and Lett have developed a "trouble shooting guide" that describes the problem, lists possible causes, and suggests treatments.[20]

Impact of Individualized and Small-Group Instruction on the Traditional Instructional Program

The advent of individualized and small-group instruction is beginning to influence the mainstream of second-language learning. Only a few teachers will ever manifest a total commitment to these innovations, but many will incorporate specific techniques in their teacher-centered classrooms. Considering the daily responsibilities of the average teacher, it would be unreasonable to expect any more.

The greatest impact on individualized and small-group instruction will come from the ongoing revision of standard second-language textbooks. Teachers are much more likely to make use of an individualized activity if it is included in the text than if they must themselves design the activity. During the past few years, authors of several texts have included individualized and/or communicative activities, at least as options for classroom use. A selected list of these texts is included here along with a brief commentary.

18. *Teaching for Communication in the Foreign Language Classroom*, ed. Schulz.

19. Barbara Gunderson, "Cooperative Structure in the Foreign Language Classroom," in *Teaching for Tomorrow in the Foreign Language Classroom*, ed. Reid E. Baker (Skokie, Ill.: National Textbook Co., 1978) pp. 37-52.

20. Patricia C. Boylan and John Lett, Jr., "Communication and Grouping: A Marriage Made in Heaven . . . And How to Test Its Outcomes," cited in Westphal, "Teaching and Learning: A Key to Success," p. 135.

Roger Colombe, *Voix et Visages de la France*, Teacher's Edition (Chicago: Rand McNally and Co., 1974). This Level I French text is accompanied by a *Study Guide and Workbook* that consists of fourteen individual booklets designed to guide the student systematically through all material contained in the text. For the teacher who wishes to individualize instruction, it provides a basis for small-group and individual activities and saves a great deal of time previously spent preparing homemade study packets. In a more traditional setting, the *Study Guide and Workbook* may be used as a basis for homework assignments and for make-up and/or reinforcement work. The Teacher's Edition includes an article entitled "Individualized Instruction" as well as descriptions of thirteen different learning games, most of which involve small groups.

Albert Valdman et al., *Son et Sens*, Teacher's Annotated Edition (Glenview, Ill.: Scott, Foresman and Co., 1977). Although the text is primarily designed for a teacher-centered approach, it is adaptable to individualized or small-group instruction. The Teacher's Edition includes a segment entitled "Individualizing a Lesson," which presents a complete study guide for one unit, and provides the teacher with a model for developing study guides for other units. Each unit in the student text includes an "Auto-Test," a definite carryover from individualized instruction.

Jean-Paul Valette and Rebecca M. Valette, *French for Mastery*, Teacher's Edition (Lexington, Mass.: D. C. Heath and Co., 1975). The book is designed for whole-class instruction but it contains numerous features that reflect individualized and small-group instruction. The beginning of every chapter in the *Workbook* includes specific student objectives. Both the tape program and the *Workbook* consist almost completely of self-correcting exercises. Many of the textbook activities are designed for two or more students with additional small-group exercises included in the workbook. Each chapter contains a set of self-tests, for which the answer key is followed by a "diagnosis" section that pinpoints the student's weaknesses and prescribes specific sections for remedial study. The Teacher's Edition includes charts showing how lesson plans for a given segment of a chapter might be varied to reflect different learning rates and interests. In addition to a section on performance objectives, the Teacher's Edition contains suggestions on how to individualize instruction with the text, including a learning activity packet and steps to developing others.

Gerald E. Logan, *Deutsch: Kernstufe* (Rowley, Mass.: Newbury House Publishers, 1976). This first-year German book is designed for use in conventional classroom settings and in individualized or independent learning programs with no adaptation or extra teacher work necessary. The text consists of a core component that is strictly limited to discrete grammar points and five complements to the text including everyday expressions, culture, pronunciation, composition exercises, and review lessons. The complements contain "daily length" lessons that may be combined in a variety of ways with the core program.

William E. Bull et al., *Spanish for Communication: Daily Lesson Plans* (Boston: Houghton Mifflin Co., 1972). This text represents an attempt at producing teacher-proof materials. It is an integrated system composed of a series of programmed student texts and daily lesson plans. *Spanish for Communication* is a continuous sequence and each of the 405 lessons in the four-level sequence has been planned in detail. The programs in the programmed student texts are to be used as systematic, preclass preparation assignments. They are self-correcting, individualized activities that require fifteen to twenty minutes of the student's time before class. The daily lesson plans come in such minute detail that they resemble an actor's script. Every minute of class time is accounted for. The authors claim that these materials are easily adaptable to individualized instruction because the daily programs and lessons make individual rates of progress possible, permit frequent reliable evaluations, and allow the teacher to be aware of the content of each of the minimal steps in the sequence the student is following.

Patricia O'Connor, *Entre Nosotros* (New York: Holt, Rinehart and Winston, 1975). This text is for the second level of a two-year sequence. Each unit consists of three different and separate subunits or series and is intended to meet the needs of the many ability levels common in intermediate courses. Nothing in subunit A of each of the units is dependent upon material included in subunits B or C. Students may proceed horizontally or vertically. Series A contains reinforcement and review of familiar vocabulary and grammar with slight expansion of Level I material. It represents the minimal for some students and is independent of Series B and C. Series B constitutes the core of Level II and is dependent on Series A but independent of C. It includes some review of Level I with considerable expansion of vocabulary and structure covered in Level I. Series C is dependent on A and B. It includes no grammar but rather reinforces material in Series A and B. It is designed to interest and challenge students with high aptitude or students with Spanish background.

In addition to textbooks such as these, the teacher also has access to an abundance of supplementary materials, many of which are already individualized or easily adaptable to individualized or small-group instruction. A new series of readers in French, German, and Spanish provides teachers with an abundance of communciation activities, most of which are readily adaptable to small-group instruction.[21] Levno[22] and Snyder[23] provide high-interest cultural materials in French and Spanish respectively that are accompanied exclusively by individualized learning activities. The Materials Center of the American Council on the Teaching of Foreign Languages offers a long list of supplementary materials, including several extremely well-designed learning activity packets on a variety of cultural topics.[24]

If teachers wish to adapt instruction to meet the needs of the individual student, materials are beginning to appear that will permit them to do so without extensive supplementary preparation. The key to the implementation of differentiated instruction thus becomes the proper selection of materials based not only on projected course goals and students' needs but also on the teacher's ability and need. Considering the daily tasks of the typical teacher, the latter factors are as important in textbook selection as are students' needs.

Probably the most comprehensive and systematic instrument available for the evaluation of textbooks is found in a recent work by Johnson.[25] The instrument considers two major areas for evaluation: text content and factors beyond content. Each area is divided into several categories as follows:

Text content: approach to skills teaching and learning; presentation of language; pronunciation/phonology; grammar; exercises and drills; vocabulary; communicative activities; culture; scope and sequence; adaptability and flexibility; supplementary materials; tests.

Factors beyond content: organization for school schedules; lesson and

21. Patricia Boylan et al., *Cara a Cara: A Basic Reader for Communication in Spanish* (New York: Holt, Rinehart and Winston, 1977); Gilbert A. Jarvis et al., *Connaître et se connaître: A Basic Reader* (New York: Holt, Rinehart and Winston, 1976); Renate A. Schulz et al., *Lesen, Lachen, Lernen: A Basic Reader* (New York: Holt, Rinehart and Winston, 1978).

22. Arley W. Levno, *Rencontres Culturelles: Cross-Cultural Mini-Dramas* (Skokie, Ill.: National Textbook Co., 1977).

23. Barbara Snyder, *Encuentroes Culturales: Cross-Cultural Mini-Dramas* (Skokie, Ill.: National Textbook Co., 1975).

24. A list of available materials may be obtained by writing ACTFL Materials Center, 2 Park Avenue, New York, N.Y. 10016.

25. Carl H. Johnson, "Choosing Materials That Do the Job," in *Building on Experience-Building for Success,* ed. Phillips, pp. 67-92.

end vocabulary; use of English; instructions for the teacher; layout; experience and expertise of author(s); evidence in development and research; biases; costs.

Such an exhaustive evaluation of several textbooks in order to select the most appropriate is time-consuming. It is time well spent, however, if the text selected becomes the instrument through which the teacher is able to keep abreast of four to five daily preparations and meet even partially the needs of individual students.

Conclusion

If one were to read completely the professional literature of the last decade in second-language learning, one would encounter many innovative programs focusing on any one of numerous curricular and/or instructional variables. There are glowing subjective evaluations of the success of these programs and one might even be tempted to believe that this literature is a reflection of the entire profession.

Unfortunately, however, the literature in reality represents only the exemplary programs developed by the innovators who, according to Rogers, represent the first 2.5 percent of a group to adopt a new idea.[26] In fact, a careful examination of the literature will reveal that many of the same programs are cited over and over again. This does not necessarily imply that effective instruction fails to exist outside of these programs. It should serve, however, as a caution to help leaders in the profession temper the degree to which they can expect or even suggest instructional change. Reality dictates the fact that both curriculum and instruction are determined primarily by the choice of available materials. Since the typical teacher lacks both the time and the ability to initiate change, it becomes the responsibility of the leaders in the profession to influence the inclusion of proven instructional innovations in ready-made classroom materials and to persuade teachers to use those materials in everyday classroom activities.

26. Everett M. Rogers, "What Are Innovators Like?" in *Change Process in the Public Schools* (Eugene, Oreg.: The Center for the Advanced Study of Educational Administration, University of Oregon, 1965) EDRS: ED 011570.

CHAPTER V

TESOL: Teaching English to Speakers of Other Languages

JAMES E. ALATIS

English is the most widely taught foreign language in the world. The teaching of English is therefore a vast undertaking. Vast undertakings require organizations, and organizations, as is well known, require acronyms. Hence TESOL has become the acronym that is most widely used in America to refer to teaching English to speakers of other languages.

Within TESOL a distinction is made between two acronyms: TEFL, teaching English as a foreign language, and TESL, teaching English as a second language. Marckwardt first called attention to the distinction the British have traditionally made between TEFL and TESL. In the case of TEFL, literary and cultural goals predominate and use of the language as an active communicative tool is minimized. In TESL, on the other hand, the primary goal of instruction is the achievement of a high level of communicative competence in English, sometimes developed to a point of balanced bilingualism or, not infrequently, English dominance over the native language.[1]

American usage has moved historically from TEFL to TESL

1. Albert Marckwardt, "English as a Second Language and English as a Foreign Language," *PMLA* 78, no. 2 (1963): 25-28.

Note: I am indebted to the work of many professionals who have helped shape TESOL over the years. I have relied in particular on TESOL surveys by two of my colleagues: David P. Harris's "The Future of ESOL: Continuity or Generation Gap," in *Essays on Teaching English as a Second Language and as a Second Dialect*, ed. Robert P. Fox (Urbana, Ill. National Council of Teachers of English, 1973), pp. 67-81, and William E. Norris's *TESOL at the Beginning of the '70s: Trends, Topics, and Research Needs* (Pittsburgh, Pa.: Department of General Linguistics and University Center for International Studies, University of Pittsburgh, 1971).

to TESOL. TESOL has the advantage of encompassing both terms. At the same time, its choice reflects the development of the profession from one whose major concern was foreign students to one whose primary focus is domestic learners of English who cannot accurately be described as foreigners.

TESOL is also the acronym for Teachers of English to Speakers of Other Languages, an independent professional organization established in 1966. The organization was created out of professional concern over the lack of a single, all-inclusive professional organization that might bring together ESOL teachers and administrators at all educational levels. The formation of the organization was a sign of TESOL's maturity as a profession. It is worth looking back to where TESOL has been in order to understand where TESOL, both the field and the organization, is today and where it is likely to go in the future.

Any attempt to trace the development of English as a second language in the United States must begin with the relationship between linguistics and language teaching. Teaching English as a second language has been an educational activity in the United States for over 300 years. Its first "students" were the American Indians, and one may note the ironic coincidence that one of the profession's most important concerns remains the teaching of English to American Indians. The coincidence is made more remarkable when one realizes that the early anthropological linguists, such as Boas, Sapir, and Bloomfield, based their linguistic theories on studies of the American Indian languages. These linguists collected and analyzed samples of speech and formulated hypotheses on language from the analyses. The methods and findings they derived were eventually extended to the study of the more commonly known languages, including English. Thus, English-teaching methodology profited greatly from linguistic science, a twentieth-century outgrowth of the study of American Indian languages. The wheel has come full circle.

A major contribution of modern linguistic science to English teaching was the application of scientific analysis to the language, including an analysis of the system of mutually contrasting basic sounds (phonemes) and an analysis of the grammar.

Another major contribution was the emphasis on the study of

the contrasts between the learner's mother tongue and the language being learned. This notion of contrastive analysis is the most important distinguishing feature of the approach advocated by Charles Fries. Fries and those who followed him insisted as well on the importance of contrastive analysis of the target and source cultures. Although contrastive analysis has seen periods of disfavor, its current position as a complementary discipline to error analysis underscores the strength of its basic contribution to applied linguistics.[2]

Developments in linguistic theory, particularly as they have affected TESOL methodology, are discussed in greater detail below. Here we intend to trace in some detail the history of the TESOL profession in America since its inception in the 1940s. The phrase "in America" is a key one; it is important to note that Great Britain, by this time, already had a century and a half of experience in teaching English abroad. However, the late entry of the United States into the field was in one sense her greatest asset, since it meant that her efforts in TESOL were, from the very outset, under the direction of people with training in linguistics. Such was not the case with the Western European nations, which already enjoyed a history of language teaching experience and considered the new linguistic concepts "as objectionably American as the variety of English spoken in the United States."[3]

In the 1940s, the United States initiated wide-scale participation in English language teaching abroad as well as the establishment of the first intensive TESOL programs at home. TESOL abroad received its impetus from the establishment of adult education projects in Latin America under our Good Neighbor Policy. TESOL efforts at home were concentrated on the development of intensive courses for the foreign students who were attending colleges and universities in the United States. The establishment of the English Language Institute at the University of Michigan in 1941 marked the first intensive, linguistically oriented TESOL program in the United States.

2. Jan Svartvik, "Introduction," in *Errata: Papers in Error Analysis*, ed. Jan Svartvik (Lund, Sweden: CWK Gleerup, 1973), pp. 7-15.

3. Albert Marckwardt, "Teaching English as a Foreign Language," in *Language Development*, Selected Papers from a Ford Foundation Conference on the State of the Art (New York: Ford Foundation, 1968), p. 21.

By the end of World War II, as a result of the expansion of national interests, American TESOL activities had spread to the Near East, the Far East, and parts of Europe. The 1940s provided the groundwork for what was to become a major educational concern.

The 1950s marked a decided increase in TESOL activities. The exchange program of the U.S. State Department had expanded to include over twenty countries, more English institutes had been established within the universities, and instruction had been extended to the non-English-speaking elementary and secondary school children in the American educational system.

Largely because of the lack of coordination and communication among the myriad government agencies that became involved in English teaching activities as a result of the sudden and widespread growth, the Center for Applied Linguistics was established in 1959 as an extra-governmental body designed to provide a channel of communication among the government agencies and the universities.

By the 1960s, TESOL had become a worldwide endeavor. The U.S. Information Agency conducted adult English classes in over fifty countries and held short-term seminars and workshops for local teachers in countries throughout the world. By the mid-1960s, over 2,000 Peace Corps volunteers were teaching English in over forty countries. The Fulbright program assigned 115 professors and teachers to English programs in the educational institutions of 22 foreign countries. The Ford Foundation and Rockefeller Foundation also assisted in the development of training facilities overseas.

On the domestic scene, American colleges and universities were serving a greatly increased number of students from abroad. By the end of the decade, there were over 90,000 foreign students served by programs in some 150 colleges and universities. However, the development of greatest significance in this decade was the profession's change of focus from the adult, university-level foreign student to the American school-age child.

In 1964, the federal government officially recognized the thousands of children, either immigrant or native born, whose mother tongue was not English and who, therefore, needed specialized instruction in English if they were fully to understand and participate in American cultural, social, and economic life. Testimony before the House General Subcommittee on Education in 1967 revealed that, of the three million non-English-speaking students in American schools, only about one million were receiving English language instruction. The myth of the melting pot was being dispelled by a truer version of the facts, the existence of a multilingual society. Attitudes toward the role of non-English languages in American society began to be reexamined. As Fishman suggested, bilingualism in the language of one's immigrant parents began to enjoy the acceptance, even status, that formerly had been restricted to bilingualism acquired in more elite social settings, for example, from a Harvard education or from study abroad.[4]

Major groups of children who needed assistance in English included American Indians and children from families who had immigrated from Latin American countries.

Consideration of the number of Spanish-speaking children attending school in just one city may give some sense of the dimensions of the effort required to correct the educational injustice. In New York City in 1967 there were approximately 200,000 children of Latin American origin, of whom about 88,000 were rated as seriously handicapped in their use of English.[5]

Increasing arguments for the recognition and acceptance of a multicultural and multilingual society, and concern that all children be provided equal educational opportunity, culminated in the Bilingual Education Act of 1968, designed to meet the special needs of large numbers of children of limited English-speaking ability in the United States. Subsequently, the Bilingual Education Act of 1974 was to provide the first definition of a bilingual education program: "instruction given in, and study of, English and to the extent necessary to allow a child to progress effectively through the educational system, [in] the native language of the children of limited English-speaking ability."

The Constitution of the National Association for Bilingual

4. Joshua Fishman, "The Implications of Bilingualism for Language Teaching and Language Learning," in *Trends in Language Teaching*, ed. Albert Valdman (New York: McGraw-Hill, 1966), pp. 122-23.

5. Mary Finocchiaro, "Teaching the Spanish-speaking Child in New York City," in *On Teaching English to Speakers of Other Languages*, Series III, ed. Betty Wallace Robinett (Washington, D.C.: Teachers of English to Speakers of Other Languages, 1967), p. 58.

Education (NABE), an organization established in May 1974 at the International Bilingual Bicultural Conference, provided another definition of bilingual education: "The continuous use and preservation of *two* languages and their corresponding cultures. One of the two languages must be English." The NABE statement, by contrast with the definition offered in the 1974 Bilingual Education Act, stresses native language maintenance. Both, however, insist on the importance of education in English. Thus, in the United States, bilingualism is inextricably intertwined with TESOL.[6] Any bilingual education program in the United States must include an effective TESOL component; conversely, any TESOL program must take careful account of the child's native language. TESOL provides a strategy for the teaching of standard English to children for whom there exists a language barrier to education. Bilingual education encourages the provision of transitional or maintained education in the child's native language.

Although TESOL professionals have been accused of fostering "cultural imperialism" and "linguistic aggressiveness" by those who feel that instruction in English is intended to replace the child's mother tongue as the language of communication, such accusations stand in direct opposition to the principles espoused by specialists in the TESOL field. Largely because of the history of TESOL's close association with linguistics, professionals have always held to an "additive" rather than a "subtractive" philosophy in teaching English.[7] That is, they have attempted to add a new register of language to a student's repertoire rather than to eradicate or replace a register that the student already possessed. TESOL professionals do not attempt a large-scale language switch, but are concerned with maintaining the student's contact with the mother tongue. TESOL stresses that the children for whom bilingual education is required are not backward, mentally inferior, or stupid, but simply speakers of other languages. TESOL has opposed the isolation of

6. *Position Paper on the Role of English as a Second Language in Bilingual Education* (Washington, D.C.: Teachers of English to Speakers of Other Languages, 1976). Copies of this paper may be obtained from TESOL, 455 Nevils Building, Georgetown University, Washington, D.C. 20057.

7. See Wallace Lambert, "Culture and Language as Factors in Learning and Education," in *Education of Immigrant Students,* ed. A. Wolfgang (Toronto: Ontario Institute for Studies in Education, 1975), pp. 55-83.

such children in "special education" classes or in special classes for the socially and emotionally disturbed and has insisted that teachers must be educated to respect the potential strengths of the linguistically (and culturally) different, rather than be armed with a set of mythologies, masquerading as theories of social science, that only discourage the students' participation in formal education. TESOL professionals have insisted that bilingual education is not synonymous with "remedial English" or "remedial reading" or "compensatory education," but consists of a highly specialized form of English instruction.

From these remarks it is obvious that the question of bilingual education is not simply one of appropriate legislation or adequate funding. Implementation requires trained, dedicated professionals, and access to appropriate methodology. As a case in point, in 1975, when the influx of Vietnamese and Cambodian refugees brought 50,000 school-age children to America, the urgent question became how best to provide for their educational needs.[8] The answer to the question involved consideration of the cultural as well as the linguistic differences that presented obstacles to effective classroom instruction. The linguistic differences would seem simple enough to deal with if the solution were thought to be found by the straightforward application of methodology, for example, by isolating the features of structure and pronunciation which differ in the two languages. Even if this were the case, we would have remained woefully unprepared, since contrastive analysis presumes the existence of linguistic studies of both languages, and in the case of Cambodian, Lao, and Thai such studies were not available. In any case it was obvious that knowing the language differences alone was not sufficient. As we have said before, American linguistic theory was based on the principle that language cannot be divorced from culture, and often it is the cultural differences that present the most serious obstacles to learning. On the one hand, even differences that seem obvious are complex. Take, for example, the "translation" of names, which was problem enough for European immigrants to

8. *A Manual for Indochinese Refugee Education* 1976-77, prepared by the staff of the National Indochinese Clearinghouse for HEW (Arlington, Va.: Center for Applied Linguistics, 1976), p. 1. The remarks that follow, citing experiences of Indochinese in America, rely heavily on information drawn from this manual.

this country, let alone for Indochinese. Added to the difficulty of decoding unfamiliar sounds is the unfamiliarity with certain customs, for example Vietnamese and Cambodians write their surnames first. Married women retain their given names. Such practices are guaranteed to wreak havoc with ordinary public school records.

On the other hand, the less obvious differences are more likely to be misunderstood because potential explanations, even sympathetic ones, are framed within the reference of one's own cultural bias and expectations. Here the *Manual for Indochinese Refugee Education* cites an example of educational expectations. Vietnamese parents place a strong emphasis on "book learning" and often hope their children will go on to university studies. In the classroom, however, the children display a "passive" approach. Conditioned by a sense of respect for their elders, they are reticent to ask questions and to disagree with or ask help from the teacher. This general unfamiliarity with the methods employed in American classrooms, compounded by the difficulties with the new language, can lead teachers to conclude that the child is incapable of doing the work. An extreme instance of this failure in the classroom is the case of a Laotian boy, a senior honor student in Laos, who six months later as a refugee high school student in Washington, D.C. found himself the recipient of three successive warning notices in biology, the result of his inability to speak English and of the teacher's failure to recognize the true source of the problem.

Painful anecdotes such as these lead us to a conclusion we have already stated, but which bears repetition: teachers as well as students must be educated. To illustrate the point even more clearly, let us turn to a fairly recent development in the field of English language teaching referred to as SESD—Standard English as a Second Dialect. SESD applies to those many thousands of American children and adults whose academic and occupational success and social mobility are severely restricted by their native English dialects and by their difficulties in dealing with the written word. The concept of SESD derives from sociolinguistic research, which has shown that not only are there widespread and orderly grammatical, phonological, and lexical features that characterize "Black English" dialect, for example, but also that there exists extensive dialectal variation within what is referred to as "standard English." [9] Socio-linguists conclude that varieties of English are legitimate, stable dialects of a single language, each with its own linguistic structure and its own area of appropriateness and special usefulness. The application of this research to TESOL methodology reinforces the "additive" principle, which underlies the TESOL approach to bilingual education and extends it to encompass bidialectalism. The students are asked not to discard their own dialects, but to acquire another and to acquire as well the instinct for using the dialect most appropriate in a given situation.

The implications of a professional approach to nonstandard dialect in a classroom that resounds with varieties of English are revolutionary. Unlike the exponents of the "verbal deprivation theory," [10] who characterize such students as deprived and deficient in verbal ability, TESOL professionals consider them equal in intelligence and facility for learning.

Such an attitude places heavy responsibilities on teachers of English. As Allen suggests:

The teacher of English as a second language in this country has to teach within the framework of English diversity; there is no one functional variety or dialect always suitable. The teacher of English as a second dialect has to accept the child's first dialect without prejudice, and then go on to help the child gain control of some variety of standard English that will broaden his area of communication—both productive and receptive. [11]

A corollary to recognition of the student's native language or dialect is stress on the learner's needs and motivations in the development of learning strategies. One foreign language professional remarked, only half-jokingly, "an ounce of motivation is

---

9. Ralph W. Fasold and Walt Wolfram, "Some Linguistic Features of Negro Dialect," in *Teaching Standard English in the Inner City*, ed. Ralph W. Fasold and Roger W. Shuy (Arlington, Va.: Center for Applied Linguistics, 1970), pp. 41-86.

10. A theory expounded by Carl Bereiter and Siegfried Engelmann in *Teaching Disadvantaged Children in the Preschool* (Englewood Cliffs, N.J.: Prentice-Hall, 1966).

11. Harold B. Allen, "Attitudes of the ESL and the SESD Teacher," in *Essays on Teaching English as a Second Language and as a Second Dialect*, ed. Fox, p. 91.

worth a ton of pedagogy." The question of motivation becomes particularly significant in SESD programs in the United States. Many nonstandard English speakers are passively bidialectal; that is, they comprehend standard English forms and successfully communicate with standard English speakers. Where, then, is their motivation to learn the standard dialect? Virginia French Allen states that it is the responsibility of teachers to

help [the students] face certain disagreeable facts—the fact that they have yet to master the kind of English required for success in school, the fact that there are new speech habits to be acquired, the fact that important decisions may go against them if they do not learn another way to talk.[12]

Psycholinguists like Wallace Lambert, Richard Tucker, and their colleagues at McGill University relate motivation to "instrumental" and "integrative" reasons for learning a second language. Robinett has made use of this principle to construct a continuum that differentiates English learners according to goal:

EFL appears at that point where English is looked upon as a cultural acquisition and the native language is dominant. "Instrumental" ESL, to use Lambert's term, is further along the continuum because English is being learned for a specific functional purpose, but the native language is still dominant. ESL as "integrative" is acquired because it is necessary, often because it is the language of instruction in the schools or because it is the language which is recognized as the common means of communication between peoples of various languages in a given country. Bilingual education comes next because both English and native language are viewed as necessary and useful, and equal emphasis is placed on both. ESOD (English as a second or other dialect) is closest to standard English.[13]

Since Robinett's article appeared, TESOL has added two domains: adult education and applied linguistics. Each of the domains can be more precisely defined through use of the concept of instrumental versus integrative. Norris has suggested that both instru-

---

12. Virginia French Allen, "A Second Dialect is Not a Foreign Language," in *Linguistics and the Teaching of Standard English to Speakers of Other Languages or Dialects,* ed. James E. Alatis (Washington, D.C.: Georgetown University Press, 1969), p. 194.

13. Betty Wallace Robinett, "The Domain of TESOL," *TESOL Quarterly* 6 (September 1972): 202.

mental and integrative reasons may be present in varying proportion in nearly all English language learning situations.[14] Elaborating
on both Robinett and Norris leads to the inclusion of both integrative and instrumental positions for each of the projected domains,
yielding the modified continuum shown in figure 1.

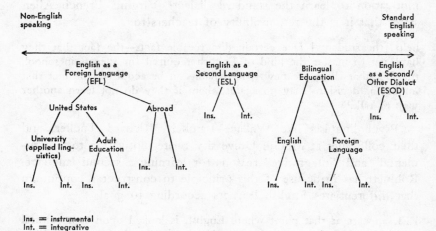

Ins. = instrumental
Int. = integrative

Fig. 1. Differentiation of English speakers according to goal
Source: Adapted from Betty Wallace Robinett, "The Domains of TESOL," *TESOL Quarterly* 6 (September 1972): 202.

Stress on learners' needs and goals introduced a new perspective
to classroom learning strategies. We have already seen that TESOL
began to turn to its sister disciplines, sociolinguistics and psycholinguistics, for assistance in defining linguistic and educational goals
for the language learner.

It is worthwhile tracing the history of TESOL methodology
from its first very close links with linguistic theory to its present
interdisciplinary stance. In its beginnings, TESOL methodology was
set within two major theoretical frameworks: descriptive linguistics
and behaviorist psychology. Descriptive linguistics stressed the
value of contrastive analysis; behaviorist psychology treated language as a set of habits learned through repetition of patterns.
TESOL professionals felt fairly confident in this approach and
were concerned primarily with developing more and fuller con-

14. William Norris, *TESOL at Beginning of the '70s.*, pp. 2-3.

trastive analyses, more and better teaching materials, and more extensive teacher-training facilities.

By the close of the 1960s, however, the transformational-generative school had usurped the place of descriptive linguistics as the most widespread and influential movement in American linguistics. This revolution had serious consequences for professionals in the field, since generative-transformational grammarians challenged the structuralists' assumptions about the nature and system of language, assumptions that were held to be fundamental to contemporary language teaching methods. In particular, they called into question the very premise that linguistics has any direct bearing on language teaching.

In the meantime, behaviorist psychology was coming under fire from psychologists and psycholinguists who argued that student attitudes, goals and motivation, as well as sociocultural patterns, should be primary considerations in language learning. As mentioned above, it was teachers of SESD who laid particular stress on these variables when faced with the evidence that difficulties in learning for Mexican-American and American Indian children were not cognitive but sociocultural. As a consequence of the upheaval wrought by the "discrediting" of the very principles upon which TESOL methodology had been founded, professionals concluded that, while the findings of linguistic research might be applied in teaching, the actual methodology must draw upon other disciplines, particularly sociolinguistics and psycholinguistics.

Sociolinguistics is defined as "the study of the characteristics of language varieties, the characteristics of their functions, and the characteristics of their speakers as these three constantly interact, change, and change one another within a speech community." [15]

Psycholinguistics seeks answers to the question "How is language learned?" The importance of a cognitive theory and its relevance to student goals and motivation may be seen from remarks by Jakobovits, who says that in order to be able to "decide upon the innovations in instructional procedures and materials which are to render foreign language teaching more effective . . . the teacher must come to have a proper understanding not only of psycholog-

15. Joshua Fishman, *Sociolinguistics* (Rowley, Mass.: Newbury House, 1970), p. 4.

ical theory and research per se, but of the process whereby psychologists themselves come to formulate these theories." [16]

Obviously, such an understanding requires far more of the teacher than native competency in the language. It also requires more than a B.A. in English literature or a certificate from a state teachers' college, however valuable literature and professional education courses may be to the well-educated TESOL professional. Unfortunately, despite the widespread need for professional English language teachers, a distinguishing characteristic of the TESOL field has always been a dearth of qualified personnel.

In April 1964, the U.S. Office of Education commissioned a nationwide study of the needs, practices, methods, and materials used in English as a second language in the United States. The results of this study pinpointed the principal features of the problem, namely inadequately prepared teachers and unsuitable materials. The report revealed that teachers entrusted with the teaching of English to children of non-English-speaking backgrounds were almost totally unprepared for their work. Of the elementary and secondary school teachers sampled, 91 percent had no practice teaching in ESL; 85 percent had no formal study in methods of teaching ESL; 75 percent had no formal training in English phonetics, morphophonemics, or syntax; 61.8 percent had no training in general linguistics.[17]

With these data in hand, it was now possible to support assertions that professionally educated teachers of English as a second language were needed; that their education should include components of fact and theory and practice; that new kinds of textbooks must be prepared, particularly for such culturally distinct groups as the Indian children in the Southwest and illiterate non-English-speaking adults; that educational administrators must treat more professionally the complex nature of English language instruction. The *TENES* report contributed greatly to the eventual recog-

16. Leon Jakobovits, *Foreign Language Learning: A Psycholinguistic Analysis of the Issues* (Rowley, Mass.: Newbury House, 1970), p. xvi.

17. Harold B. Allen, *TENES: A Survey of the Teaching of English to Non-English Speakers in the U.S.* (Urbana, Ill.: National Council of Teachers of English, 1966), pp. 28-30.

nition in the United States of TESOL as a professional discipline in its own right.

However, fifteen years after the TENES survey, how does the profession stand? Let us first consider again the extent to which English is a foreign language in the United States. An estimated 28 million persons (one in eight) in the United States have non-English language backgrounds; 10.6 million of these have Spanish language backgrounds. An estimated 2.4 million persons in the United States do not speak English at all. Further, contrary to general belief, most of these persons (two out of three or 18.5 million) are not foreign but native born.[18]

One must add to the numbers of this established population the steady influx of immigrants and refugees, which is likely to grow greater if current efforts to revise the refugee laws succeed in establishing a new yearly quota of at least 50,000 refugees (10,000 more than present legislation permits).[19] Statistics suggest that the United States is no less in need of professional ESL teachers than it was at the time of the *TENES* survey. Yet in 1976-77, of an estimated 102,000 public school teachers of English as a second language, only three out of ten had taken even one course in teaching ESL.[20]

One cannot plead too strongly that serious attention be paid to professional training for teachers of English as a second language. In its guidelines for the certification and preparation of those teachers, the TESOL organization states that it is important for teachers of ESL/EFL to have the experience of learning another language, that a training program to achieve this end is both possible and desirable, and that such a program will ultimately produce an improved ESL component and therefore an improved Bilingual Education program.[21]

18. Dorothy Waggoner, "Non-English Language Background Persons: 3 U.S. Surveys," *TESOL Quarterly* 12 (September 1978): 247, 249.

19. Christopher Dickey, "Carter Seeking Major Revision of Refugee Laws," *Washington Post*, 8 March 1979, Section A, p. 1, column 1.

20. Waggoner, "Non-English Language Background Persons," p. 247.

21. *Guidelines for the Certification and Preparation of Teachers of English to Speakers of Other Languages in the United States* (Washington, D.C.: Teachers of English to Speakers of Other Languages, 1975). Copies of this pamphlet may be obtained from TESOL at the address given in footnote 6.

The particular strength of professionally trained ESL teachers is their ability to assist immigrants and refugees to adjust to and function within American society, while at the same time recognizing and affirming the importance of the native languages and cultures. In this regard it should be stressed that TESOL programs are clearly in the national interest. It should be equally clear that TESOL programs are also in the international interest. This statement is not intended as an espousal of the "let 'em learn English" approach to international relations. Nonetheless, it is an indisputable fact that English has become the world's most widely taught foreign language. Professionals in the language teaching field encourage foreign language instruction for everyone; for a great many people, English is a foreign language, and for political and historical reasons a very important one. Foreign language professionals view with justifiable alarm the decline in support of English teaching abroad. At the same time, they view with no less alarm the failure among Americans, both at home and abroad, to consider seriously the importance of foreign language learning. Ferguson has made the point that although the United States is the world's leader in quality research on language acquisition in first and second languages, it is probably the world's poorest consumer of that research.[22] Professionals are keenly aware of the principle of reciprocity in language learning and have been careful to point out that they did not expect the rest of the world to learn English while Americans remained complacently monolingual.

Thus it may be seen that, just as the fields of TESOL and Bilingual Education are inextricably intertwined, so are the fortunes of TESOL professionals tied to those of the entire foreign language profession. Unfortunately, it has often been the case that interrelated fields such as TESOL, bilingual education, linguistics, international studies, and foreign language education have neutralized each other's efforts because of a lack of cohesiveness among their professional organizations. TESOL professionals must learn to work together with other professionals in language and international studies toward a common goal. The myriad language and area

22. Charles Ferguson, "Language and Global Interdependence," in *Language in American Life*, ed. E. Michael Gerli et al. (Washington, D.C.: Georgetown University Press, 1978), p. 31.

study organizations must integrate their efforts in order to avoid the proliferation, duplication, and internecine conflicts that consume energy and prevent the formation of effective programs.

Unfortunately, language professionals have habitually reflected, not shaped, the interests of the public. If the profession is to acquire and maintain intellectual strength and influence, it must create a new concept of the professional and a new concept of a single professional entity. The professional organizations represent a constituency of over 100,000 people, whose most important immediate assignment is the education of the public officials—in particular, politicians, lawmakers, judges—whose decisions affect so profoundly the affairs of the profession. Particularly on the domestic scene, it is unrealistic of the federal government to increase immigration quotas without providing the necessary resources to accommodate the language needs such a policy creates. It behooves us also to present to the American public the strongest case possible for language and area studies in order to convince the government that TESOL programs deserve extensive and extended support. Recent events suggest that such support may be forthcoming. In particular, the establishment of the President's Commission on Foreign Language and International Studies suggests that some attention is being paid to the language needs of the American people. Furthermore, contrary to its original intentions, the Commission recently announced its decision to add two fields of language study to its considerations: English as a second language and bilingual education. It remains to be seen whether the results of the Commission will effect a reversal of the trend toward reduced commitment to English language instruction abroad and diminished foreign language studies at home. Nonetheless, TESOL professionals should be encouraged by the Commission's recognition both of the interrelatedness of ESL and bilingual education and by the inclusion of English language teaching within the wider field of foreign language instruction.

CHAPTER VI

Bilingual Education

ANTHONY GRADISNIK

Background of Bilingual Education in United States

Bilingual education is not new in the United States. School laws in the 1800s in Ohio (1839), Wisconsin (1846), Colorado (1867), Oregon (1872), Maryland (1874), and Minnesota (1877) dealt specifically with the language issue in the curriculum either as a medium of instruction or as a subject to be taught.

While emphasis at present is on Spanish as the leading minority language in bilingual education, in the 1800s German was receiving the greatest attention, especially in the Midwest. But even as far west as Oregon, and as early as 1872, state legislation permitted public schools in which instruction was given completely in German. Bilingual schools in Milwaukee (1846), Cincinnati (1840), and Baltimore (1874) reflected the intense desire by the German population to have their children be instructed in and maintain the German language. The extent of the German language influence is indicated by the Wisconsin law of 1846, which recognized only those Milwaukee schools as public that at least taught English as subject matter.[1] Even in Missouri, where the state law required instruction in English, the 1887-88 report of the State Supervisor of Education testified that the German population was so large and influential in some school districts that instruction was mainly or entirely in German.[2] In addition to the public schools, many non-public schools, mainly the parochial schools, were bilingual. The first generation of Germans not only considered their own private parochial schools to be superior to the common schools of the day,

1. Heinz Kloss, *The American Bilingual Tradition* (Rowley, Mass.: Newbury House, 1977), pp. 86-87, 158-59, 180, 190-91.

2. Ibid., p. 89.

but also as places where their children could maintain their language and cultural traditions.

The rationale given by German-Americans to support the use of the German language in the schools of the 1800s closely resembles that used to justify the existence of modern "maintenance" programs in bilingual education. They argued that German was important as an international language, that its use in schools made sense for children from German-speaking families, and that it was also very enriching for children from English-speaking families.[3] Bruce, a Milwaukee historian and educator, defended the use of German, stating that "the bridge upon which the immigrant passed from foreignism, let us say Germanism, to Americanism, was a foreign language . . . and that language (German) did more to anchor the German-born on American ideas than could have been accomplished through the English language."[4]

Before modern programs for bilingual education began to make their appearance in the 1960s and the early 1970s, the teaching of English as a second language, not bilingual education, was the approach employed to provide for the special language needs of non-English-speaking children. Little, if any, attention was paid to the special language needs of children with limited proficiency in English. Actually, it was not until the 1960s that programs for the teaching of English as a second language began to be widely extended throughout the United States. New York City had pioneered with special instruction in English for children of the many different ethnic and language groups continually arriving in that city. But in most cities such instruction was, if not entirely negligible, at least in the embryonic stages of development in 1960.

As a result of the migration of thousands of Cubans to Florida in 1963, the Dade County Public Schools adopted bilingual education as the best approach to meet the special educational needs of the children of Cuban refugees. Started first on a voluntary basis at the Coral Way School, the program soon became so popular that it was extended to other schools. An evaluation of pupils' achievement found that pupils in the bilingual program performed as well

3. Ibid., pp. 93-94.

4. William George Bruce, *A Short History of Milwaukee* (Milwaukee, Wis.: Bruce Publishing Co., 1936), p. 67.

as those in a control group in the regular curriculum. In addition, the Spanish-speaking pupils were learning to read and write in their native language and English-speaking pupils had the advantage of learning a second language.[5] The Dade County bilingual education program, the first in modern times, contributed greatly to the reawakening of interest in bilingual education. In 1964, other bilingual education programs in Spanish-English were initiated in Texas at the Nye School, outside Laredo, and in the San Antonio Independent School District. Before federally funded bilingual projects were sponsored under the Bilingual Education Act of 1968, fifty-six bilingual programs were already in operation and extended from Calexico, California, to Hoboken, New Jersey. In 1969, a year after the passage of the Bilingual Education Act, seventy-six bilingual projects were approved by the U.S. Office of Education for funding under Title VII of the Elementary and Secondary Education Act. Most of them were for Spanish-English programs.[6] In 1977, there were 518 bilingual education projects funded under Title VII, representing sixty-seven different languages and dialects, including Arabic, Cherokee, Chinese, French, Greek, Italian, Pennsylvania Dutch, Polish, Portuguese, and Yiddish.

Federal funding for bilingual education programs has been concentrated mainly at the elementary school level. *Los Olvidados*— the forgotten ones—are the students at the high school level. There has been little encouragement from the U.S. Office of Education for the implementation of high school programs. Only thirty-two school systems, located in just ten states and Puerto Rico, had a federally funded bilingual program for high school students in 1972-73.[7] That number has not grown much since, even though newly arrived, non-English-speaking high school students have such

5. Mabel Wilson Richardson, "An Evaluation of Certain Aspects of Academic Achievement of Elementary Pupils in a Bilingual Program: A Project" (Coral Gables, Fla.: University of Miami, 1968), mimeograph.

6. Theodore Andersson and Mildred Boyer, *Bilingual Education in the United States* (Austin, Tex.: Southwest Educational Development Laboratory, 1970), pp. 18-20.

7. Anthony Gradisnik, "*Los Olvidados:* Meeting Bilingual Education Student Needs at the Secondary Level," in *Report of the Central States Conference on the Teaching of Foreign Languages,* ed. Frank Grittner (Skokie, Ill.: National Textbook Co., 1974), p. 85.

a short time to learn English and other high school subjects before their high school careers are over. Too often they drop out of school before receiving a diploma. Consider, for example, a fifteen-year-old, newly arrived, non-English-speaking Puerto Rican student. In a high school without bilingual education, he takes such subjects as history, mathematics, and science, in classes where English is the medium of instruction. He spends a year or two vainly trying to read words he cannot understand. Frustrated because he cannot understand what is going on, he finally drops out. Had he been programmed into a class in English as a second language and into bilingual classes where he would have had the advantage of learning and understanding subject matter taught in both English and in his native language, the boy might have completed high school.

Why Bilingual Education?

A proposal to introduce a program in bilingual education raises such questions as: What will a bilingual approach offer that cannot be offered by instruction in English alone? Is bilingual education pedagogically sound? Will children learn better? What happens to the child's ability to understand, speak, read, and write English? Why should a school system change from instruction in English only and include another language as a medium of instruction? Some staunch opponents of bilingual education ask if it will threaten the American way of life by reducing the prominence of the English language as a unifying force. They point to the possible perils involved in using a bilingual policy to perpetuate cultural separatism and enclaves based on language, mentioning the divisions between the English- and French-speaking cultures in Canada as cases in point.

Those who support the introduction of bilingual education take the view that such an education is the right of all children, not only of those who speak no English. They do not regard bilingual education as a compensatory or remedial program. They insist that instruction in English as a second language is not bilingual education, although bilingual instruction that includes instruction in English as a second language is regarded as the preferred model for instructing students of limited English proficiency.[8] They regard the linguistic and cultural differences of children as assets rather than liabilities and they see bilingual education as providing an opportunity for enrichment that capitalizes on these characteristics. They deny that it is the intent of programs in bilingual education to segregate children who are linguistically and culturally different from the rest of the school population. Rather, they see it as desirable for children of all ethnic backgrounds to be integrated so as to reap the greatest benefits of cross-cultural exchanges with peers.[9]

Supporters of bilingual education also argue that its opponents ignore the way Americans have lived linguistically and culturally, since throughout the nation's history the kind of education parents have chosen for their children has depended upon the time, the place, and the situation. They point out that the America of the early 1900s was distinctly different from the complex technological society of today. At the turn of the century, immigrants did not need highly developed skills in English to get jobs and make a living. Many children were not even enrolled in school (high school was for the elite) and many manual labor jobs, not requiring the ability to read or write English, were available for those who dropped out of school.

Those engaged in bilingual education emphasize that its primary concern is to help children with limited proficiency in English develop greater competence in that language, and also that use of the child's mother tongue, as well as English, as a medium of instruction makes sound pedagogical sense. It helps the pupil bridge the language gap more effectively in his efforts to learn concepts in various subjects. Children gain more confidence as they realize that they can learn in their own language before trying to learn concepts in a language they do not yet understand. Furthermore, the study of the history and culture associated with the minority

8. See "Position Paper on the Role of English as a Second Language in Bilingual Education," *TESOL Newsletter* (Washington, D.C.: Georgetown University, September, 1976), p. 14.

9. Albar Peña, "Bilingual Education: The What, the Why, and the How," *Journal of the National Association for Bilingual Education* 1 (May 1967): 28.

pupils' mother tongue is considered essential in helping the pupils to achieve a positive identification first with their own language and culture and then to take legitimate pride in both cultures. This feeling of well-being and pride can be a positive factor in attitudes of minority children toward school and their desire to learn. The close correlation between a positive self-concept and successful learning experiences has been emphasized by the U.S. Commission on Civil Rights. The Commission has recorded numerous instances of how an English-only curriculum has had negative effects on the attitudes of minority-language children toward themselves. Testimony included comments from Hispanos who said that they were ashamed of their background because of the way they were taught and that the "no Spanish" rule added to their feeling of discouragement.[10] The relationship of a student's self-concept to success in school was also documented in the Coleman Report of 1966, in which it was found that minority-language children generally had a tendency to doubt their capability to achieve success and, even more than English-speaking students, they doubted their ability to learn.[11]

The Commission on Civil Rights has endorsed bilingual education as an important means for providing equal educational opportunity for students with limited or no proficiency in English. It has emphasized that bilingual education also helps to attain another valuable objective—"the enrichment of the education of children of all socioeconomic levels and racial-ethnic groups through learning two languages and two cultures."[12]

Proponents of bilingual education also stress that a child should not have to sacrifice his rich native language and culture to achieve meaningful participation in a society whose language and culture is different from his own. Furthermore, they see bilingual education as consistent with the concept of "options for learning," which enables parents to have freedom of choice as to the educational alter-

10. Kathleen A. Buto et al., *A Better Chance to Learn: Bilingual-Bicultural Education* (Washington, D.C.: United States Commission on Civil Rights, 1975), pp. 33-36.

11. James S. Coleman, *Equality of Educational Opportunity* (Washington, D.C.: U.S. Government Printing Office, 1966), pp. 288-90.

12. Buto et al., *A Better Chance to Learn*, p. 4.

natives they prefer for their children. Since instruction in English only has not in the past provided sufficient successful experiences for minority-language children whose proficiency in English is limited, bilingual education offers parents an alternative.

Advocates of bilingual education also remind critics that there have been beneficial changes in home-school relations, in great part due to the bilingual education movement. Prior to the first Bilingual Education Act in 1968, few parents of minority-language children were aware of or involved in their school's educational program or activities. But in the past few years, increased parental involvement and visible concern and support for their children's educational development have resulted in improved home-school relations in school districts throughout the country. In addition, school administrators, teachers, and counselors appear to have an increased sensitivity and a deeper understanding of the needs of the minority-language child.

Toward Federal Support for Bilingual Education

EARLY SUPPORTERS OF BILINGUAL EDUCATION

In the 1960s, the movement for bilingual education was the result of a combination of historical events, political pressures, civil rights activism, and a new ethnic consciousness. It took certain political and educational leaders to awaken Congress and the public to the educational needs of children who were dropping out of school at a rate higher than other children. Senator Yarborough of Texas is often called the father of bilingual education. As chairman of the Special Senate Subcommittee on Bilingual Education, he pointed out that

The failure of our schools to educate Spanish-speaking students is reflected in comparative drop-out rates. In the five Southwestern states . . . Anglos fourteen years of age and over completed an average of twelve years of school compared with 8.1 years for Spanish-surname students. I regret that my own state of Texas ranks at the bottom with a median of only 4.7 years of school completed by persons of Spanish surname, according to the 1960 census.[13]

13. U.S. Congress, Senate, Special Subcommittee on Bilingual Education of the Senate Committee on Labor and Public Welfare, *Hearing on S. 428*, 90th Cong., 1st Sess., 18 May 1967, pp. 1-2.

The efforts of Senator Yarborough and other senators and congressmen laid the groundwork for the first bilingual education bill ever passed by the U.S. Congress. When signing the Bilingual Education Act of 1968, President Johnson emphasized that the legislation was a new effort to prevent dropouts since it provided a "better start—a better chance in school" for children of Latin and Indian descent.

Other supporters of bilingual education had been busy bringing into sharper focus the urgent need for a modern bilingual education program, which they thought was long overdue. Andersson emphasized that one of our sins in education is the failure to respect the languages and cultures of our minority children, whether Hispanic, Eskimo, Navajo, or Hawaiian. Referring to the National Defense Education Act of 1958, which provided thousands of dollars for developing and improving the language proficiency of nonnative Spanish teachers, Andersson deplored the irony of the fact that nothing was being done to maintain and develop further the language skills of Spanish-speaking children.[14]

A. Bruce Gaarder, a staunch advocate of the maintenance of native language, emphasized the absurdity of an educational policy that resulted in the spending of about $1 billion annually to teach languages in schools, colleges, and universities while virtually nothing was being done to maintain and develop the native language skills of children.[15] Fishman, one of the most knowledgeable investigators of bilingualism, language maintenance, and language shift in the United States, urged that measures be taken to establish a policy of planned reinforcement of language maintenance. He also recommended the establishment of a commission on biculturalism (or bilingualism) in American life, the establishment of bilingual public schools, and the establishment of a Department of Language Maintenance in the U.S. Office of Education.[16]

Fishman's recommendation for a federal bilingual office bore fruit. In 1969, an Office for Spanish-speaking American Affairs was

14. Theodore Andersson, "A New Focus on the Bilingual Child," *Modern Language Journal* 49 (March, 1965): 155-60.

15. *Hearing on S. 428*, p. 54.

16. Joshua Fishman, "The Status and Prospects of Bilingualism in the United States," *Modern Language Journal* 49 (March 1965): 143-55.

established in the Office of Education under the direction of
Armando Rodriguez. With the expansion of its responsibilities and
functions, that office was later designated as the Office of Bilingual
Education, with Josué González as its director. Another important
development was the creation of the National Advisory Council
on Bilingual Education. The Council is the central nerve of the
bilingual education movement in the nation. Its function is to advise
the Secretary of Health, Education, and Welfare as to general
regulations and matters of policy in bilingual education. Reflecting
a more global perspective in its report to the President and the
Congress in 1975, the Council significantly and deliberately accepted in 1975 the substitution of "bilingual multicultural education"
for "bilingual education."[17]

FEDERAL LEGISLATION ON BILINGUAL EDUCATION

Title VII of the Elementary and Secondary Education Act
of 1965 has been amended on three different occasions to include
legislation pertaining to bilingual education. With the Bilingual
Education Act of 1968, the federal government deliberately gave
official support to bilingual education for the first time. In 1974
and again in 1978, Congress amended the Act. The Bilingual Education Acts of 1968, 1974, and 1978 do not compel schools to establish
bilingual programs. Rather, schools are provided opportunities to
receive federal funding if they are fortunate enough to have their
project proposals accepted.

The main purpose of legislation on bilingual education is to
provide equal educational opportunity mainly for minority children of limited English proficiency in programs that are designed
to help them achieve competence in the English language while using
their native language. Programs funded under the Bilingual Education Acts are to use both English and the child's mother tongue
as mediums of instruction and instruction is to include an appreciation for the cultural heritage of such children.

The Bilingual Education Act of 1978 reflects a significant change
in the definition of pupils who are to benefit from the law. It now
specifies children of "limited English proficiency" rather than

17. National Advisory Council on Bilingual Education, *Annual Report*
(Washington, D.C.: the Council, November 1, 1975), p. 8.

"children with limited English-speaking ability." This change allows inclusion of minority pupils who have difficulty reading and writing English as well as those with difficulties in understanding and speaking the language. Before a decision was reached to use the term "limited English proficiency," there was much discussion of alternative terms such as "limited English ability," "limited English language skills," "limited English language proficiency."

In all three of the Bilingual Education Acts, Congress has shied away from any legislation advocating "maintenance" of language skills. Bilingualism for children, as contrasted with bilingual education, has not been an objective of congressional legislation. Instead, the intent has been to provide "transitional" bilingual education in which further instruction using the native language is not required once a student is fully functional in English. Yet, a 1974 survey by the National Education Task Force de la Raza revealed that 87 percent of the bilingual education programs advocated maintenance programs and considered their programs to be of that type.

In addition to ignoring the maintenance of native language skills of minority children, Congress also emphasized in 1974 that, "in no event shall the program be designed for the purpose of teaching a foreign language to English-speaking children."[18] In the Bilingual Education Act of 1978, Congress continued to reflect a "transitional" stance in regard to minority-language children by emphasizing that federally funded programs must provide

measurable goals for determining when those children no longer need such assistance and provide, from state and local sources, for necessary follow-up services to sustain the achievement of the children after they have left the program, except that if any child is enrolled in a bilingual program assisted under this title for two years that child shall have an individual evaluation establishing the need for continued services.[19]

This last provision clearly requires school districts that receive federal funds to establish some type of "entrance" and "exit" criteria to determine when a minority child has acquired sufficient English language skills and is no longer considered to be of "limited English proficiency."

18. Bilingual Education Act, 1974, U.S. Public Law 93-380, Sect. 703.
19. Congressional Record, House, 10 October 1978, p. H12174.

The Bilingual Education Act of 1978 appears to be more liberal in permitting children whose language is English to acquire some measure of second-language understanding. It provided that:

In order to prevent segregation of children on the basis of national origin in programs assisted under this title, and in order to broaden the understanding of children about languages and cultural heritages other than their own, a program of bilingual instruction may include the participation of children whose language is English, but in no event shall the percentage of such children exceed 40 per centum.[20]

By inserting the provision, "to broaden the understanding of children about languages and cultural heritages other than their own," Congress may have anticipated the forthcoming report of the President's Commission on Foreign Language and International Studies. The Commission, authorized in 1978 by President Carter, was created because the United States was not meeting its obligations under the 1975 Helsinki Accord to strengthen and improve foreign language and area studies. One of the charges given to the Commission was to "review existing legislative authorities and make recommendations for changes needed to carry out most effectively the Commission's recommendations."[21]

The President's Commission is presently engaged in public hearings throughout the nation. Its recommendations could well have far-reaching legislative implications for bilingual education if it chooses to encourage the "maintenance" type of bilingual program as a viable means of nurturing and further developing a child's native language skills. Support for this approach has also been made a part of the "Resolutions on Language in American Education," jointly prepared by the American Council on the Teaching of Foreign Languages, the Modern Language Association, and the Center for Applied Linguistics. These organizations urged the President's Commission to support the resolutions, including the proposal that, "to develop existing language resources, the schools should offer students from non-English-speaking backgrounds the opportunity to study their home language."

20. Ibid., p. H12173.

21. *Federal Register* 43 (April 25, 1978): 17457.

Even though federal legislation does not provide funding under Title VII of the Elementary and Secondary Education Act for "maintenance" programs, the present Director of the Office of Bilingual Education, Josué González, is a staunch advocate of the maintenance concept. In an interview with the National Association for Bilingual Education, González stressed that school districts could and should supplement Title VII funding with local funds in order to make a maintenance program possible.[22] The Board of School Directors of the Milwaukee Public Schools did just that in 1974 when it officially endorsed a maintenance-developmental type of bilingual education from kindergarten through grade twelve.

In addition to the Bilingual Education Acts, other federal legislation and administrative regulations, court decisions, and state laws have given support to the right of children of limited English proficiency to equal educational opportunities through bilingual education. Legal pressures have caused many school districts to reexamine closely their practices in curriculum and instruction to ensure equal educational opportunities for these children. In addition, school systems are faced with budgetary pressures, since they risk the loss of federal funding if they are found to be in noncompliance with guidelines of the Office of Civil Rights.

Two federal laws have had a great influence on bilingual education. First, schools receiving federal funding are actually contractually bound under the Civil Rights Act of 1964 not to engage in discriminatory practices. One form of discrimination that could lead to forfeiture of federal funds is the failure to make appropriate provisions for minority-language children with limited proficiency in English. Second, the Equal Educational Opportunities Act of 1974 is quite specific in providing for the needs of children of limited English-speaking ability. It requires an educational agency to take appropriate action "to overcome language barriers that impede equal participation by students in its instructional programs."

Unlike the federal Bilingual Education Act, which provides funding opportunities but does not mandate bilingual education, various states have established laws requiring that bilingual pro-

22. *NABE News* 2 (November 1978): 1.

grams be established when the need exists. In 1969, when the first federal bilingual programs went into effect, no state had mandatory bilingual education legislation. In 1971, Massachusetts became the first state to legislate the establishment of transitional bilingual education programs. It also provided the needed financial assistance to help local school districts. Texas, Illinois, and New Jersey followed with bilingual legislation in 1973. As of August, 1978, according to information available from the National Clearinghouse for Bilingual Education, at least twenty states had enabling legislation for bilingual education. This clearinghouse, authorized by the Education Amendments of 1974, provides a long-needed service as the principal national information center for collecting, analyzing, and disseminating information on bilingual education.

THE COURTS AND BILINGUAL EDUCATION

In *Lau* v. *Nichols*, a class-action suit filed on behalf of some 1,800 non-English-speaking Chinese students against the San Francisco Unified School District, it was charged that these students were being denied meaningful instruction because they could not understand the language of the classroom. In its unanimous opinion in 1974 in this case, the U.S. Supreme Court relied solely on the Civil Rights Act of 1964, which bans discrimination based on grounds of race, color, or national origin in any program or activity receiving federal financial assistance. The Court ruled that the San Francisco schools had violated Title VI of the Civil Rights Act and could not argue the lack of discrimination because the Chinese students were provided with the same educational treatment as other students. The Court said:

Under these state-imposed standards there is no equality of treatment merely by providing students with the same facilities, textbooks, teachers, and curriculum; for students who do not understand English are effectively foreclosed from any meaningful education.[23]

The court went on to rule that "the district must take affirmative steps to rectify the language deficiency in order to open its instructional program to these students."

23. *Lau v. Nichols,* 414 U.S. 563 (1974).

This landmark decision of the Supreme Court was also important in that it upheld the authority of the Office of Civil Rights of the Department of Health, Education, and Welfare to issue rules, regulations, orders, and interpretations regarding educational programs for children of limited English-speaking ability. The Office of Civil Rights Memorandum of May 25, 1970, requiring federally funded school districts "to rectify the language deficiency in order to open its instructional program to these students," was specifically referred to by the Supreme Court.

In the summer of 1975, following the decision in *Lau* v. *Nichols,* the Office of Civil Rights issued a statement that is now commonly referred to as the "Lau Remedies." It held school districts accountable for identifying and providing for the special language needs of minority children who were non-English-speaking or who had limited English proficiency. Although the Lau Remedies appeared to stress bilingual education as a principal remedy, a memorandum of the Office of Civil Rights to its regional directors in April, 1976, attempted to clarify the policy of the Office by stating that "the Lau Remedies are not exclusive; however, when a district varies from the suggested OCR Remedies, a burden is placed upon that district to show that the Remedies submitted in the plan will be effective to cure the violations."[24]

Teitelbaum and Hiller, attorneys who have been extensively involved in litigation on equal educational opportunity and bilingual education, believe that, although the *Lau* decision did not expressly endorse bilingual education, it

legitimized and gave impetus to the movement for equal educational opportunity for students who do not speak English. *Lau* raised the nation's consciousness of the need for bilingual education, encouraged additional federal legislation, energized federal enforcement efforts, led to federal funding of nine regional "general assistance *Lau* centers," aided the passage of state laws mandating bilingual education, and spawned more lawsuits.[25]

24. Lloyd R. Henderson, "Memorandum to Directors, Office of Civil Rights, Regions I-X," April 8, 1976.

25. Herbert Teitelbaum and Richard J. Hiller, "Bilingual Education: The Legal Mandate," *Harvard Educational Review* 47 (May 1977): 139.

Other court cases since the *Lau* ruling have more specifically identified bilingual education as a court mandate. In the case of *Serna* v. *Portales Municipal Schools* (1974), the U.S. Tenth Circuit Court of Appeals held that children of limited English-speaking ability had a right to bilingual education. Of significance, too, was the ruling that English-dominant Chicanos and Anglo students also were to receive some bilingual instruction. In *Aspira of New York, Inc.* v. *Board of Education of the City of New York* (1974), the Court prescribed a bilingual program for those students who can learn more effectively in Spanish at the same time that they are receiving intensive instruction in English. The school board was required to develop an improved method of assessing and identifying students with English language difficulties. The Court also rejected immersion as a technique of second-language learning for minority children. A decision rendered by the district court in the case of *Rios* v. *Read* (1977) involving the school district of Patchogue-Medford, Long Island, resulted in acknowledgment by the court that the school district did provide a remedial program for limited-English children and did have a bilingual department. But the court also observed that increasing the quantity of bilingual programs was "meaningless without a concomitant emphasis on the quality of instruction."[26]

Bilingual Education in Controversy

THE EPSTEIN REPORT

In the short time since it appeared in 1977, a report by Epstein has had a tremendous impact on policy makers and has caused leaders in bilingual education to assess carefully the philosophy, implementation, and evaluation of bilingual education programs.[27] Formerly education editor for the *Washington Post*, Epstein spent six months as a journalist-in-residence with the George Washington University Institute for Educational Leadership. His assignment

26. Ibid., pp. 147-50.

27. Noel Epstein, *Language, Ethnicity, and the Schools: Policy Alternatives for Bilingual-Bicultural Education* (Washington, D.C.: Institute for Educational Leadership, George Washington University, 1977), p. vi.

was to investigate bilingual education in the United States through extensive interviews with policy makers, critics, and advocates, as well as to examine thoroughly the works of educators, linguists, anthropologists, sociolinguists, political scientists, historians, and others. Epstein's work was intended to provide an "extensive synthesis, examination of policy alternatives, and a paper that would unravel complex issues for decision makers."

At the invitation of the Institute for Educational Leadership, José C. Cárdenas, Executive Director of the Intercultural Development Research Association, San Antonio, Texas, long recognized as a leader in bilingual education, prepared a critique of Epstein's report that is included in the publication. The following selected quotations from both authors reveal differences between them on a few of the controversial issues related to bilingual education:

Epstein	Cárdenas

On legal requirements for bilingual education

There is no federal legal requirement for schools to provide bilingual or bicultural education. (p. 2)	Though the Supreme Court in *Lau* v. *Nichols* did not provide such legal requirement, it must be remembered that the plaintiffs made no such request in the case. . . . Other court cases have resulted in much more explicit interpretations of federal law in regard to bilingual education. (p. 76)

On federal expenditures

After nearly nine years and more than half a billion dollars in federal funds . . . the government has not demonstrated whether such instruction makes any difference in the students' achievement, in their acquisition of English, or in their attitudes toward school. (p. 1)	On the other hand, traditional educational programs for minority children expend billions of dollars a year with a most remarkable consistency of failure and are replicated year after year at federal, state, and local expense with not only no evidence of success, but rather with substantial and conclusive proof of failure. (p. 81)

On cultural maintenance programs

It is also clear that bilingual-bicultural advocates want to provide such instruction to students who are proficient in English. They oppose using the native language only temporarily as a bridge to English instruction. Rather, they long have sought to give equal importance to the mother tongue and culture, pressing for what are called language and cultural "maintenance" programs. (p. 3)

Though most bilingual education advocates give highest priority to children of limited English-speaking ability, they share an ideal in which American schools will value other languages to the point of teaching them in our schools and maintaining and developing them in the case of language minorities. In many years of involvement in minority education, I have never heard the term or encountered the concept of "cultural maintenance programs." (p. 81)

EVALUATIONS OF BILINGUAL EDUCATION

One of the most controversial aspects of bilingual education has been the lack of effective evaluation and data-gathering procedures. Responding to a congressional mandate in 1974 to assess the effectiveness of Title VII bilingual programs, the Office of Education contracted with the American Institutes of Research (AIR) to make an evaluation in both the cognitive and affective domains. The $1.5 million study involved thirty-eight Spanish-English projects that were in the fourth and fifth year of federal funding. The AIR finding that the programs "did not appear to produce gains in student achievement over and above what would be expected . . . (in) a traditional classroom" brought sharp criticism. For example, Gray identified various weaknesses of the study, such as:

the failure to distinguish between the effects of good programs and weak programs; (the treatment of) bilingual education as an undifferentiated whole, which it is not; the short pre- and posttest design over a five-month period; (the) unreliability of teacher assessment of students' language ability; (the) inappropriate use of the Comprehensive Test of Basic Skills to assess English reading ability with limited-English and monolingual Spanish speakers.[28]

28. Tracy Gray, "Response to the AIR Study: Evaluation of the Impact of the ESEA Title VII Spanish/English Bilingual Education Program" (Washington, D.C.: Center for Applied Linguistics, April 18, 1977).

Because of the lack of solid evaluation procedures and results, the Bilingual Act of 1978 contained the provision that "by September 30, 1980, the Secretary shall develop evaluation and data-gathering models, which take into account linguistic and cultural differences of the child . . . and shall include allowances for variables."

Planning and Developing a Bilingual Education Program

Up to a few years ago, many school districts had no thought of implementing a bilingual education program. However, a combination of circumstances—an influx of children who did not speak English and had limited proficiency in the language, the Civil Rights "Remedies," pressure from parents and the community, state bilingual legislation, or perhaps a critical self-examination by the school district—has caused many school boards to consider whether or not a bilingual education program was needed in their districts.

Schools that question whether a bilingual education program is needed should also ask whether their children with limited-English proficiency are really being provided with equal educational opportunities. Are their language needs being adequately met by the present program? Are they achieving as well as the English speakers in learning subject matter and in learning to read English? Are the children happy, at ease, and ready to learn? Is the ratio of drop-outs from high school for these students out of proportion in comparison to their English-speaking peers? Are there bilingual teachers on the staff to meet their special instructional needs? Are parents actively involved in determining the kind of education they want for their children?

Leaders in bilingual education point out that some bilingual education programs do not achieve positive results because of failures in implementation rather than because the concept of bilingual education is faulty. Of paramount importance in planning and developing a bilingual program is the establishment of a sound management system under the leadership of a bilingual project director who is responsible for the overall success of the program. Working in cooperation with the supervisory staff, principals, teachers, and Bilingual Advisory Council, the Director takes appropriate action to overcome any obstacles that may jeopardize the attainment of the objectives of the program. A crucial component of the management system is the selection of capable teachers who are truly bilingual and well-trained in the philosophy and rationale of bilingual education and in the methods and techniques of second-language learning.

SUGGESTIONS FOR IMPLEMENTATION OF
BILINGUAL EDUCATION PROGRAMS

Based on the experiences of school districts that have established successful bilingual education programs, the following procedures for implementation appear to be basic and potentially fruitful:

1. Start with a small program and gradually enlarge it each year. A nucleus of experienced teachers, the acquisition of and familiarity with bilingual books and materials, good programming procedures and lesson planning will make the first year's task less monumental.

2. Provide for continuity so that eventually a program from kindergarten through grade twelve will be established. Having a "maintenance" bilingual program extending through every grade not only nurtures the bilingual potential of students; it also makes it easier to provide for the needs of non-English-speaking pupils no matter when they arrive or at what grade level.

3. Establish a bilingual advisory committee of parents at the neighborhood school level as well as at the district-wide level. Encourage active involvement of parents in evaluating the bilingual program. Involve high school students as members of the advisory council.

4. Establish a bilingual newsletter to keep everyone informed of school, city, state, and national developments in bilingual education.

5. Involve curriculum specialists from the State Department of Public Instruction to serve as an educational resource team to critique the program and make recommendations for its improvement.[29]

29. Anthony Gradisnik, "Bilingual Education Can and Does Work: The Milwaukee Story," in *Teaching for Tomorrow in the Foreign Language Classroom*, ed. Reid E. Baker (Skokie, Ill.: National Textbook Co., 1978), p. 64.

It is clearly evident that there is no one model for bilingual education programs that is applicable to all school districts. Small school districts without a large number of minority-language children have a problem in providing for the language needs of the one, two, or three newly arrived, non-English-speaking pupils who sporadically enroll in school. Too often, nothing is done to provide even a minimum program of instruction in English as a second language. Yet, the needs to learn English, the problems of cultural adjustment, the frustrations, and the search for identity are every bit as real for these pupils as for the non-English-speaking pupils in the southwest or the northeast where the numbers may be greater.

To meet the needs of these "isolates" who enroll at different times, school districts might consider designating one elementary school teacher and one secondary school teacher to serve as specialists in English as a second language or as bilingual teachers when needed. These teachers, with a reduced teaching assignment, could be assigned to other administrative or counseling tasks when no pupils with limited English proficiency are enrolled. They would need to prepare themselves as specialists in teaching English as a second language or as bilingual teachers by undertaking advanced study and by extensive reading in those fields. Another alternative for the school district is to employ qualified retired teachers as language consultants on a part-time basis.

MODELS FOR PROGRAMS OF BILINGUAL EDUCATION

Some of the models for programs of bilingual education from which school districts may choose are the following:

1. *The self-contained classroom,* with one bilingual teacher assisted by a bilingual aide. This is considered a most desirable arrangement.
2. *Team-teaching.* Two teachers, one bilingual and one monolingual, pool their teaching strengths. Such a program provides for flexibility, individualization, and opportunities for large-group interaction.
3. *The integrated full-day program.* Pupils from different classes are "pulled out" and given special instruction in subjects by a bilingual teacher.
4. *The departmental model.* In this model, which is popular at the junior and senior high school levels, students receive instruction in

subjects from different bilingual teachers in different rooms. Integration with other students is essential.

5. *A nonbilingual teacher assisted by a bilingual aide.* This teaching situation is considered the least desirable.

6. *A district-wide center for newly arrived non-English-speaking pupils.* School districts faced with the problem of providing "transitional" bilingual education for children of ethnic and minority-language groups that are small in number might consider establishing a center as a "magnet school."

A successful district-wide center has been established in the Milwaukee Public Schools. All newly arrived, non-English-speaking pupils in grades one through six are assigned to the Center for one year of language orientation. The pupils are assigned to regular classes but are "pulled out" for help in the English language from a specialist in the teaching of English as a second language. The budget provides for employing resource consultants in language from the community or local university on an hourly basis to tutor pupils in subjects in their native language. The length of time each child spends daily in the Center depends on the pupil's special language needs. Free transportation to the school is provided.

IMMERSION PROGRAMS IN SECOND-LANGUAGE LEARNING

A completely different kind of approach in bilingual education is designed specifically for the *majority*, not the *minority*, language child. Commonly referred to as a program of "immersion," this exciting new approach to second-language teaching began in Canada in the 1960s and has achieved outstanding success and popularity. In 1976-77, it was estimated that over 13,000 pupils in seventy-five Quebec schools were enrolled in immersion programs.

One of the most carefully researched second-language projects has been the early immersion program that began in an elementary school at St. Lambert, Quebec, in 1966. Begun at the insistence of English-speaking parents, the program aimed at developing functional French skills by having French, a second language for these children, used as the medium of instruction, not as the object of instruction. Unlike the traditional approach to second-language teaching, children in an "early immersion" program receive their instruction in subjects exclusively in the second language for the first two or three grades.

The results of an evaluation of the St. Lambert program at the end of grade four, for pupils who had started in kindergarten, revealed that the experimental pupils were at the same level in English reading, listening comprehension, and knowledge of English concepts as pupils in the English control group. In addition, they achieved favorably in French when compared to their French-speaking peers.[30]

In the United States, immersion language programs have been initiated slowly—too slowly, if one considers the positive results of Canadian evaluations. These results showed that children can achieve functional second-language ability without sacrificing any skills in English reading or achievement in subject learning. Then, too, American cities involved in desegregation planning, based on the establishment of specialty schools, might well consider establishing an early immersion language program in one of the elementary schools as a city-wide option for learning.

The immersion approach, based on the Canadian St. Lambert model, has proven to be very successful in the following five city public schools and one college experimental school in the United States: Culver City, California (1971)—Spanish; Silver Spring, Maryland (1974)—French, Spanish; Milwaukee, Wisconsin (1977)—German, French; San Diego, California (1977)—Spanish; Hayward, California (1976)—Spanish; Campus School, State University of New York, Plattsburgh (1976)—French.

If the immersion program has been so successful in Canada and the United States for English-speaking majority-language children who are learning a second language, why could not the same procedure work well for Spanish-speaking minority-language pupils in learning English? Lambert, the evaluator for the St. Lambert Project who is widely recognized for his research on minority-language children, has explained why this premise is not valid. He identifies two types of bilingualism: "subtractive bilingualism" and "additive bilingualism." If the minority child's native language is replaced to some degree by the majority language, it has a subtractive effect on the child. In some cases, such children may

30. Wallace E. Lambert and G. Richard Tucker, *Bilingual Education of Children: The St. Lambert Experiment* (Rowley, Mass.: Newbury House, 1972), pp. 203, 204.

develop low levels of achievement in both languages. In "additive bilingualism," where the child's first language is the dominant or majority language in the culture, the use and acquisition of a second language is an added achievement for the child and cognitive learning is more evident.

The immersion approach to second-language learning is being carefully reviewed by the President's Commission on Foreign Languages and International Studies. The immersion approach is attractive because it offers excellent opportunities for interdisciplinary and multidisciplinary studies, since the second language is incorporated into the processes of learning the subjects in the school program. Immersion also offers an excellent vehicle for cementing an alliance between global education and second-language learning.

Concluding Statement

Bilingual education is here to stay. Despite scathing attacks against it, bilingual education will survive and continue to play an important role in school districts where its implementation has been carefully planned and parent and community involvement encouraged. There is no doubt that publications such as Epstein's controversial *Language, Ethnicity, and the Schools* have caused soul searching by those involved in bilingual education and have exerted a decided influence on federal officials and legislators concerning bilingual education. As scrutiny of bilingual education by federal, state, and local authorities becomes focused more and more on accountability, more "error-proof," hard-data evaluation will be insisted upon, resulting in stronger bilingual education programs with multicultural overtones. Federal and state legislation, administrative regulations, and court decisions have had a decided impact and will continue to guide the direction and destiny of bilingual education into the 1980s.

A closer liaison and keener cooperative spirit, long overdue, will solidify the working relationships between those involved in bilingual education, those in the foreign language field, colleagues in the teaching of English as a second language, and members of the various language and bilingual education professional associations. They will become increasingly aware of the urgent need and the exciting potential that a united front offers in advancing second-language learning in the United States and in meeting the challenges of critics, legislators, and the general public.

CHAPTER VII

Foreign Language Study at the Postsecondary Level

FRANK G. RYDER

Trends can be reversed. In the halcyon days of the National Defense Education Act, few expected to see the field of language study in sharp decline with dropping enrollments in undergraduate and in graduate programs, casting a pall over all of postsecondary education. During the 1960s, leaders in the profession should have questioned the steady inflation of faculties and graduate admissions. Few did, and the prosperity did not last. But why should our current adversity be permanent? Is it time to question the gloom?

The gloom, to be sure, is deep. It culminates in almost macabre projections. In the 1980s, only 10 to 20 percent of our Ph.D.'s in the humanities will get academic jobs. The fifteen largest graduate departments of English could alone fill every job opening in the field for a decade, from universities to two-year colleges.[1] Given the steady state of enrollment in four-year colleges and universities, it is apparent that such projections imply not just trouble in the job market; they imply nothing less than the atrophy of postsecondary education as a whole. Without new people where will the new ideas come from? If the situation is that bad, contrary opinion is vain; heroic means of life support should be turned off.

The Nature of the Problem

Deterioration can of course proceed so far as to be irreversible. Some thoughtful observers argue that this is the case with universi-

---

1. Cited by M. G. Scully, "In Grad Schools, Unhappy Trends," *Chronicle of Higher Education*, 24 April 1978, p. 7. Allan Cartter reviews the underlying general trends in an article with Dorothy G. Harrison and Ernest R. May, "Preliminary Reports from the Higher Education Research Institute," *ADE and ADFL Bulletins*, special joint issue (September 1976): 66-72.

ties in countries like Italy. The irrationalities of number, structure, finances, and spirit have created an ever-increasing internal disorder, a kind of entropy, and the system may soon cease to work. American education, however, is historically characterized by resources of flexibility and recuperation, and the patient, although currently in crisis, should not be buried. We must be grateful to those who, on good grounds, warn us. As for the Cassandras—or the Polyannas —of the long-range statistic, we might propose a discount of at least half—or a bit less for the sanguine, rather more for the voices of doom. We all think like Calderón's Astolfo in *Life is a Dream*:

> What a great
> Astrologer would be one who foretold
> Nothing but harms, since there's no doubt at all
> That they are always due!

ELECTIVES AND REQUIREMENTS

Even with discount we face a future of crisis. Yet crises, unlike prosperity, require action and therefore permit the exercise of logic and astute planning. The first challenge is to identify the true locus (or loci) of our problem. Some of the dreary statistics are secondary or derivative; no good comes from reciting them all. Leaders in education must be prepared to worry selectively. For example, why must we take the erosion of degree requirements in foreign language to be either critical or primary? Many institutions, by intent or inadvertence, maintained their requirements through the days of intellectual anarchy and failed leadership—("Pick any courses you want: I can't tell you what to take."). Those days are gone and surviving requirements will probably not be abrogated. New ones may well be added. The cafeteria is closing and the dietitians are taking over. Harvard's core curriculum is a portent and a stimulus to other institutions. Basic demands will be made, headed by the truly modest proposal that we should be literate. Refusing to tolerate bottomless affront to our mother tongue may be the largest single impetus for remedial measures against other forms of ignorance. Reintroduction or lengthening of the foreign language requirement is altogether conceivable. If that is a testimony to the importance of foreign language in the world today and among the intellectual furnishings of a civilized American, that is

fine—so long as the requirement is not unique but in the company
of other necessities. If it serves to protect us alone and to perpetuate
and sanctify what we are now doing, it is not fine but a great
shame. In nature the unchallenged organism dies. In education it
becomes dull.

THE GROWTH OF TWO-YEAR COLLEGES

By contrast, enrollment figures for foreign languages in the
two-year colleges are the objective correlative of a genuine emer-
gency, not because Spanish now holds an absolute majority of
elections, exceeding by a wide margin French, German, Russian,
Italian, Latin, Japanese, Chinese, and all the rest together,[2] but
because all foreign languages together constitute a merest crumb
on the pie chart for the one growing segment of American education. Cosand long ago predicted that the two-year schools would
in the mid-1980s be an instructional home to over half the students
in higher education.[3] That promises to be one of the accurate
predictions. Right now one can extrapolate to an approximate
4,500,000 students in two-year programs (compared to about 7,300,-
000 in four-year programs), and of these 4.5 million a minuscule
18,000 take German; 36,000, French; 94,000, Spanish.[4] One percent
of 4,500,000 is 45,000. That surely defines a crisis.

THE RELATIONSHIP BETWEEN GRADUATE
AND UNDERGRADUATE PROGRAMS

Our educational system may not be a sacred edifice but it is
in a real sense a wall against chaos and barbarism. Small cracks
at crucial junctures can be serious, especially if they escape notice.
How many of us are aware of the rapid deterioration at the hinge
between college and graduate school? So much hue and cry has
been raised over the glut of Ph.D.'s and the shortage of jobs that
we have failed to notice what has happened at the foot of Parnassus,

2. *MLA Newsletter,* Winter 1978.

3. J. P. Cosand, "The Community College in 1980," in *Campus 1980,* ed.
Alvin Eurich (New York: Delacorte, 1968), pp. 134-48.

4. "Twenty-year Trends in Higher Education," *Chronicle of Higher Education,* 13 November 1978, p. 13.

partly as a consequence of all the hue and cry. No one, relatively speaking, is starting the climb.

THE ENROLLMENT CRISIS

Few of us realize how acutely sensitive a system becomes as it approaches minimal population. This is the case with graduate programs in foreign language. The threshold of administrative malaise concerning student numbers seems to lie around five or ten. Below that, in class size, in advanced degrees per year, in admissions to the graduate department, the fiscal heart beats more slowly and pumps less blood. The faculty argues against procrustean decisions by the number. But number is a real thing. If a department admits four students per year (and all survive—highly unlikely), and each takes four courses at a time, and the department offers five courses each semester, and it takes the student three years to get his course work done, then there will be ten students on the average in each course. If the department offers six courses, there will be eight in each. If the student takes only three courses at a time, there will be seven or six. If the department admits only three—or if only that many survive—there will be seven or six, or five or four. Somewhere it ceases to be a course or a seminar. Somewhere critical mass is not attained and the whole operation breaks down. And even the most sanguine faculty member cannot argue against the significance of one figure: zero. Visits around the country confirm the approach to that unenviable statistic at two kinds of institutions, the very good small graduate programs and those frankly marginal in attractiveness. Departments that are both large and good may not have to worry—yet. Figures from the Association of Departments of Foreign Language, registrations for the *Graduate Record Examination*, and simple observation confirm large declines in applications everywhere.[5] I do not question for a moment that, faced with a vacuum, universities and departments will lower standards and admit the walking dead. The temptation

5. The beginning of the decline was noted as early as 1971 in the *ADFL Bulletin* 3 (September 1971): 9. From 1970 to 1971 applications showed a drop of 18.4 percent at 102 Ph.D. departments and of 23.9 percent at 146 M.A. departments. American Council on Education figures showed that the total number of *Graduate Record Examinations* taken in French, German, and Spanish declined from 2650 in 1975-76 to 2150 in 1976-77.

is great; and the punishment for having insufficient students is terrible: no teaching assistants for the beginning work, anemic graduate courses and crippled seminars, and what is for some the threat of having to teach undergraduates all the time. In sum, a crushing blow to our modus operandi and our ego.

Graduate students still in the pipeline—the metaphor is customary but undignified—will continue to come out the other end. But there will be no siphon effect if there is no water, and for some universities the flow will dry up. Of some of these we will say it was a mercy. The shortage of jobs can of course be prolonged if professors continue to teach until age seventy, ignoring all inducements for early retirement and all human beings but themselves. The American Association of University Professors says the seventy-year limit will cause serious problems well into the 1980s. Even this irritant will diminish, however, and especially in foreign languages (but probably not in English, history, and the other *Massenbetriebe*) it is barely possible to see an end to the Ph.D. glut. Are we prepared?

THE QUALITY OF DOCTORAL PROGRAMS

A final point at which the statistical picture is threatening relates intimately to the above. It is hard to get figures for Spanish and French, but those for German are clear, probably typical, and thoroughly alarming. Sixty-five American departments list themselves as offering the Ph.D.[6] Of these, seven have only two full professors, six have only one, and one has none. As to the number of departments offering the Ph.D., it is two or three times too large. As to the number of full professors, unless there is some inverse relationship between promotion and excellence, those fourteen departments (over 20 percent of the roster) have somehow failed to comprehend the demands, the dignity, and the legitimate price of graduate instruction. They should forthwith abandon their pretense.

THE ENROLLMENT PICTURE AND THE NEEDS OF SOCIETY

We customarily identify as our principal crisis the battered state of enrollments in college foreign language classes. In the

6. "Personalia 1978-79, German Departments in the U.S.A.," *Monatshefte* 70 (Fall 1978): 255-80.

sense that fewer young people escape the prison house of monolingualism, the decline is indeed a tragedy. But if we mean only that our courses are underelected, the tragedy is, ironically, less acute and the crisis is in part of our own making. We do a poor job of demonstrating, of translating into reality, the deep intellectual relevance of our discipline. More often we make no attempt at all. The remedies available for such negligence are all the more deserving of urgent attention because it is not inconceivable that the external situation, in the four-year colleges at least, will rectify itself before we have rectified our negligence. Not merely are requirements apt to reappear; the very establishment of the Modern Language Association Task Forces,[7] supported by the Rockefeller Foundation, and most recently of the President's Commission, is almost reminiscent of the days of William Riley Parker, the post-Sputnik era. The impetus this time is less specifically from outside the language teaching profession and it is less a single trauma that initiates the action. It stems rather from a growing awareness of certain grave developments in this country and in the world around us.

FOREIGN LANGUAGES AND INTERNATIONAL REALITIES

Those developments, remote as they seem to be, deserve to rank among the trends that bear critically on our situation in the foreign languages. The United States has, in a word, changed from a creditor nation to a debtor, from a comparative stronghold of monetary integrity to a solicitor of alms-like currency props, from a nation proud of exporting its business ventures, products, and acumen to a nation on the block, its businesses, houses, even its farm land for sale at bargain prices—and all this with respect to nations whose languages we scarcely deign to learn. It is well that such economic relations become a two-way path, but it is a shame to have it happen without our volition and to see the needle of the compass swing quite so violently. Above all, it is pathetic that we must negotiate monolingually in defense of our fiscal independence.

7. See "Report of the Task Force on Institutional Language Policy," *ADFL Bulletin* 10 (November 1978): 1-11. This is required reading for those who make policy in the foreign language field.

THE GROWING ECONOMIC DEPENDENCE OF AMERICA

If all this seems extreme, consider that our balance of payments deficit runs at about $25-30 billion a year and that we end up owing the largest part of it to those who speak a different language. In 1974, Europeans, most of them speaking English as a second language, invested $16 billion in the U.S.; middle-easterners invested almost $2 billion.[8] It can safely be said that virtually no one speaks *their* languages. Why bother? The purchase of American properties is impossible to follow statistically, although nervous efforts are being made in most states and at the federal level to do so before we are bought out. In an adaptation of the title of Charles A. Reich's *The Greening of America*, one of our most widely read magazines headed a recent cover "The Buying of America."[9] Of course, we do not have to learn the languages of the people doing the buying because if they come over they will learn ours.

FOREIGN LANGUAGES AND THE NEEDS OF SCHOLARSHIP

Another facet of our now dated pride is, one hopes, the notion that American science can go it alone. Without a doubt, the devastation of German science, starting with the Nazis, and the weakening of French, Russian, and English capacities for research, attendant upon the second world war, left us preeminent. There was an international survey many years ago that found no truly advanced work in the life sciences going on anywhere else but in Sweden and Israel. Perhaps that was a high point. The Smith-Karlesky report now confirms a serious weakening of our capabilities for research,[10] and the presidents of the Massachusetts Institute of Technology and the California Institute of Technology have voiced their alarm.[11] Much of what they say is directed against inadequate support for American research, but in the meanwhile

8. Figures taken from Claus Reschke, "Career Education at the College Level: A Modest Proposal," *ADFL Bulletin* 9 (September 1977): 43-47. One can assume that the figures for 1979 are much larger.

9. *Newsweek,* 27 November 1978.

10. See *New York Times,* 1 June 1977, p. 10.

11. Anne C. Roark, "U.S. Commitment to Scientific Research Deteriorating Rapidly," *Chronicle of Higher Education,* 13 November 1978.

West European, Russian, and Japanese research has been growing. The two trends taken together are ominous. The chilling hybris engendered by our earlier, unquestioned superiority has left us little equipped in spirit or language to deal with growing bodies of research in science and the social sciences. Our scholars often cannot read new or reestablished journals, they cannot participate in overseas meetings except (in both cases) by courtesy of the remnants of enforced deference to the English language, a kind of imperialism no less odious for being more subtle. We have come to expect the same deference from presidents, ministers, diplomats, and business leaders all over the world. They pay us this tribute nightly on our television news. Why should they? Do we reciprocate? We can derive little consolation from the fact that this is part and parcel of the far broader affront of monolingualism, a monolingualism that has become the distinguishing mark of every aspect of our relationship with the rest of the world.

Curricular Experimentation and Declines in Enrollment

It would be well to conclude this list of significant trends with one that is more flattering. The degree and range of curricular experimentation at the level beyond the beginning courses (four-year and two-year) during any one of the years of our anxiety is incomparably greater than anything we accomplished during the decade of our complacency. The variety of new courses, new formats of topic or approach, new combinations with other disciplines, new cooperative teaching ventures, whole new sequences of study in foreign language, and new ventures in translation is spread on the records of, for example, the Association of Departments of Foreign Languages and its *Bulletin*. No reasonably imaginative teacher of foreign language could read these lists and descriptions without finding something to emulate. It is altogether inspiring. There are to be sure the occasional wrenching analogues to Woody Allen's famous course "Yeats and Hygiene: The poetic work of W. B. Yeats is examined against a background of good dental care." But for the most part the innovation is sensible and impressive. It matters little whether the course is "Spanish for Nurses" in a Texas junior college or "French Culture through Literature" in a St. Louis community college; the incorporation of individual language programs at Indiana University not just into Comparative Literature but into West European Studies; or Dartmouth's approach to Russian cultural history as the record of two cities: Leningrad and Moscow. These and hundreds of courses like them are testimony to a profession alive and aware of its mission. The shadow side is that such praise can be accorded neither to elementary undergraduate language courses nor to graduate work as a whole. Related directly to the last point (about elementary courses) and paradoxically to the burden of the preceding paragraph is the alarming drop that almost annihilates enrollments at the end of the beginning sequence. Even where this juncture does not correspond to the end of the requirement, the drop is by orders of magnitude. It is so well attested that statistics would be salt in the wound. If our more advanced undergraduate work is so varied and so good, why do students fail to sign up? The answer may be all too clear. When students pick electives, past experience weighs more than hope or anticipation. To put it mildly, their experience in beginning foreign language has not been an epiphany. Even with a generous discount for an unfavorable climate, the teaching of beginning language courses has been such as to make further study a dispensable challenge.

This is one person's view of the figures and trends that bear most unmistakably upon our well-being: not the erosion of requirements but the unexamined return to them; the precipitous drop in elections after first year; the remarkable vitality of the college curriculum after the beginning courses; the failure of foreign language in two-year colleges; the drop in applications to graduate schools in the foreign language field and the consequent imperiling of all programs, good and bad; the excess of graduate programs over the level needed; the changed role of the United States in the world balance of commerce and research.

Solutions to the Problems of the Past

Anyone in a position to make decisions for the future of foreign language study in higher education must have a list of this sort and must devise corresponding strategies, agenda for maximum effort in the hope of maximum effect. The following proposals represent only one form such an effort might take.

MEETING THE LANGUAGE NEEDS OF THE TWO-YEAR COLLEGES

The situation of foreign language in the two-year colleges must be addressed soon, not just because it is ipso facto unacceptable but because more and more students will proceed into the third and fourth year of college by transfer, not internally, so to speak. This happens extensively in California. If it were to happen nationally our college undergraduate programs, especially our programs for majors, would suffer profoundly.

It is extremely hard to find points of leverage for policy making in two-year colleges, and much effort must be local. As a first step, all undergraduate departments of foreign language should appoint a liaison member for junior and community colleges in the region, and the departments should cultivate the friendship and interest of the language teachers in those colleges and of administrators who might be instrumental in the introduction of new programs. Teachers in two-year colleges should be invited to all events sponsored by universities, from Spanish tables to Russian lectures. Departments with teaching assistants should propose internships, *free*, to test our new offerings in two-year colleges. The Association of Departments of Foreign Language should increase its activities involving junior colleges—much has already been done—and should be the agent for the cultivation of contact with the American Association of Community and Junior Colleges. Graduate departments of sufficient size must consider a degree or certificate program to train teachers for two-year colleges. The Ph.D. program in Language Literature, and Pedagogy at the University of Virginia, designed to provide teachers of English for such colleges, is an analogy. In a field characterized by shortages of jobs, this program has a shortage of candidates available for jobs. Funds can virtually be counted on if we will act. Opportunities abound, but optimism is not warranted. Each of us knows colleagues unaware of the nature and function of a community college, even when one exists five miles away.

DEVELOPING RELEVANT BEGINNING COURSES

To stop the frightening attrition that marks the advance from beginning courses to true electives, we need only take advantage of our advantages. Fortunately the field of foreign languages has an inherent attraction, even a humanistic urgency, matched by few disciplines. One might not guess so from the content and tenor of beginning courses. We must take two giant steps: articulate the basic purposes of language study; make early language work accord with those purposes and with the mental level of our students.

In the process of defining what foreign languages are about, we will gain not just the benefits of successful propaganda but an orienting point for our teaching. How can teachers teach anything without having a sense of its historical and present justification in American education, of why they are teaching it, under what aegis, with what goal in mind? What, in Dante's word, is the anagogical meaning of our undertaking? The communication of a body of information or the inculcating of a skill is not in itself a sufficient end, at least not in any humanistic enterprise. Teachers who look back at their careers and can say only that what they did in all those years was "teach German" should be depressed.

REDEFINING THE PURPOSES OF FOREIGN LANGUAGE PROGRAMS

Let us ask ourselves what the deepest wellsprings of our own purpose have been. And having found an answer, let us not conceal it from our students. But it is not enough to say that each of us will express his own, different rationale and that this is both inevitable and good. It would be better to work toward some consensus, better to identify, at least for debate, certain transcendent goals. I propose two. One will appear abstract, the other is happily concrete. The concrete one has more immediate persuasiveness; it will probably do more immediate good. Working toward it will aid in the pursuit of the other less tangible but no less important goal. It can capture the interest of even the most skeptical and elusive student.

The reason we study a foreign language and the spirit in which we do it are both existential concerns. Both center on another person, another human being, and that person is somewhere in France or Martinique or Louisiana, in Mexico or Spain or San Diego, in Germany or Austria or Switzerland, wherever. This is no trivial statement. The object of the kind of communication we teach is two-fold: for our students it is the satisfying of boundless sociability, of a desire to know the world and the people in it. For their partner in the ideal conversation, or in any conversation taken in its ideal dimension, it is something else. It is the tribute of being acknowledged in one's essence as manifested in one's language, the fundamental respect involved in a complex humanizing gesture the negative of which is the monolingual insult: "I'm too busy to learn your language; you learn mine." This last is in a literal sense hybris. As has been suggested, it is also irony of historic dimensions. The more that teachers of foreign language stress this concrete, personal goal in explaining their profession, the more they will prosper. For they are the natural custodians of the means to its attainment, more than any teacher of history or geography or political science. We must never let our students forget either the intangible humanizing spirit of the bilingual act or the concrete pleasures of the "I-Thou" relationship in a foreign language on foreign—or different—soil.

PROVIDING FOREIGN STUDY EXPERIENCES

Reminding oneself forcefully of one's goal and following rigorously the dictates of logic will entail some striking secondary obligations. To take the extreme: unless all we have said is to remain a pious hope, an abstract wish, every student at every level should have the personal experience of talking extensively with native speakers of the language he is studying. That means "foreign study" for everyone? Yes, in a sense. Pie in the sky of Academe? No.

Conventional programs of foreign study are varied and numerous. They deserve continuing support and they deserve to prosper. Unfortunately, most of them come too late. Third-year programs can only in the most tenuous way enlighten the first-year student. From our point of view as teachers, they cannot effectively serve as a counter to the massive drop in elections after intermediate work. They preach, albeit effectively, to the converted. But every college with a mini-term, or whatever it is called, has the opportunity to bring students into foreign environments, and this can happen in the first or second year. Between Christmas and the beginning of many a second term is time for a whole credit-bearing course in France or Austria—not to mention sightseeing, plays, skiing—and several universities avail themselves of this precious time. More should.

But are not these adventures costly and will not the ideal therefore be attainable by only a few colleges? Not necessarily. Community support can and should be sought for the foreign experience. That takes time. But meanwhile, for many languages a nearer and immediately accessible goal exists. Some such places have been mentioned; others are possible. Communities or government agencies might very well endow a pilot program to bring the language students of two- or four-year colleges into extended contact with these even nearer "foreign" destinations: Lafayette, La., Maine, Montreal, Québec—all are in greater or lesser degree "francophone." And where is the nearest settlement of Vietnamese refugees? Especially for the French communities in America, the waves of bicultural/bilingual work, much of it funded by the federal government, has prepared our way, with trained personnel, well-developed programs, and staffs of people who speak "standard French" along with local forms of the language. Vietnamese French, it happens, can be very good—if by good we mean Parisian. The pressures of language-oriented tension, a sobering demonstration of the existential importance of language itself, are nowhere more apparent than in Québec.

Spanish is especially fortunate. There is not only Mexico and before long Cuba. What of the Spanish communities in Florida? It is also possible to walk several blocks on Fourteenth Street in New York City before hearing the first word of English. To object that this is not the Spanish we teach is a curiously elitist argument in a field that practically pioneered the recognition of actual use as a criterion of usage.

German and Russian face a greater challenge. Yet remarkably enough it is Russian at the high school level that provides the most dramatic recent evidence of what can be done to fill the gap. If not a natural community of native speakers, then a made-up one, a sociological construct! Jefferson County in Colorado recently reported more students of Russian in its public schools than the entire state of Ohio. The key was a Russian language camp on week-ends.[12]

When we get to the motivational "bottom line," as jargon has it, everything depends on what one takes as a categorical imperative. If internationalism as the guiding motivation of the bilingual effort is as important as here suggested, and if foreign language teachers are the guardians of that aspect of education, then we will find ways to do what is necessary.

Once we have determined upon the primary effort, a whole complex of international activities will suggest itself, creating a support environment, directed toward the language experience itself. Two-year colleges have been more imaginative here than senior institutions. A recent article in the *ADFL Bulletin* reported on an Intercultural Communications Program at a community college in St. Louis, with new and special courses such as "Films and People," "Enjoying Foreign Films," "Cultures through Literature," "French (or Latin-American, Spanish, German) Civilization," "Techniques of Translation," "Cultural Patterns in Spanish Art." [13] Also described were workshops or lecture-demonstrations on "Chicanos and Farm Labor Organizations," "Linguistic Differences between English and American," "Contrastive Analysis of German," and "American Educational Systems." The U.S. Department of Health, Education, and Welfare backed this program.

Humanistic Values of Foreign Language Study

The other article of faith by which we orient our effort is less immediately appealing but almost more fundamental. It constitutes our principal claim to educational validity in the intellectual sense, in the domain of the individual mind, just as the feature of internationalism constitutes our greatest benefaction in the domain of "attitude" and the "inspirational." This focussing point is the unique revelation, through the study of foreign language, of the nature of

12. Leon L. Twarog, "Beyond Survival: The Role of FL Programs in the High Schools and the Two-year Colleges," *ADFL Bulletin* 8 (March 1977): 13.

13. Richard Kalfus, "Intercultural Communications," *ADFL Bulletin* 8 (March 1977): 21-22.

language itself, language as the sole ordering mechanism by means of which all human beings deal with reality. Language is our primary system for reducing to a pattern and controlling the otherwise disjointed, hopelessly multifarious universe we confront. Through language we impose the basic marshalling categories of space and time, being, becoming, and causation. The crucial point is that the patterns differ distinctively from language to language. It is therefore not inaccurate to say that reality itself for a speaker of Japanese is different from our reality. It is not simply a matter of perception. Saying that, we would imply that reality is something fixed and that language is a sort of contingent and inaccurate approximation to it. This is not so. Consider what it means to have in Japanese half a dozen verb endings to choose from—from which choice *must* be made—in any given mood or tense before one can finish a spoken sentence. Or what it means to have several pronouns for "I" and several for "you." Relative level of social standing, degrees of familiarity, shades of deference or brusqueness, irony—all are *part* of the interpersonal reality of the speaker of Japanese, in a way simply not true of the speaker of English. Consider the role that language plays in the whole egalitarian movement of present-day America, especially in the amelioration of the role and position of women. Japanese women face a language with far greater obstacles to the surface manifestation of equality than the generic "he" or the chair*man*-spokes*man* syndrome. *They* have typically feminine verb endings, suffixes, and pronouns to deal with, plus mandatory tonal differences. And much of this linguistic skew is invidious to women. Even German and French can hint at some of these differences. What is the effect of Gottfried Keller's persistent reference to *Mädchen* as *es*? Why is Mark Twain's story of the flame consuming the fishwife so funny—*she* eating *it* up? What unfamiliar terrors and subtle ecstasies lurk in the developing French or German acquaintanceship as it progresses from *vous/Sie* to *tu/du*?

THE SECOND LANGUAGE AS A BRIDGE TO UNDERSTANDING ONE'S OWN LANGUAGE

It is virtually self-evident that such an appreciation of language as the vehicle of human perception, understanding, and control cannot be gained from contemplation of one's own language. In it, all seems obvious and inevitable. Only when a student discovers that the speaker of another language takes the world apart and puts it back together again in a radically different fashion, even in the same language family (in our case Indo-European), does he realize the relativity of perception, the contingent nature of what we call the real, and the centrality of language.

These observations are intimately related to the previous argument concerning internationalism. Moravcsik and Juilland put it well:

It is important to study the religion, history, and philosophic reflections of foreign cultures. But in trying to understand people with different symbol systems and different ways of expressing themselves, nothing serves to transcend cultural barriers better than the learning of a language other than one's own.[14]

What all this implies is a great deal of work: the revising of most texts, the creation of new bodies of auxiliary material. As it is, we are ill-equipped to use these powerful weapons of motivation for the betterment of our students and of our professional position. We need ammunition. We need a well-designed inventory of persuasive examples where the lexicon reveals the different realities perceived by different cultures, for example, Whorf's treasure trove of studies of Indian languages and cultures that make no distinction between (and have no different words for) space and time, and therefore seem hyper-modern;[15] the shared discrimination of Eskimos and skiers as they label different kinds of snow with terms such as "corn," "powder," and so forth; Cook's observation that French lacks a word for "privacy" and English a term corresponding to *Gemütlichkeit*;[16] the bearing upon the Spaniard's attitude toward "cruel" bull fighting of the fact that, as Lado notes, his lan-

14. Julius Moravcsik and Alphonse Juilland, "The Place of Foreign Languages in a Curriculum for Liberal Education," *ADFL Bulletin* 8 (May 1977): 10-12.

15. Benjamin Lee Whorf, *Language, Thought, and Reality: Selected Writings of Benjamin Lee Whorf*, ed. John B. Carroll (New York: Wiley, 1956).

16. R. F. Cook, "Foreign Language Study and Intellectual Power," *ADFL Bulletin* 8 (May 1977): 7.

guage separates human and animal "legs" (*piernas*, *patas*), "necks" (*cuellos*, *pescuezos*), and so on.[17]

Would it not be profitable to have a list of grammatical anomalies to speculate about? What is the significance or effect of the (in)famous German syntactical rule which says that the more closely related two verbal elements are the farther they will be apart in main clauses? (Language humor in German capitalizes on the annihilation of whole strings of eulogy by a postponed *nicht* or the dismay of a speaker who, at the end of an ornate predicate, cannot remember which separable prefix he was going to use.) Or what are the implications of the curious frequency of the postponed subject in Russian sentences? Or for that matter, how does any language get along without the verb "to be?" These and other features of language would not be chosen to serve mere curiosity, although there is nothing wrong with that, but to illustrate the fundamental relation of language to cognition and to the defining of attitudes.

THE ROLE OF LITERATURE IN THE LANGUAGE PROGRAM

Much the same can be urged of literature. Not only is it the highest, most complex manifestation of language, exhibiting the manipulation of speech forms in the service of art. It is also a kind of truth or true statement, often as true as we can get, about the human condition, treating man not in his collectivity (as the social scientists do), but as an individual or a recognizable kind of individual in a specific yet generically valid situation. Deprived of literature, we are deprived at one extreme of the middle ground between isolated perceptions of our own isolated lives or casual perceptions of others, and at the other of the generalizations, the essentially statistical or "collective" observations of the social sciences.

Program Needs: Staff, Curriculum, and Materials

There are certain implications of asserting such broad aims as the heart of our teaching enterprise. The most drastic have to do with planning, with materials, with organization of the curriculum, but above all with the training of teachers. If graduate schools of

17. Robert Lado, *Linguistics across Cultures* (Ann Arbor, Mich.: University of Michigan Press, 1957), p. 116.

arts and sciences overemphasize literary and cultural abstractions, schools of education underemphasize the intellectual relevance of language. And neither, it seems, can articulate our purpose. Somewhere our future teachers must be given the ability, the impetus, and the wherewithal to explain the significance of language and the true nature of literature and of cultural difference.

THE EDUCATION OF GRADUATE STUDENTS

Such training is but one aspect of the widening and intensification necessary to graduate education in general. We must prepare graduate students for every role they will fill as teachers, not just for the writing of scholarly articles and the presentation of literary history or critical theory, and not just for the teaching of French, German, or Spanish 1-2, either. They must, as has been said, become defenders of the faith. They must also learn how to teach introductory literature and culture and basic linguistics. They must learn how to lecture and how to give papers at meetings, how to do team teaching, how to organize courses in translation or to incorporate foreign language materials in broad courses such as "World Literature." [18] They must be aided in understanding and extending the place of our discipline in their individual institutions and in the educational system of this country. All this is easy to say and necessary to do. Hardly a graduate institution in the United States does the job.

IMPROVING LANGUAGE PROFICIENCY

Something else follows from our categorical imperative, and that is a steep increase in the level of competence we expect from teachers in the use of the language itself, particularly its spoken form. These days of our professional discontent, the days of shortage, are precisely the time for redefining standards in expectation of our restoration to grace. We can strive valiantly to improve present methods in the classroom, we can try to expand and improve present programs—and these efforts will help. But many of

18. For a fuller statement, see my article, "Changes in Graduate Training," *ADFL Bulletin* 7 (November 1975): 3-8, and, on German in particular, my "The Present and Future Shape of Graduate Programs," in *German Studies in the United States*, ed. W. F. Lohnes and Valters Nollendorfs (Madison, Wis.: University of Wisconsin Press, 1976), pp. 121-27.

the variables are beyond our control, and success is not guaranteed. The one point at which we have full control is that of admission to graduate study.

Here, draconian as it may be, we can refuse to admit those whose weaknesses (particularly in speaking) would, if transferred to students, impair their ability to function in the higher spheres we have staked out as ours. We should change procedures for admission. We ought to use writing samples, tapes, interviews, not just the hackneyed pattern of transcript, letters, and scores on the *Graduate Record Examination*. Somehow it should also be possible to warn colleges how high our expectations are. It will be harsh, but far less harsh than if we fail someone for linguistic deficiency when he is already part way through graduate study—and it will be a mercy to future students.

Asking high competence in the spoken foreign language is not tantamount to preferring native speakers. The danger is real that we may do so, in the legitimate search for fluency, but if we do we will suffer. A judicious number of our teachers should doubtless be native speakers, but not too many. One thing a native speaker can never be is a complete "role model," proving in the flesh that an American can learn and use a foreign language. There are those who, forgetting this, would fill our departments with Germans and Spaniards, saying that their German or their Spanish is exemplary. How much credit is one supposed to get for speaking his mother tongue? Ideally we should search among our applicants for those American young people who have already developed, or who approximate, true fluency. They exist and they will be, as teaching assistants and ultimately as colleagues, our best role models.

It will be said that we cannot tighten standards when our applications are slowing down. We can, first because the few applications we are getting tend also to be better, and second because we must in any event reduce radically the number of graduate programs.

IMPROVING TEXTBOOK AND OTHER INSTRUCTIONAL RESOURCES

A final word must go to the issue of instructional resources in early language work. Dispassionate review of all kinds of elementary and intermediate material, from books to audio-visual aids, will lead, if we are honest about it, to something approaching despair. Two flaws mark tape after tape, book after book: quantitatively they are unmanageable, qualitatively they are beneath the appropriate level of intellectual dignity.

Sheer quantity is represented at its most intractable in college texts at the introductory level.[19] Their bulk is such that few can be finished in a year. Either we cut or we run over into the second year. The latter alternative has the effect of prolonging what is in many ways an embarrassment, especially given the nature of our materials: elementary language work almost halfway through college. The reason for such heroic length is in itself laudable: a striving for reasonable completeness and clarity in grammar and for adequate practice of the morphological and syntactical patterns presented. Indeed some of our beginning texts are of great linguistic sophistication, but the very attaining of this high quality has led to quantitative excesses. Such materials, intellectually impressive but lengthy, are obviously preferable to those that are both long and inept, but they make formidable demands upon our patience. We must remind ourselves that in a real sense grammar is virtually infinite, with subpatterns and variations of such abundance that they cannot all be taught; some must be relegated to the great reference grammars— and even they are not exhaustive. So no beginning text can be "complete." But we must also realize that the truly crucial patterns of a language are relatively few and that even among these few there is a spectrum of conspicuousness. Who would not settle for a generation of students who regularly picked the right one of the three basic verb positions in German sentences, even if they did not get the double infinitive right, or the future perfect? And a final realization: grammar is rarely a goal in itself. The more time we devote to it, the less time we have for literature, cultural readings, writing, advanced conversation, and, one suspects, the fewer students we will retain. It is quite possible that the next wave of successful introductory texts will be very brief grammars, concentrating on patterns of the highest frequency, and giving intensive but not exhaustive practice. The assumption will be that teachers

19. See also Helen P. Warriner, "High School Foreign Language Texts: Too Much between the Covers to Cover," *Foreign Language Annals* 11 (October 1978): 551-57.

can supply further drill, that students will move swiftly into reading and other ventures, including travel, where the acquisition of grammatical control will not cease but will become more effective because it is better motivated.

It is fervently to be hoped that new texts will try to exhibit an awareness of the age and intelligence of their clientele, and of the kinds of materials in other disciplines that are presented concurrently with ours. What is a student to think when he spends one evening on Milton or Faulkner, on the *Federalist Papers* or Plato's *Dialogues*, and spends the next learning other dialogues composed of fictive inanities in a European bus or reading *ersatz*, bowdlerized "stories"? This is not to attack situational phraseology of a practical sort. Such sentence and phrase units are essential. But anyone who knows languages knows that it is only by *force majeure* that they can also be made to carry the burden of grammar. Situational utterances are by nature formulaic and peculiar, not generic. Nor is it an attack on the reading of stories. But in the name of our dignity as teachers of young adults, let us apply our efforts not to making up cute episodes about Armand and Suzette or Kurt and Inge but to searching out texts both real and simple.

SUMMARY

Everything we do is determined by the principles we take seriously. What would we do, how would we teach, what materials would we write or choose if we agreed on certain fundamental standards? To make our offerings on the entire postsecondary level as attractive as possible (within the bounds of legitimacy) we might work toward agreement on the following principles.

The reality principle. Leave pure fiction where it belongs: in literature. Let foreign language instruction be alive, transmit actuality, deal insofar as possible only with "originals." Stop making up things. Instead, select real newspaper articles, real geographical or historical materials, real literature. (Literature offers few problems. Especially among modern writers, lexical and syntactical simplicity is often a preferred mode, a kind of metaphor or metonymy for directness and urgency of understanding. Think of Brecht or Prévert.) Where imitation is necessary, let it be, as Aristotle said, "of a certain magnitude." Write dialogues with substance and appropriate dignity—that does not mean with owlish solemnity. Try to use phrases that will serve the students when they reach the ultimate reality of foreign travel, residence, and study. Encourage them to attain the reality. (The other principal reality is more elusive but no less real: what language is, what literature does, what "contrastive culture" means.)

The maturity principle. An end to demeaning materials! Accepted by students, they foster a pathetic view of language and language learning. Viewed with appropriate skepticism, they lead to cynical amusement and rejection. In a far more rigorous sense than the common one, this means we need graded readings and graded materials. "Graded" is commonly a word for "condescending" and means aiming a level or two beneath the student's intelligence and dignity. It should mean: studiously selected so as to be just a step or two above, leading upward without discouraging.

The pleasure principle. What has been advocated thus far may sound overly serious, "not much fun." That is the opposite of the intention. We should keep always in mind what Whitehead said in his *Aims of Education*.[20] The early stage of learning in any field is the stage of enthusiasm. Precision and discipline follow. Reading good things is a pleasure; playing with language, in skits or at weekend camps, is fun; manipulating words in free writing is a game. Language learning probably affords more of a playing field for *homo ludens* than almost any other study. No methodology, no training can inculcate this awareness; it must, eventually, be felt. But it can be cultivated. We can repeat to ourselves and we can use as a criterion of selection and retention the axiom that pleasure and enthusiasm are the particular touchstones of our enterprise. Our work and we ourselves must show that it is exciting to learn a language.

20. Alfred North Whitehead, *The Aims of Education* (New York: Macmillan Co., 1929), pp. 28-30.

CHAPTER VIII

Evaluating the Second-Language Learning Program

REBECCA M. VALETTE

Evaluation plays a key role in any program for learning a language. In selecting and preparing the appropriate evaluation instruments, teachers and administrators are obliged to clarify their objectives and assess the relevant variables: the students, the teachers, the nature of the instruction, and the nature of the subject matter being taught. In interpreting the data derived from the evaluation instruments, teachers and administrators learn about the parameters of the program and its effectiveness. In this chapter, attention is focused on three major areas: determining students' characteristics, measuring students' achievement, and evaluating the instructional program.

Determining Characteristics of Students

An effective second-language program takes into account the nature of the students enrolled, building on their strengths and compensating for their weaknesses. Students' characteristics may be grouped in four categories: language aptitude, preferred learning style, attitude, and prior language experience.

LANGUAGE APTITUDE

Carroll has defined aptitude as the amount of time needed to master a task.[1] All other factors being equal, students with high language aptitude will learn a new language more readily than those with low language aptitude. All students, except the mentally retarded, possess the capacity to learn a second language.

1. John B. Carroll, "The Prediction of Success in Intensive Foreign Language Training," in *Training Research and Education*, ed. Robert Glaser (Pittsburgh: University of Pittsburgh Press, 1962), p. 122.

Over the past sixty years, research on language aptitude has been based on the assumptions that (a) certain talents or abilities (loosely termed "aptitude") contribute to the ease with which a student learns a foreign language; (b) language aptitude is unevenly distributed in the population; (c) degree of aptitude may be measured quantitatively; and (d) the nature of aptitude may vary as instructional objectives change, for example, from learning to speak a language to learning to read or translate.

Currently there are three aptitude tests commercially available in the United States, each designed for a somewhat different age group: (a) the *Carroll-Sapon Modern Language Aptitude Test* (MLAT), 1959, for high school students and adults; (b) the *Pimsleur Language Aptitude Battery* (PLAB), 1966, for junior and senior high school students; and (c) the *Carroll-Sapon Elementary Language Aptitude Test* (EMLAT), 1967, for elementary school students.[2] Each of these tests requires about one hour of administration and consists of several sections, some of which are recorded on tape. The answer sheets may be machine scored and yield part scores as well as total scores. All three tests are accompanied by manuals and tables of norms to guide administrators and teachers in interpreting students' performance.

Aptitude tests may be used to predict which students are most likely to succeed in mastering a second language quickly. If candidates for a class are of similar intelligence and equally well motivated, then measured aptitude becomes an important factor in selecting students for a language course in which there are limited openings. While a high degree of selectivity may be a feature of the Army Language Schools, for instance, this same selectivity does not characterize American secondary education. Moreover, the typical school population is not homogeneous with respect to general intelligence and motivation. Hence, aptitude is but one of several factors that are useful in predicting success in a language course. It is important that aptitude tests *not* be used to keep students out of a language program, especially if they are motivated and want to learn.

Tests of language aptitude can be profitably used to group

2. All three tests are available from the Psychological Corporation, 757 Third Avenue, New York, NY 10017.

incoming students in relatively homogeneous classes. Students with high overall aptitude are often able to enter an accelerated section, while those with low overall aptitude need a slower pace.

PREFERRED LEARNING STYLE

In recent years, foreign language educators have realized that individualizing instruction according to learning pace may respond to differences in aptitude (where aptitude is defined as the time needed to learn a task), but that such individualization does not take into account differences in students' learning styles. It is also true that teachers have preferred teaching styles, and that the most effective language program is one where teaching and learning styles complement one another.

Inventories of learning style for second-language classes are still at the experimental stage. The *Edmonds Learning Style Identification Exercise* has been developed by Reinert for use in the Edmonds School District in Washington State. On this twenty-minute recorded test, students indicate whether each of fifty familiar English words gives rise to a visual image, a written word, a physical reaction, or whether the sound of the word conveys the meaning directly. An analysis of the responses indicates whether students have a pronounced preference for a specific learning mode (pictures, need to see the language written out, need for movement or activity) and whether they have the ability to derive meaning from sound directly.[3]

Papalia has experimented with a matching pair of inventories, one to be taken by the student and one to be filled out by the teacher on the basis of classroom observations. After both forms have been completed, the teacher and student meet for an interview and try to determine the optimum learning conditions.[4]

Caution is needed in interpreting the results from inventories of learning style. Not only do all students have several different learning styles, depending on the task to be mastered, but their preferred learning styles change over time. Furthermore, some

3. Harry Reinert, "One Picture is Worth a Thousand Words? Not Necessarily!" *Modern Language Journal* 60 (April 1976): 160-68.

4. Anthony Papalia, *Learner-Centered Language Teaching* (Rowley, Mass.: Newbury House, 1976), pp. 12-47.

students may try to please the teacher and hence not answer all items with total candor. It is recommended, therefore, that the results obtained from such inventories be tempered with observational data.

ATTITUDE AND MOTIVATION

Students with a high positive attitude toward second-language study and a strong motivation to master the language will obviously do better than students with a negative attitude and no motivation. One must distinguish, however, between initial motivation prior to language study and ongoing motivation. Once students have begun their language courses, their degree of motivation seems to be a function of their success in the course. For many language students motivation seems to decline in the face of difficulty.

In their research on why students study a second language, Gardner and Lambert postulated a distinction between an "integrative motive" and "instrumental orientation."[5] The learner who wishes to be identified with another linguistic group exhibits an integrative motive. Such a person often wants to reside in the country where the language is spoken, enjoys contact with speakers of the second language, and consequently also learns the language readily. Persons with a negative integrative motive do not want to be identified with those who speak the language under study. Such students often resist learning the new language. Students with an instrumental orientation are learning the second language for a specific purpose. Usually they feel that there are economic or social advantages to be gained by acquiring the new language. Gardner and Lambert have developed a short measure of motivation consisting of eight reasons for studying the second language. Students indicate the extent to which they agree or disagree with each statement.[6]

Data from the *Foreign Language Attitude Questionnaire*, developed by Jakobovits, can help teachers (a) "find out how the

5. Robert C. Gardner and Wallace E. Lambert, *Attitudes and Motivation in Second-language Learning* (Rowley, Mass.: Newbury House, 1972), pp. 12-15.

6. Ibid., p. 148. This measure is part of a longer battery that measures attitudes and motivation.

students really feel about the various aspects of the foreign language curriculum"; (b) change aspects of the instructional process where it is pedagogically feasible and desirable to do so; and (c) "correct erroneous ideas, unrealistic expectations, or negative attitudes that the students may hold."[7] The questionnaire has two forms, one for students who have already studied a second language and the other for those beginning second-language study.

PRIOR LANGUAGE EXPERIENCE AND PLACEMENT

In placing incoming students in a foreign language sequence, the program administrator also needs to know whether the students have had prior language experience either in the language to be studied or in another language. In forming language classes consisting of students with no prior language experience, the administrator can use information from aptitude tests, learning style inventories, and attitude questionnaires. The data such instruments provide can be helpful in organizing courses and course content to meet students' needs.

Students who speak a second language (other than the one under study) and students who have formally studied a second language in school will usually progress more rapidly in a beginning course than students without this added linguistic experience. This advantage is particularly marked in the case of students who know a language related to the one they are learning. For instance, students who speak French will find Spanish much easier than those students who know only English. If students with a second-language background are identified at the outset, they should be placed in an accelerated course.

It is pedagogically unsound to place students with no exposure to the language being learned with students who have had prior language study. For instance, seventh-grade students who have studied Spanish in elementary school should not be placed in the same classes as students with no Spanish experience. Both groups suffer. The true beginners are timid in the presence of classmates

7. Leon Jakobovits, *Foreign Language Learning: A Psycholinguistic Analysis of the Issues* (Rowley, Mass.: Newbury House, 1970), p. 294. The *Foreign Language Attitude Questionnaire* is available from the Northeast Conference on the Teaching of Foreign Languages, Box 623, Middlebury, Vt. 05753.

who appear fluent, while the students with some knowledge are frustrated by having to begin all over again.

Most schools that receive large numbers of students with prior language experience have developed their own systems for placing them effectively. Since placement is always carried out in relation to a specific curriculum and sequence of courses, there are no commercially available language tests that can be adapted to all situations.

At the university level, students are sometimes allowed to place themselves. After reading the course descriptions and noting prerequisites, they select the class that best corresponds to their needs and background. When large numbers of students are placed at the beginning of a term, students should be permitted to change courses after an initial period if they or their teachers find they have been poorly placed.

Measuring Students' Achievement

Most of the research and writing in the area of second-language testing focuses on the measurement of students' achievement.[8] How much have the students learned in their language courses? Second-language learning is a complex enterprise that cuts across the three domains: cognitive, affective, and psychomotor.[9] In the cognitive domain, students must learn new vocabulary and grammar, as well as rules of syntax and norms of usage. In the psychomotor domain they must acquire new habits of pronunciation and, in the case of languages such as Arabic and Chinese, new systems for writing. In the affective domain, students must have the desire to communicate with others.

8. The main handbooks on foreign language testing are: John L. D. Clark, *Foreign Language Testing: Theory and Practice* (Philadelphia: Center for Curriculum Development, 1972); David P. Harris, *Testing English as a Second Language* (New York: McGraw-Hill, 1969); Robert Lado, *Language Testing: The Construction and Use of Foreign Language Tests* (New York: McGraw-Hill, 1964); and Rebecca M. Valette, *Modern Language Testing*, 2d ed. (New York: Harcourt Brace Jovanovich, 1977).

9. Rebecca M. Valette and Renée S. Disick, *Modern Language Performance: Objectives and Individualization* (New York: Harcourt Brace Jovanovich, 1972).

SKILL-GETTING AND SKILL-USING

The process of acquiring a second language is comprised of two kinds of activities, which Rivers has named "skill-getting" and "skill-using."[10] In skill-getting, the students are learning new items of vocabulary, new grammatical patterns, new rules of usage. In tests of skill-getting, students are tested on their knowledge of vocabulary items, verb forms, sentence patterns, and perhaps pronunciation and spelling. In skill-using, students are using the communication channels, singly or in combination: listening comprehension, where the focus is on understanding what is being said; speaking, where the focus is on expressing oneself so as to communicate with speakers of the language; reading comprehension; and written self-expression.

In tests of skill-getting, the emphasis is on correctness: Was the right word used? Did the verb have the correct ending? Was the accusative case used appropriately? Were the direct object pronouns in the proper position? Was the sound "*ü*" properly pronounced? Was the past participle correctly spelled? The skill-getting activities lend themselves readily to highly reliable tests. One can easily make up a language test with a large number of items (standard tasks and multiple tasks), set a time limit (standard conditions), and develop an unambiguous answer sheet (standard scoring).

In the tests of skill-using, the emphasis is on communication. Skill-using tests are of high validity, for most language teachers will insist that their ultimate goal of instruction is to develop the communication skills. With tests of listening comprehension and reading comprehension, it is possible to select passages (standard tasks) prepare several questions on each (multiple tasks), set a time limit (standard conditions), and develop a right-wrong answer sheet (standard scoring). With tests of self-expression, whether in speaking or writing, it is much more difficult to develop a standard scoring procedure.

10. Wilga Rivers, *A Practical Guide to the Teaching of French* (New York: Oxford University Press, 1975), p. 4.

CRITERION-REFERENCED AND NORM-REFERENCED TESTING

In criterion-referenced testing, the students' results are reported with reference to preestablished criteria: Does the student control the pronunciation system of the language? Can the student form the present tense of regular verbs? Or, at a higher level, can the student speak the language well enough to meet routine needs of a tourist? One of the problems in second-language testing is that, aside from the rating scale of the Foreign Service Institute,[11] there is no nationally accepted set of criteria delineating the various levels or stages of language acquisition. In fact, the first recommendation of the Modern Language Association Task Force on the Commonly Taught Languages was that an "outline of realistic proficiency goals by stage of achievement" be developed.[12]

In norm-referenced testing, the student's performance is reported in relationship to other students, for example, members of the same class, students in the same school district, students in schools throughout the nation who have had two years of German. Results are translated into grades, percentile rankings, or standard scores. Scores on norm-referenced tests are useful in comparing performance between groups, but do not provide information on level of achievement.

RELIABILITY AND VALIDITY

The biggest problem in objective evaluation in foreign languages is how to reconcile the requirements of reliability and validity. Tests of skill-getting can have a high degree of reliability. Language learning, however, is not the sum of myriad parts: it is not by learning 1000 grammar rules, 1000 verb forms, and 3000 items of vocabulary, for instance, that one can suddenly read, speak, or understand the language. Communication is a distinct phenomenon, and communication skills must be specifically tested.

A test is *reliable* if it consistently provides comparable scores. The features of a reliable test are standard tasks, multiple tasks,

11. *Absolute Language Proficiency Ratings* (Washington, D.C.: Foreign Service Institute, November 1968). The FSI oral proficiency scale is reprinted in Valette, *Modern Language Testing*, pp. 157-61.

12. "Report of the Task Force on the Commonly Taught Languages," *ADFL Bulletin* 10 (September 1978): 2.

standard conditions, and standard scoring. A test is *valid* if it measures what it sets out to measure. A speaking test that asks students to read a paragraph aloud and then yields a score on pronunciation is not a valid measure of the students' ability to speak the language. In assessing commercially available language tests, an administrator or teacher should study the types of items and how the test is scored.

TYPES OF TESTS OF SECOND-LANGUAGE ACQUISITION

Items that test second-language acquisition focus either on skill-getting, that is, on the elements of language (vocabulary, grammar, pronunciation, and spelling), or on the active use of one or more language skills: listening comprehension, speaking ability, reading comprehension, and writing ability.[13]

Skill-getting. Most teacher-made tests and a large portion of the items on many of the commercial tests assess the students' control of vocabulary, grammar, pronunciation, and spelling. The trend is toward testing these elements of language in context, and toward excluding wrong forms.

In a vocabulary item, the student is asked to produce or identify a specific word or expression. These items may range in difficulty from very simple to very difficult. Many standardized tests are characterized by what is termed a "vocabulary bias." In such a test, the students with a sizeable vocabulary are favored over those with a good command of grammar.

Grammar is most frequently tested via the written language. On teacher-made tests, the students usually complete blanks or transform sentences according to a model. On standardized tests using a multiple-choice format the students are required to choose the correct response. Knowledge of grammar may also be tested with listening tests where students are to distinguish, for instance, between single and plural forms or between present and past tenses. Spoken tests of grammar are usually administered informally in the classroom. In some schools, students record their responses to questions on grammar in the language laboratory.

On tests of pronunciation, the students may recite material

13. For more information on the types of items used in second language tests, see the handbooks mentioned in footnote 8.

which they have memorized (a dialog, for example), repeat sentences after the speaker, or read material aloud. Tests of this sort are given informally in the classroom, or more formally under standard conditions in the language laboratory.

Dictation tests based on familiar material are frequently used as tests of spelling. In addition, spelling is usually considered part of most tests of vocabulary and grammar, in which case an item not spelled properly is counted wrong or may receive only partial credit, depending on the scoring system. The concern has been expressed that some teachers may be overstressing the importance of spelling in second-language learning.

In the 1960s, the "pure" test (containing only one language skill) was favored over the "hybrid" test (including two or more skills). This concern with "pure" tests is reflected in the commercially developed language test batteries, which have four parts corresponding to the skills of listening, speaking, reading, and writing.

Skill-using. In tests of listening, the students hear a recorded passage and answer questions. If the passage is long and if the questions are based on specific details, an added element, such as the ability to retain information, may influence the scores. (Even in one's native language one can hear and understand a phone call, for example, and not recall all that was said.) On commercial listening tests, the questions about the recording are usually presented in a multiple-choice format.

In tests of speaking, the students are asked to talk on a specific topic or narrate the story conveyed by a series of drawings. The scoring of such tests is time-consuming, and hence expensive.

Tests of reading comprehension in a second language are similar in format to reading tests in English. The students are presented with a passage followed by related questions. On tests devised by teachers or textbook publishers, these questions usually require written responses. On commercial tests, the questions are in a multiple-choice format.

On tests of writing at the elementary level, students write short paragraphs, dialogs, or letters. At more advanced levels, longer compositions are required. The key to a good writing test is the development of a workable and reliable scoring system.

In a conversation or interview test, the student must demonstrate both listening comprehension and speaking ability. The teacher usually plays the role of the interviewer, and then evaluates the student's performance at the end of their conversation. It is often better if two teachers administer the test, one doing the interviewing and the other the scoring. The accuracy of the scoring can be heightened by recording the interview and scoring it at a later time. In interview testing, it is essential to develop a scoring sheet that lists the aspects to be evaluated and the weight assigned to each.

AVAILABLE LANGUAGE TESTS

The language tests available commercially fall into three groups: the norm-referenced, four-skills batteries, which schools can purchase and administer as they wish; the standardized annual tests, which are given on specific dates and in specific locations; and the tests that accompany instructional materials.

Four-skills batteries. The four-skills batteries currently available were developed in the 1960s. Although critics have pointed out weaknesses in these tests, they are still widely used because they have not been replaced by newer tests. These batteries are (a) the *MLA Cooperative Foreign Language Tests,* 1963, available in levels L and M (after two and four years of high school instruction) for French, German, Italian, Russian, and Spanish;[14] and (b) the *Pimsleur Modern Foreign Language Proficiency Tests,* 1968, available in levels One and Two (after one and two years of high school instruction) for French, German, and Spanish.[15]

Over the past ten years, teams of teachers in Europe have collaborated to develop test batteries for use in certifying the language skills of students in adult education programs. The student who passes this test battery receives a certificate of basic proficiency. These *"Zertifikat"* tests are available in French, Spanish, English, and German, and are being distributed in the United States through the Goethe House.[16]

14. Available from Addison-Wesley Publishing Co., South Street, Reading, Mass. 01867.

15. Available from the Psychological Corporation, 757 Third Avenue, New York, N.Y. 10017.

16. Available from the Goethe House, 1014 Fifth Avenue, New York, N.Y. 10028.

Standardized and annual tests. The majority of the standardized tests in foreign languages are prepared and administered by the Educational Testing Service. These tests include the *College Board Achievement Tests* (in French, German, Hebrew, Russian, and Spanish), *The Test of English as a Foreign Language*, the *College Board Advanced Placement Tests* (in French, German, and Spanish), and the *Graduate Record Examinations* (in French and Spanish).[17] The state of New York prepares its annual *Regents High School Examinations* in French, German, Hebrew, Italian, and Spanish. These are administered only to students in high schools in New York State.[18]

Tests accompanying instructional materials. Most publishers of secondary school basic foreign-language textbooks offer testing programs to accompany their texts. Such tests may be used as departmental final examinations, or as a part of the departmental final, throughout the school system. It is essential, however, that the language teachers evaluate such tests carefully before using them in order to determine whether the test content reflects the objectives of the course.

GLOBAL MEASURES OF LANGUAGE PROFICIENCY

One of the most promising areas of current research in language testing is that of "global" tests. Global tests are built on the premise that the better one understands a second language, the more accurately one can reconstitute a spoken or written message. Global tests are easy to prepare, quick to administer, and can be scored quickly and reliably. Several schools are experimenting with global tests as placement tests for incoming students.

In the global dictation tests, students hear an unfamiliar passage that is read one sentence at a time. Writing out the text under these conditions requires comprehension, retention, and writing skills. The ability to remember longer sentences and write them down accurately is a function of language ability.

The noise test is a type of dictation in which comprehension

17. For more information, contact the Educational Testing Service, Princeton, N.J. 08540.

18. Retired forms of the Regents examinations are available from Amsco School Publications, Box 351, Cooper Station, New York, N.Y. 10003.

is made more difficult by adding static, or "white noise," to the dictation tape. The candidates either write out their answers or choose the correct form from among three or four options in a multiple-choice format.

The cloze test is a written test where the student reconstructs an incomplete message by filling in missing words. First a selection is chosen which is at the reading level of the students. The entire first sentence is presented, and then every fifth or sixth word is deleted. In the "exact word" scoring method, the student receives credit only for providing the exact word from the original text. In the "appropriate word" method of scoring, students also get credit for providing an acceptable synonym which fits the text syntactically and grammatically.

Evaluating the Instructional Program

The nature and quality of the instructional program is a crucial factor in second-language courses, because, with the exception of classes in English as a second language, the students' primary and in many cases only contact with the language under study is through the school. There are three main areas that should be evaluated: the staff, the facilities, and the curricular materials.

EVALUATING THE STAFF

The effective second-language teacher is one who guides the students in their mastery of the language and inspires in them the desire to strengthen or at least maintain their skills once they have left the classroom. To accomplish these goals, the teacher must know the subject matter, establish a good rapport with students, and develop an effective classroom style.

The foreign language teacher should feel at ease speaking the foreign language and should be able to use the language accurately. In the early 1960s, the Modern Language Association sponsored the development of a battery of *MLA Proficiency Tests for Teachers and Advanced Students*. These tests, available in French, German, Italian, Russian, and Spanish, consist of seven parts: four language sections which evaluate the skills of listening, speaking, reading, and writing; and three sections testing knowledge of culture, knowledge of linguistics, and professional preparation.[19] Although in need of revision, these tests provide an objective evaluation of teacher proficiency. New York State, for instance, uses these examinations to grant credit for the External Regents Degree and to certify language teachers who have not acquired their skills in a formal university program.

In 1978, the Educational Testing Service made its *Oral Proficiency Interview* available to the public. The candidate has a twenty-minute oral interview with a trained examiner. The tape recording of the interview is subsequently evaluated by trained scorers, and the candidate's command of the language is reported on a scale from 0 to 5.[20] Schools hiring new language teachers should encourage prospective candidates to provide results of the *Oral Proficiency Interview*, for only in this way can an administrator who is not fluent in the second language be certain that the prospective teacher has appropriate mastery of the language.

Rapport with students. The affective component of language teaching cannot be underestimated. The good teacher is fair, self-confident, possesses a sense of humor, and is dedicated to the students' intellectual and moral growth. Although there is not a test designed to evaluate skills in this area, enrollment figures may provide some indication of how students view a particular teacher. Also, certain observational techniques and questionnaires that can provide feedback from students can provide evidence regarding the degree of rapport between the teacher and the class.

Teaching style. The growing interest in students' learning styles has naturally led to a concern with teaching styles. Some teachers feel at ease with an open-style classroom where many activities are occurring simultaneously, while others prefer a more structured, teacher-centered classroom. To help analyze teacher-student interaction in a teacher-centered classroom, Moskowitz has developed the FLint (Foreign Language Interaction) system.[21]

19. Available from the Modern Language Association, 62 Fifth Avenue, New York, N.Y. 10011.

20. For more information, contact the Educational Testing Service.

21. Gertrude Moskowitz, "Interaction in the Foreign Language Class," in *Sensitivity in the Foreign Language Classroom*, ed. James W. Dodge, in *Reports of the Working Committees* (Middlebury, Vt.: Northeast Conference on the Teaching of Foreign Languages, 1973), pp. 13-57.

If the goal of a second-language program is to enable students to communicate in that new language, certain facilities and learning conditions should be available: small classes, homogeneous grouping, specialized classrooms, and accessible recordings.

The Modern Language Association has recommended a maximum class size of twenty in courses where the emphasis is on the development of conversational skills. Students need the opportunity to interact with one another and with the teacher, and this becomes exceedingly difficult with more than twenty students in a class.

Although it is possible to schedule two classes (such as third- and fourth-year French) into the same classroom with the same teacher at the same period, this type of heterogeneous grouping cuts effective class time by 50 percent. The rate of language acquisition is substantially reduced in mixed classes.

The most effective foreign language teachers use a great variety of activities. It is much easier for a language teacher to make a broad use of realia (such as magazines, posters, records, games, readers, transparencies) if all classes are taught in a foreign language classroom. The teacher who must travel from room to room finds it impossible to carry around a wide selection of materials.

Recent research into second-language acquisition stresses the importance of listening to authentic speech. Students should have access to recorded materials, either via a language laboratory, preferably one allowing for individual control of the tapes, or via tape recorders and cassette players in the classroom. If the school has facilities for duplicating tapes, students can take foreign language cassettes home for additional listening practice.

EVALUATING THE CURRICULAR MATERIALS

The focus of the instructional program is determined by the curriculum, the textbooks, and the testing program. Usually the curriculum is stated in general terms, and is open to differing interpretations. Therefore, in evaluating a second-language program, the administrator will do well to study the textbooks and how they are used, as well as the tests and the grading systems.

Studying the curriculum. It is usually difficult for school ad-

ministrators to evaluate a second-language curriculum. The task
can be made easier, however, by requesting that the department
provide answers to the following questions for each course or
level of instruction:

What percentage of the curriculum in terms of instructional
emphasis is concerned with skill-getting? With skill-using?

What percentage of the curriculum is focused on the oral skills
of speaking and listening? On reading and writing? In some
cases, one might want to make a four-way distinction among
the skills of listening, speaking, reading, and writing.

Is cultural material added for occasional enrichment or does the
study of culture and civilization constitute a regular part of
the program? In the latter case, what percentage of the curriculum focuses on culture and what percentage on language?
Culture and language are frequently interwined, but some programs contain a special cultural strand with specific content.

Evaluating the instructional materials. In 1974, Carroll reviewed
the research on learning theory and concluded with a set of guidelines for writers of instructional materials.[22] These guidelines,
transformed into questions, may be used as a checklist by committees reviewing instructional materials for use in foreign language classes. For example, do the materials:

1. contain lesson objectives addressed to the students?
2. visually draw attention to important elements in the lesson?
3. contain understandable descriptions of how the language
   works?
4. contain exercises with clear instructions and presented in
   meaningful contexts (not merely pattern drills or a series
   of unrelated sentences)?
5. include self-tests with answer keys and guidelines for review?

22. John B. Carroll, "Learning Theory for the Classroom Teacher," in
The Challenge of Communication, The ACTFL Review of Foreign Language
Education, vol. 6, ed. Gilbert A. Jarvis (Skokie, Ill.: National Textbook Co.,
1974), pp. 144-45.

6. contain meaningful presentations of new material that build on prior learning?
7. contain sufficient examples of new patterns so that the student can draw conclusions about rules of grammar?
8. contain frequent activities for review?
9. contain extra readings and extra activities for listening so that students can develop comprehension skills?
10. contain suggestions for activities for self-expression?

If the instructional materials do not contain all the above features, the teacher may want to supplement the text by preparing additional components and using ancillary materials.

Evaluating the tests and the grading system. In reality, the manner in which course grades are assigned reflects course objectives more accurately than either the curriculum guide or the instructional materials. There is a tendency to base student grades more heavily on skill-getting behaviors than on skill-using (free and semiguided skits, compositions, conversations; ability to understand new readings and unfamiliar recordings).

By using a chart such as that shown in table 1, teachers and administrators can assign the relative importance to be given to the various learning activities and language skills in determining grades for individual students.

TABLE 1

SCHEME FOR ANALYSIS OF THE GRADING SYSTEM IN FOREIGN LANGUAGE CLASSES, WITH ILLUSTRATIVE WEIGHTS GIVEN (IN PERCENT) TO SKILL-GETTING AND SKILL-USING IN VARIOUS ACTIVITIES

ACTIVITY	PERCENT OF FINAL GRADE				
	SKILL-GETTING		SKILL-USING		TOTAL
	WRITTEN	ORAL	WRITTEN	ORAL	
Outside preparation	10	5	5	—	20
Class participation	5	10	2.5	2.5	20
Cultural projects	—	—	5	5	10
Quizzes and tests	10	5	—	5	20
End-of-term test	20	5	5	—	30
Total	45	25	17.5	12.5	100

EVALUATING OVERALL EFFECTIVENESS

The overall effectiveness of a second-language program can be measured against external standards and also in terms of its contribution to the school curriculum. The performance of students on national and standardized tests allows a school system to evaluate its program from year to year and to determine how well students are doing in comparison to students in schools throughout the country. The *MLA Cooperative Tests* and the *Pimsleur Tests* provide norm-referenced scores in the areas of listening, speaking, reading, and writing. These tests should not be given, however, until after two or three years of secondary school language study. Scores on the Foreign Language Achievement Tests and the Advanced Placement Tests administered annually by the College Board provide an objective evaluation of students' performance against national standards. In New York State, the Regents Examinations fulfill a similar function. The various associations for teachers of specific languages (French, German, Spanish and Portuguese) hold national competitions in the spring for students of all levels. Only students of teachers who are members of the association are allowed to participate. The winning students, their teachers, and their schools are announced in June.

An analysis of enrollment trends within the school system may help to reflect the effectiveness of a second-language program. What percentage of the students in the system are taking second-language courses? What percentage of the students enrolled in the first-year courses continue to a second year? to a third year? to a fourth year? to the advanced classes? What percentage of the students are enrolled in two language courses? What percentage of the students would have liked to enroll in a language course but could not because of scheduling or other difficulties?

Conclusion

Language tests, like tests in any other curriculum area, are not always of the highest validity and reliability. Furthermore, the test administrator should take into account that the score received by a given student on a single test, unless that score is very high or very low, usually does not provide a true measure of that student's ability. Nevertheless, tests and evaluation instruments, when properly utilized, can provide useful information about the second-language program.

CHAPTER IX

The Education and Reeducation of Teachers

HELEN L. JORSTAD

Introduction

Patterns of education for teachers of foreign language have tended to reflect prevailing practices in the teaching of language. Prior to the Civil War, methods used in modern language classrooms were carbon copies of methods used in teaching classical languages in order to make the study of modern language a respectable part of the curriculum.[1] Thus, translation was one of the principal activities of the classroom, as well as thorough dissection of the language in order to teach its grammar. Gradually emphasis shifted to the teaching of all four skills in modern languages. In the four-year (or longer) language programs of the day, these aims were possible. In 1899, the report of the Committee of Twelve of the Modern Language Association paved the way for consideration of language programs that were shorter than four years.[2] The committee's suggestion that in extreme circumstances a two-year program would suffice led to the adoption of that duration as the norm rather than as an exception. The virtual demise of foreign-language programs prior to and during World War I only encouraged the relegation of language study to the bottom of any curricular considerations for some time to come. Two-year programs purporting to teach students to listen, speak, read, and write another language were, of course, doomed to failure, and in 1929 the Coleman report recommended that, since only two years of language study were generally offered and since development of

1. Frank M. Grittner, *Teaching Foreign Languages*, 2d ed. (New York: Harper and Row, 1977), pp. 1-2.

2. *Report of the Committee of Twelve of the Modern Language Association of America* (New York: Heath, 1901).

oral facility is not possible in such a short program, reading should be the focus in the study of foreign languages.[3]

Teacher education programs during these years were unlikely to produce teachers who could teach more than the reading of a foreign language, in any case. Generally, programs consisted of a background in general education and a requisite number of credits in language study. Since language programs in college followed the general procedures of high school programs in preparing students principally to deal with literature, prospective teachers were likely to have had very little experience in understanding or speaking the languages they would be teaching. Even though a few teachers might have tried to emphasize listening and speaking skills in their classrooms, it was difficult for them to do so because of their lack of training and because they themselves often could barely understand or speak the language they were teaching.[4]

This situation led Freeman to ask in 1944, "What constitutes a well-trained modern language teacher?" [5] He suggested the following as essentials: correct pronunciation, oral facility, knowledge of grammar and syntax of the language, mastery of vocabulary, and a complete background in culture, civilization, and modern-language pedagogy—no small order for college or university training programs that were not consciously stressing those aims for their students. As a result, in a speech seven years later to the National

---

3. Algernon Coleman, *The Teaching of Modern Foreign Languages in the United States* (New York: Macmillan Co., 1929). This report is the most famous of the seventeen volumes in the entire Carnegie-sponsored study completed in 1927. In his volume, *The Training of Teachers in the Modern Foreign Languages* (New York: Macmillan Co., 1930), Charles M. Purin reported that inadequate teacher preparation was the rule.

4. For a review of language teaching during that period, see also Richard J. McArdle, "Teacher Education, Qualifications, and Supervision," in *Britannica Review of Foreign Language Education*, vol. 1, ed. Emma Marie Birkmaier (Chicago: Encyclopedia Britannica, 1968), pp. 259-80; Howard B. Altman and Louis Weiss, "Recent Developments in the Training and Certification of the Foreign Language Teacher," in *Britannica Review of Foreign Language Education*, vol. 2, ed. Dale L. Lange (Chicago: Encyclopedia Britannica 1970), pp. 239-73; and David E. Wolfe and Philip D. Smith, Jr., "Teacher Education for New Goals," in *Foreign Language Education: A Reappraisal*, ed. Dale L. Lange and Charles J. James (Skokie, Ill. National Textbook Co., 1974), pp. 97-126.

5. Stephen A. Freeman, "What Constitutes a Well-trained Modern Language Teacher?" *Modern Language Journal* 25 (January 1941): 293.

Federation of Modern Language Teachers Associations, Freeman could still say that colleges had no standard training syllabus for prospective teachers and that they provided instead a variety of unrelated major or minor courses "which have little value in preparing a teacher." [6] He urged that the various associations of teachers (of French, German, Spanish and Portuguese) give attention to special problems of recruiting teachers, training them, and overseeing their placement. Little progress was evident in 1954, when Parker pointed to the continuing decline in standards for the education and certification of teachers of modern languages.[7]

In 1952, the Foreign Language Program of the Modern Language Association of America was established to help bring about unity among various segments of the language-teaching profession and to begin to take corrective action. A statement of qualifications for secondary school teachers of modern foreign languages was issued in 1955 outlining "minimal," "good," and "superior" levels of proficiency for teachers of languages in seven areas: aural understanding, speaking, reading, writing, language analysis, culture, and professional preparation.[8] That statement was the basis upon which the language programs under the National Defense Education Act, including the development and standardization of proficiency tests for teachers, were built. The work of Freeman and others provided a model for helping the profession redirect its efforts. The statement of qualifications was endorsed by every language organization and by the American Council of Learned Societies. It still serves as the major statement of guiding principles for continued development of proficiency standards for programs of teacher education.

These early efforts to improve the teaching of languages, in combination with world events, resulted in federal funding of programs as well as considerable public attention. Between 1958, when Sputnik was launched, and 1968, when the major funding of pro-

6. Stephen A. Freeman, "What about the Teacher?" *Modern Language Journal* 33 (April 1949): 255-67.

7. William R. Parker, *The National Interest and Foreign Languages* (New York: UNESCO, 1954).

8. The statement was first published in the *Bulletin of the National Association of Secondary School Principals* 39 (November 1955): 30-33 and was reprinted in the *Modern Language Journal* 50 (October 1966): 372-74.

grams expired, the National Defense Education Act provided money for schools throughout the country to purchase laboratory and other equipment and for teachers at all levels to secure retraining both in the United States and in countries where the languages they taught were spoken. As a result, teachers were able to improve their language skills and their teaching methods. At the same time, proficiency tests for teachers were developed and standardized at the NDEA Institutes for teachers.[9] It seemed possible, finally, for language teaching to be revitalized permanently, with stress moving again to the development of the skills of listening, speaking, reading, and writing through long sequences of language study beginning in the elementary schools. The need for large numbers of language teachers for the programs at all levels, from elementary schools through senior high schools, led to a relaxation of standards as colleges and universities recruited teachers to fill the needs. Yet teachers during and since that time have probably been better equipped to handle training in language skills than they were prior to Sputnik. More and more states moved toward the approach of "approved programs" for licensure of teachers, in which completion of an institutional program approved by state departments of public instruction was to be the basis for certification instead of a simple listing of some number of specified courses. Many institutions established stringent requirements for levels of language proficiency and for specific school-based instructional components before recommending candidates for licensure. In the meantime, however, explosive events on college campuses in the 1960s resulted in the curtailment of language requirements for entrance and/or for graduation in many schools, first at postsecondary levels and later in secondary schools. Language teachers responded by creating courses and programs designed to help meet individual students'

9. *MLA Cooperative Foreign Language Proficiency Tests* (Princeton, N.J.: Educational Testing Service, 1961). The tests were formerly known as the *MLA Foreign Language Proficiency Tests for Teachers and Advanced Students*. Descriptions of the development and norming of the tests may be found in Miriam M. Bryan (*DFL Bulletin* 5, no. 1 [1966]: 4-7), in Wilmarth Starr (*PMLA* 77 [September 1962]: Part 2, 31-42), and in Charles T. Meyers and Richard S. Melton, *A Study of the Relationship between Scores on the MLA Foreign Language Proficiency Tests for Teachers and Advanced Students and Ratings of Teacher Competence* (Princeton, N.J.: Educational Testing Service, 1964).

needs and to appeal to students' interests in an effort to enlist customers for their services.

Research on the Education of Language Teachers

The most important research project involving the education of teachers of foreign or second languages was undertaken in connection with the NDEA Institutes.[10] Summer and academic year programs at major institutions throughout the country set the tone for the so-called "new key" instructional approach and they built a spirit of enthusiasm. The wide acceptance of in-service training to improve teaching skills and language proficiency made it seem possible to predict the establishment of a real "profession" of language teaching.[11] It was hoped that the new spirit and approach would be continued in teacher education programs on an ongoing basis, so that a new kind of teacher might emerge—one who was proficient in the language, knowledgable about the culture and the civilization of another people, well-versed in linguistic science and able to apply its principles in the classroom, and an excellent teacher with unbounded enthusiasm for teaching. While a few innovative programs emerged, ten years after the end of the era little remained of those soaring hopes and spirits.

Much of the research in the education of language teachers relates to teachers' proficiency in languages. Carroll measured the proficiency of 2,782 seniors majoring in French, German, Italian, Russian, and Spanish at 203 institutions in the four language skills (listening, speaking, reading, and writing).[12] Those seniors who were preparing for teaching were given additional tests on applied linguistics, culture and civilization, and professional preparation. Carroll found startling evidence that significant numbers of advanced students who were about to be graduated with majors in a foreign language were barely able to attain minimal require-

10. Summaries of the evaluations of the NDEA Institutes are contained in Joseph Axelrod, *The Education of the Modern Foreign Language Teacher for American Schools* (New York: Modern Language Association, 1966).

11. Wolfe and Smith, "Teacher Education for New Goals."

12. John B. Carroll, "Foreign Language Proficiency Levels Attained by Language Majors Near Graduation from College," *Foreign Language Annals* 1 (December 1967): 131-51.

ments for speakers of the language. He also found that students who had spent some time in a country where the language they were studying was spoken performed significantly better than those who had never travelled. He concluded that the results provided "strong justification for a year abroad" for language majors.[13] It is doubtful that Carroll's findings would be much different today, since there are still few programs that provide for systematic development of language skills as the central focus of a program for language majors. Nor is there much differentiation between programs for language and literature majors and those for prospective teachers, despite ample evidence of the need for stronger language-based programs for teachers.

In their massive Pennsylvania study, Smith and Berger found that levels of language proficiency of teachers did not have much relationship to the progress of their students in secondary school classes.[14] The study was flawed, however, by the large number of variables that were difficult to control, by the lack of effective training for teachers in the "experimental" sections of the project, and by the difficulties of definition of treatments and the measurement of results.[15] Despite the results of the study, it is hard to believe that nonfluent teachers of language can turn out fully fluent students after two, three, or even four years of language study.

Carroll's study of the teaching of French as a foreign language in eight countries did not use standardized measures of teachers' language proficiency.[16] It did, however, ask teachers to rate their own proficiency in each of the skill areas. Results showed, not

13. Ibid., p. 137.

14. Philip D. Smith, Jr., *A Comparison of the Cognitive and Audiolingual Approaches to Foreign Language Instruction: The Pennsylvania Foreign Language Project* (Philadelphia: Center for Curriculum Development, 1970). For a summary of the project, see idem, "The Pennsylvania Foreign Language Research Project: Teacher Proficiency and Class Achievement in Two Modern Languages," *Foreign Language Annals* 3 (December 1969): 194-207.

15. See "Critique of the Pennsylvania Project," *Modern Language Journal* 53 (October 1969): 386-428.

16. John B. Carroll, *The Teaching of French as a Foreign Language in Eight Countries* (Stockholm: Almqvist and Wiksell, 1975; New York: John Wiley and Sons, 1975).

surprisingly, that teachers who believed themselves fluent in speaking a second language produced students who could understand the language very well; those who judged themselves highly proficient in writing French had students who were good in reading skills. It would have been useful to have measured teachers' proficiency through standardized tests or interviews, but the results are nonetheless interesting and significant. Students in the United States were among the poorest in the study, although it should be noted that the other countries all provided many more years of language study for students prior to the ages at which they were tested. Thus, one of the major findings, that the time a student has spent learning a second language is the single most important factor in influencing proficiency, would naturally mean that students in the United States would do very poorly. Although the findings of this study have not yet been widely publicized, the data remain on file. Other analyses may shed further light on factors that make for success in language learning in a school setting and that may have important implications for teacher education.

Without examining the relationship between language proficiency of teachers and students' achievement, a number of studies have attempted to draw descriptions of successful (good, excellent) language teachers.[17] Generally, the traits that make good language teachers are not so different from those that make good teachers in general, for example, flexibility and openness to innovative approaches and materials. With regard to the language, most studies have found that time in the country where the language is spoken is the one single factor most closely related to success in the classroom. It is possible that there is a feeling of comfort with a foreign language and in a particular culture that might relate to a sort of fluency not measured by present standardized instruments. It is also possible that if that kind of fluency or comfort factor could be measured, programs could be devised both in this

---

17. For example, see Joseph Axelrod, *The Education of the Modern Foreign Language Teacher for American Schools*; Robert L. Politzer and Louis Weiss, *Characteristics and Behaviors of the Successful Foreign Language Teacher*, Technical Report No. 5 (Stanford, Calif.: Center for Research and Development in Teaching, 1969); and Gertrude M. Moskowitz, "The Classroom Interaction of Outstanding Foreign Language Teachers," *Foreign Language Annals* 9 (April 1976): 135-57.

country and abroad to help teachers attain it. With regard to flexibility and openness to innovation, teacher education programs must provide a wider assortment of alternative approaches, and help teachers to develop a personal philosophy of teaching that enables them to feel comfortable in a wide variety of situations. They should be given help in supplementing and implementing existing text materials in such a way that a natural "flow" will result in a language class that enables students to learn the language and appreciate cultural diversity more easily than in a traditional, book-bound program.

Guidelines for the Preparation of Language Teachers

Two events in the late 1960s helped the profession to determine future language needs and plan programs for teacher development. One event was the formation of the American Council on the Teaching of Foreign Languages, an organization that gave sustained attention to problems of teacher education for language programs, as well as to efforts for renewed federal attention to the study of languages and to interpretations of innovative approaches to language teaching through annual conferences, publications, and workshops for its members. The second event was the publication in 1966 of the golden anniversary issue of the *Modern Language Journal,* which contained a compilation by the editor, André Paquette, of several statements regarding language proficiency and the training of language teachers, as well as a detailing of the "Guidelines for Teacher Education Programs in Modern Foreign Languages" that were developed by the Foreign Language Program of the Modern Language Association and the National Association of State Directors of Teacher Education and Certification.[18]

The guidelines outlined the components of a model program of teacher education, including academic specialization and professional education. According to the guidelines, language teachers should be able to develop their students' control of listening, speaking, reading, and writing skills; help students understand another culture through the study of language and of ways in which that

18. "Guidelines for Teacher Education Programs in Modern Foreign Languages," *Modern Language Journal* 50 (October 1966): 342-44.

culture contrasts with the culture of the United States; develop appreciation of foreign literature; choose and use materials, methods, and equipment appropriately; work with teachers of other subjects in the school; and diagnose students' difficulties and evaluate their progress in learning a language. One section of the guidelines detailed features of programs for the education of teachers of foreign languages.[19]

While the guidelines have been followed in some instances, they have never been wholeheartedly embraced by the entire profession, partly because of the changes in the national mood. In general, college and university programs have not changed from their traditional literature-oriented base, despite the need for teachers with a broad background in linguistics, language, and culture. This dislocation is perhaps the greatest single threat to continued preparation of language teachers who can meet the needs of today's schools. These needs are often met by in-service offerings after a teacher has found employment, but preservice teachers have difficulty finding programs that give them an adequately rounded background. Moreover, many cannot today afford to study abroad without funds such as those formerly provided under NDEA. The guidelines continue to be followed, however, in some model college and university programs.

Far from being out of date, the guidelines have lost none of their relevance and contain sound advice for those responsible for programs of teacher preparation. Despite the constantly changing nature of elementary and secondary schools, teachers educated in full accordance with the guidelines should be better equipped to innovate and shape future language programs. It should be equally obvious that language departments in colleges and universities are not equipped, for the most part, to provide leadership in such a development because of a too pervasive lack of interest in teaching basic language (as opposed to literature) and because study of the present-day culture of a wide variety of peoples speaking a particular language is often not considered very scholarly. Too few language departments provide opportunities for

19. See "Exposition of Part D of the Guidelines," *Modern Language Journal* 50 (October 1966): 344-63, for a discussion of these features by noted professional language educators.

their majors to specialize in language and culture rather than in literary studies.[20] It is possible that the commission established by President Carter to prepare recommendations for improving instruction in foreign languages and area studies will make such an emphasis more widespread.[21] I turn now to suggestions for steps that could be taken to bring programs for the preparation of teachers of languages more nearly into accord with the guidelines.

CONTROL OF THE FOUR LANGUAGE SKILLS

If teachers are able to help their students develop the basic language skills, it seems axiomatic that teachers themselves should have excellent skills of reading, writing, listening, and speaking and that they should be able to use the language exclusively in all classes at all levels of instruction. An additional language competency, not generally included in the standard skills enumerated, is the ability to use appropriate language in specific situations and to be able to transmit this kind of natural use of language to students at appropriate levels.

Because language departments in American colleges and universities seem largely unable to devote adequate course time and effort to the development of a high level of competence in language, it seems clear that alternative approaches must be found. In no other curricular area does true mastery take so long to achieve, and in no other is it so important that the prospective teacher have adequate opportunities for full professional development. There is simply no other way for the quality of language teaching to be high enough so that graduates of elementary and secondary schools will have attained functional levels of proficiency in a foreign language. This is ultimately the important implication of Carroll's international study.

If American institutions are unable to meet the challenge, how

20. Warren C. Born and Kathryn Buck, comp., *Options for the Teaching of Foreign Languages, Literatures, and Cultures* (New York: American Council on the Teaching of Foreign Languages, 1978). The collection provides an impressive survey of some notable exceptions.

21. Recommendations of the Commission are to cover a wide area of concerns, ranging from global education perspectives to language study and teaching and international education.

can teacher preparation programs that recommend candidates to state departments of public instruction for licensure ensure that teachers they recommend have complete command of the languages they intend to teach? There is an alternative. It does not seem far-fetched in this day of an oversupply of teachers to recommend that extended stays in another culture be required of all language teachers as an integral part of their preprofessional preparation. A related recommendation, of course, is that programs of financial aid for such travel and study be instituted. Not only will prospective teachers have opportunities to develop language abilities they cannot now achieve, but they will also have opportunities to develop essential cultural awareness. Such study should be encouraged especially in areas where a foreign language is spoken in neighboring countries such as Canada and Mexico. A further barrier to widespread overseas study, travel, and work experiences can be overcome if a national body were to become a clearinghouse for the evaluation of credits so that credit for the study of language and culture could be counted toward a major. Competency, however achieved, should be recognized by language departments and preprofessional programs.

For the time being, language departments at the very least should (a) teach every course intended for majors with the language as the medium of instruction and with the courses organized so that students have opportunities to participate fully; (b) require all papers, tests, and exercises to be prepared in the language; (c) teach special reading skills so that students can learn to read directly in the language early in their careers (translation as a separate skill for students at advanced levels should also have a role, but not in reading classes); (d) develop significant offerings to help students acquire an understanding of present-day culture through newspapers, magazines, film, and the like; (e) offer classes in the structure of the language as well as in phonetics; (f) expand courses in conversation to major offerings at every level.

TEACHING ABOUT FOREIGN CULTURES

The guidelines recommend that teachers of languages be able to "present the language as an essential element of the foreign culture" and be able to contrast another culture with that of the

United States. As indicated in the discussion of the previous guideline, the cultural background recommended exceeds that which is generally possible for language majors to complete. The sad fact is that the "close relationship between language and culture" is not often defined for students; instead, "culture" is generally limited to study of those elements commonly conceived of as "civilization."

Nor is the language major helped to develop a process for dealing with cross-cultural stereotyping and isolation—a process which focuses on the progressive refinement of a natural succession of hypotheses about another culture. Instead, teachers leave programs of preservice training largely able to "teach as they were taught" in this area (showing slides, singing songs, or telling something about the culture—all surely legitimate activities, but more effectively incorporated into deeper cultural objectives). At no time in our history has it been more important to break down cultural stereotypes, even within our own country. Such humanistic aims for language study are often claimed, but teachers have not learned how to teach for such goals. Indeed, it seems hard to imagine how a student who has been exposed to the quaint aspects of another culture by sitting through little talks or slide programs can have developed "intercultural understanding" or "openness toward another people." On the other hand, teachers who are themselves helped to identify and work through the stereotypes they hold about other cultures can help their students see their own stereotypes for what they are—incomplete representations of a culture based on limitations of time, place, social class, urban/rural setting. There needs to be careful instruction in recognition of biases in materials of all types used by students and teachers, whether the materials are developed for curricular use or come directly from another country (for example, magazines, newspapers, children's books, realia).

TEACHING LITERATURE

Language teachers should know how to present literature from another culture so that students can understand it and appreciate its values. It would seem that American teachers of language should have no difficulty meeting this guideline, since literature is often the chief focus of preprofessional study in the language. In fact, however, while some majors are able to understand a good deal of literature on their own, for their own enjoyment, far too many are simply not able to handle the language well enough to appreciate its literature. One need simply note the large numbers of language programs in which literature courses are taught in English and in which students are asked to translate rather than to read or to appreciate the literature.

Teachers in elementary and secondary schools too often are unacquainted with the most important literature that would give them real understanding of members of another culture. They should be reading and studying children's literature, adolescent literature, poetry and nursery rhymes, game songs and chants, fairy tales, folklore—all the "literature" that is usually most fascinating to children and young people and can help them understand better the full development of the "foreign" personality—the literary allusions, the childhood literary backgrounds which form the basis for a literary tradition. Yet it would be difficult indeed to find more than a handful of courses in the United States where prospective teachers can receive such a background. They should also study folk heroes, sports heroes, comic-strip heroes, corporate symbols, and the like, to understand the close relationship between present-day culture and its literature.

Moreover, assuming that teachers develop a love for and understanding of a foreign literature themselves, model programs of teacher education need to help them to develop teaching techniques suitable for classrooms in elementary and secondary schools. If teachers teach in the way in which they have been taught, a real love for literature will probably not be forthcoming. Part of the task in this area also involves helping teachers to choose appropriate reading materials, as well as classroom aids for teaching them.

USE OF MATERIALS AND EQUIPMENT

Teachers should be able to choose and use methods, techniques, aids, material, and equipment for teaching that are appropriate to their classes. Teacher preparation programs are performing more successfully in this respect than in the others, especially when one considers the types of summer workshops offered for in-service teachers, in addition to methods courses in preservice programs. Yet in many courses the focus still tends to be on telling teachers "how to do it" and why, rather than on providing valid demonstrations of a wide range of alternative approaches. In methods courses, students should have many opportunities to try a number of possible approaches and techniques to help find those that are most productive and comfortable for them. Microteaching situations, either with peers or with students in schools, provide teachers with practice that helps them to develop means for critiquing their own teaching, the ultimate goal of any preservice or in-service program of supervision.[22]

Teacher education programs should provide as many opportunities as possible for teachers to work in schools at all levels, beginning such experiences as early as possible and continuing contact throughout the program. Methods appropriate for teaching foreign language in elementary schools should be part of every language teacher's preparation, as well as courses in teaching reading and other subject areas, since many secondary language teachers today are being moved into middle-school programs.

Despite the continued development of hardware available for teaching, it is likely that today's teacher is less able to use it for teaching languages. Publishers are not continuing to refine software possibilities to enable more creative teaching of the repetitive aspects of language. The quality of software materials used in audio laboratories has not kept pace with the rest of the media world, probably because the financial base for such development, the availability of money from federal and other sources to purchase electro-mechanical equipment and materials, has all but disappeared. Materials, text and otherwise, have likewise not changed a great deal recently, again perhaps because of a shrinking market. Accordingly, more time must be spent in language methods courses and in in-service programs in helping teachers analyze, choose, and develop teaching materials that are in tune with objectives

22. For the background of microteaching and bibliographical references to studies of microteaching for language teachers, see Ray T. Clifford, Helen L. Jorstad, and Dale L. Lange, "Student Evaluation of Peer-group Microteaching as Preparation for Student Teaching," *Modern Language Journal* 61 (September-October 1977): 229-36.

stressing the development of cultural understanding and the real use of communicative language for specific purposes, since such materials are not forthcoming from most publishers. Ideally, the development of such materials should take place within the foreign culture, so that realia and personnel resources would be plentiful and authentic.

CORRELATION WITH OTHER CURRICULAR AREAS

Teachers of languages should be able to correlate their teaching with that in other curricular areas. In most schools we have not met this guideline. It is primarily in the elementary school that efforts have been made to coordinate second-language teaching with social studies, language arts, music, art, and other subject areas—and largely due to the singular efforts of individual teachers, who may or may not have had courses in the teaching of foreign language at the elementary level. Secondary teachers are generally slower to work together to coordinate curricular offerings. Even in middle schools, where more flexibility should provide more opportunities for cooperative ventures, teachers have tended to remain isolated and to teach alone. (It is becoming more common, however, to see teachers of several different languages working together, more commonly with a vast festival or in some other nonclass activity.) In general, such isolation begins in our teacher education programs, which make few efforts to help prospective teachers understand the importance of the interdependence of the curriculum. Moreover, in many areas where the most cooperation would be possible, language teachers tend to feel they need to compete with other curriculum areas for student enrollees. Even without actually working with another teacher, however, language teachers could have some experiences that would better equip them to deal with other curricular emphases in their own classes. They might, for example, have a strong background in the social studies, especially to help them understand and use an inquiry approach to learning. They might have work in the sciences and the history of science so that they could understand efforts in other countries to deal with problems of energy conservation and of ecology. The wider the language teachers' background, the more able they are to help students develop language as an ancillary skill, useful in working in any curricular area.

EVALUATION OF STUDENT PROGRESS

Teachers should be able to use latest approaches to the evaluation of student progress and the diagnosis of problems. A concomitant understanding is the role of so-called "error" in developing a mastery of language skills. Most prospective teachers do not study testing and evaluation in a structured way. In many programs, despite this deficiency, testing shapes the teaching program to the extent that much of the already limited classroom time is spent dissecting and talking about minute points of grammar, since that area of language is most commonly tested. Many programs that are ostensibly preparing students for functional use of language make little or no effort to test such functional use. Unfortunately, this is likely to be even more prevalent as competency testing becomes more widespread in high schools, since present nationally standardized tests, which can be used as guides, tend to stress discrete grammar and vocabulary items rather than the communicative use of language in either spoken or written modes. Teachers certainly should have enough background to analyze proposed tests and to suggest appropriate alternatives based on closer congruence with the real goals of good language programs.

OTHER USES FOR THE GUIDELINES

Although the guidelines were designed to provide direction for the development of preservice programs for the preparation of teachers, they are also helpful in planning programs of in-service training. Teachers in service should have time to maintain and improve their language skills and to deepen their understanding of foreign cultures. They should have opportunities to develop testing programs that will assist in the diagnosis of the difficulties students encounter in learning a language and in the proper placement of students, as well as in the measurement of proficiency and achievement. Time should be provided so that language teachers can work with teachers in other instructional areas. They also need time for the development of curricular materials and for experimentation with innovative approaches to the teaching of language.[23]

The guidelines may also be used to give direction to the selection of teachers who are well prepared to teach foreign language. Those who hire teachers should seek evidence of the applicant's attainment of the specific skills suggested by the guidelines. Direct references from all the units with which the applicant has worked —language departments and departments of education—should be sought. If all employers insisted on excellence and on the certification of real attainment of skills, teacher education programs would have to strengthen their focus on total preparation.

Needed Research

There are a number of areas related to the preparation of language teachers where further research would be helpful. In addition to the needed research previously suggested in this chapter, it would be useful to have studies of the best ways to select candidates for participation in teacher education programs. It is possible that we should consider not admitting anyone who does not already have wide experience here and abroad in the requisite areas or who does not have well-developed language skills and understandings. Since the skills require a long time to develop, it may be unrealistic to expect prospective teachers to learn to teach a language while their own abilities are intermediate at best. We may also find that prospective teachers need to love students and the people whose language they teach as much as or more than they love to dissect the language. It may well be that those who merely love grammatical analysis should not be encouraged to go into teaching unless they are willing to spend time developing the skills suggested by the guidelines by direct work with young people so that language teaching may be seen in a more realistic perspective.

There should be funding for the establishment of a number of model programs that would seek the best combinations of demonstration, practice, and internship to help teachers develop teaching skills. Such programs might require work, travel, and/or study in

23. See, for example, Charles A. Curran, *Counseling-Learning in Second Languages* (Apple River, Ill.: Apple River Press, 1976): Georgi Lozanov, *Suggestology and Outlines of Suggestopedy* (New York: Gordon and Breach, 1978); Caleb Gattegno, *Teaching Foreign Languages in Schools: The Silent Way*, 2d ed. (New York: Educational Solutions, Inc., 1972).

a foreign culture. It might be useful to experiment with a model teaching center in another country where experiences could be designed that are specifically intended to work through stereotypes within the culture as well as to provide wide opportunities to use the language for real communication.

Finally, research should continue to seek the best methods and materials for helping teachers develop and teach cross-cultural understanding, as well as the best ways of working with teachers in other curricular areas toward that end.

CHAPTER X

The Supervision of Foreign Language Teachers

CONSTANCE K. KNOP

The Purposes of Supervision

The underlying premise of this chapter is that supervision can help teachers improve their teaching and encourage the development of the skills of self-evaluation that are useful in continuing efforts to improve. The points to be made are applicable to the supervision of both preservice and in-service teachers.

Mosher and Purpel have pointed out that two basic approaches recur throughout the history and literature of supervision: the scientific approach and the democratic approach.[1] Proponents of the scientific approach hold that teaching can be analyzed to uncover successful and unsuccessful elements. The students' learning is the central criterion for determining success in teaching, even though research has yet to demonstrate the various ways in which specific teaching strategies affect students' learning. Analysis is concerned with assessment and evaluation prior to decisions about certification, retention, or merit increment. The supervisor is generally considered a member of the administrative staff whose assigned task is to maintain teaching standards.

In the democratic approach, the focus is on teachers as individual human beings. The goal of supervision is to help teachers use their talents in order to reach creative fulfillment in the classroom. To that end, different teaching strategies, new curriculum materials, and varied techniques are discussed with the teacher. The supervisor is considered a colleague who shares ideas, encourages the teacher's efforts, and gives guidance and support when necessary.

In Button's study on the history of supervision in the United

---

1. Ralph L. Mosher and David E. Purpel, *Supervision: The Reluctant Profession* (New York: Houghton Mifflin Co., 1972), p. 15.

States, both approaches recur.[2] In the period from 1870 to 1885, supervisors used the democratic approach primarily, sharing their knowledge of curriculum content with teachers less educated than they and also modeling teaching behaviors. From 1885 to 1905, supervision seemed to move toward the scientific approach in that supervisors began to analyze the teaching they observed on the basis of their own experiences and philosophies of teaching.

The most extreme form of scientific supervision appeared from 1905 to 1920, when the doctrine of social efficiency was in vogue. Under that doctrine, very specific teaching behaviors thought to lead to the increased learning of students were identified. Modeled after procedures used in factories and in the business world, supervision viewed the teacher as a factory worker, students as the material to be worked on, and learning as the product. Timed tests were established to determine the most effective sequence and techniques for accomplishing given skills or tasks. Teachers were evaluated as to how they measured up on those tests of specific behaviors.

As individuals and in union groups, teachers rebelled against a concept of supervision that they considered narrow and intimidating. As a result, supervision has ostensibly included elements of the democratic approach since the late 1920s. Some schools, however, still use supervision primarily for purposes of assessment and many teachers still harbor a mistrust of supervision as "snoopervision." Consequently, even though a supervisor may be trying to carry out the goals of democratic supervision, the teacher may be fearful of the elements of evaluation and assessment that are associated with a scientific approach.

In the literature of foreign language education, supervision has received little attention. In position papers developed by national studies, the major points raised on teacher training focus on the selection of teachers of methods courses, the content of language and education courses, and the language skills needed. While the Purin Report[3] and the Modern Language Association guide-

2. H. W. Button, *A History of Supervision in the Public Schools from 1870-1950* (Ann Arbor, Mich.: University Microfilms, 1964).

3. C. M. Purin, *The Training of Teachers of the Modern Foreign Languages* (New York: Macmillan Co., 1929).

lines for teacher education programs[4] stress the need for expert supervision, no philosophy or theory of supervision is suggested and no techniques for supervising emerge in the recommendations.

Supervision is rarely discussed in books on methodology. One of the few exceptions is found in the work of Kaulfers, who lists questions and criteria for evaluating the goals of the foreign language program, the teacher's classroom skills and evaluation of students, and the students' growth in skills, attitudes, and self-evaluation.[5] His list includes criteria for examining general classroom instruction as well as activities specific to foreign language teaching (for example, "criteria for evaluating efficiency in class management" and "criteria for evaluating the products of creative activities involving the use of the foreign language"). Nevertheless, he does not discuss approaches or techniques to use in supervising nor does he present any theoretical framework regarding the goals and values of supervision.

Handschein stresses the need for supervision, especially of new teachers, and then outlines a sequence of techniques to use in observing.[6] The approach described is both democratic and scientific, emphasizing the giving of support and encouragement to the teacher through conferences and sharing of lesson plans while at the same time insisting that supervision must go beyond sympathy and good intentions. He calls for analysis of the teacher's approach and students' learning in the light of predetermined objectives.

Hagboldt summarizes several articles dealing with the training of teachers. He supports the essential points of those articles: that careful supervision is critical in guiding student teachers and in-service teachers and that supervisors generally have insufficient training for their task.[7]

In keeping with a scientific approach to supervision, Grittner

4. Modern Language Association, "Guidelines for Teacher Education Programs," *Modern Language Journal* 50 (October 1966), 342-44.

5. Walter V. Kaulfers, *Modern Languages for Modern Schools* (New York: McGraw-Hill, 1942), pp. 373-89.

6. Charles H. Handschein, *Modern-Language Teaching* (Yonkers-on-Hudson, New York: World Book Co., 1940), pp. 356-60.

7. Peter Hagboldt, *The Teaching of German* (Boston: D. C. Heath, 1940), pp. 217-43.

suggests basic questions to raise in evaluating the foreign language program of any school, such as relating the activities of teachers and students to the stated course objectives and analyzing the students' progress in learning.[8]

Articles in foreign language journals present more concrete suggestions and techniques to use in supervision. Moskowitz has developed an instrument (FLint: Foreign Language Interaction), based on the Flanders instrument for interaction analysis, for use in analyzing interactions in foreign language classrooms.[9] The instrument contains twenty-two categories that student teachers are trained to use in observations of other teachers and in analyzing their own teaching. Moskowitz views this approach as a means of developing greater awareness and sensitivity regarding the effect of teacher behavior on students.

Bailey also advocates the use of a time-interval recording system in the observation and analysis of classroom behaviors.[10] Teacher and supervisor analyze the data gathered on four or five agreed upon behaviors and then discuss progress and change since the last observation as well as directions for future change. The approach can be adapted to behaviors specific to foreign language instruction, such as the use of English versus the use of the foreign language.

Mackey uses audio and video tape recordings of classroom interactions to analyze quantitatively the speech and actions used by the teacher and learners.[11] The teacher then plots the results on a

8. Frank M. Grittner, *Teaching Foreign Languages* (New York: Harper and Row, 1969), pp. 321-41.

9. Gertrude Moskowitz, "Interaction in the Foreign Language Class," in *Sensitivity in the Foreign-Language Classroom*, ed. James W. Dodge, in *Reports of the Working Committees* (Middlebury, Vt.: Northeast Conference on the Teaching of Foreign Languages, 1973), pp. 13-57. See also, ibid., "Interaction Analysis: A New Language for Supervisors," *Foreign Language Annals* 5 (1971): 211-12.

10. Leona G. Bailey, "Observing Foreign Language Teaching: A New Method for Teachers, Researchers, and Supervisors," *Foreign Language Annals* 10 (December 1977): 641-48.

11. William Mackey, "Graduate Education in Foreign Language Teaching" (Paper given at the Edinboro Institute of Foreign Language Teaching, Edinboro State College, Pa., October 9, 1971). ERIC ED 071 530.

sequential and cumulative time scale to obtain a quantitative profile of the classroom behaviors.

All the preceding approaches may be described as "scientific" in that they call for recording and analyzing events, behaviors, and interactions in teaching. Wolfe, on the other hand, calls for a humanistic, confluent approach to supervision, focusing on the affective domain and the emotional needs of the teacher.[12] He points out that teachers' anxieties and insecurities must be faced and worked out before teachers can be effective in the classroom.

Elsewhere I have shown how the "scientific" and "democratic" approaches to supervision may be combined by using data gathering and analysis of teaching along with supportive techniques in pre- and postobservation conferences.[13] I have suggested frequent use of audiovisual recordings to allow teachers to formulate their own analysis and evaluation of a class session and to help reduce the threatening aspect of meeting with a supervisor.

Although the works just cited are addressed to techniques and activities in supervision, none of them postulates or develops a theory of supervision. For that, we must turn to recent literature in the field of teacher supervision.

Current Approaches to Supervision

THE SCIENTIFIC APPROACH

As noted above, scientific supervision focuses on observable behaviors in the classroom, including the teacher's strategies and the students' progress, in order to analyze and assess the teacher's performance and improve students' learning.

McNeil believes that teaching can and should be improved through careful supervision.[14] In fact, he contends that supervisors have the responsibility to protect the profession and students from mediocre teachers. He begins supervision with a conference prior

12. David E. Wolfe, "Student Teaching: Toward a Confluent Approach," *Modern Language Journal* 57 (March 1973): 113-19.

13. Constance K. Knop, "Developing a Model for Student Teacher Supervision," *Foreign Language Annals* 10 (December 1977): 623-38.

14. John McNeil, *Toward Accountable Teachers* (New York: Holt, Rinehart and Winston, 1971).

to observation during which the supervisor and teacher set up criteria for determining students' learning during the class hour. The criteria are in the form of objectives stated in terms of observable behaviors. Data are gathered on learners' responses and actions in order to accumulate evidence of change and of meeting behavioral objectives. The postobservation conference focuses on determining whether or not the criteria were met. The teacher's personal or professional needs or concerns are not included in discussions. Instead, students' needs and problems or their progress in learning suggest directions for change in the teacher's behavior or strategies.

Competency-based education. Competency-based education is a manifestation of scientific supervision. Students' achievement, as seen in measurable, overt behaviors, is the primary focus in observing and evaluating the class. The competencies are presumably agreed upon by teachers and supervisors for the entire school district. In the foreign language area, Steiner has set up models for preparing behavioral objectives and generating lists of competencies.[15] She has urged classroom teachers to take upon themselves the determination of these objectives for their students. If that is not done, she believes that administrators, who know less about goals of the foreign language program, will establish them. At the State University of New York at Buffalo a guide has been developed to work toward competency-based education and supervision of student teachers in foreign languages.[16] State-prepared guidelines for competencies are available in Florida, New York, and Pennsylvania.

Use of interaction analysis. Interaction analysis, a system designed to record and categorize observable classroom behaviors, is one activity often used by supervisors in a scientific approach. Its goal, however, is not so much to assess teachers' performance as to help them understand the types of communication and interactions occurring in their classes (for example, the amount of

15. Florence Steiner, *Performing with Objectives* (Rowley, Mass.: Newbury House, 1975).

16. Anthony Papalia, *A Competency-Based and Field-Centered Teacher Education Program in French: Teacher Competencies and Evidence of Achievement* (Buffalo, N.Y.: State University of New York at Buffalo, 1974).

teacher talk as compared with student talk, the number of teacher-initiated responses as compared with student-initiated ones, the incidence of rewards, questioning, and building on students' responses). Either Moskowitz's twenty-two categories of the FLint system or Bailey's time-interval recording system could be used in making such analyses.

THE DEMOCRATIC APPROACH

Supervision as therapy. At the opposite extreme in supervision is the democratic approach advocated by Dussault.[17] His entire focus is on the teacher, whom he likens to a patient in client-centered therapy. Like the patient, beginning teachers are filled with doubts, insecurities, and anxieties because of incongruency between the "ideal teacher self" they envision and their "real" or "present teacher self," which they perceive as inadequate. In the Dussault approach, discussion in a conference consists almost exclusively of the teacher's talk about personal needs and problems with respect to the teacher role; analysis of the classroom activities or students' learning is not of much concern, unless it is affecting the teacher's self-concept. The supervisor is to give unconditional, positive regard and support at all times. Thus, the critical and analytical phase of supervision is entirely eliminated.

Among those writing in the foreign language field, Wolfe may be regarded as favoring democratic supervision. While he does not advocate the approach of Dussault, he does call for more emphasis on the affective domain in training and supervising beginning teachers.[18] He points out that most programs of teacher preparation center almost exclusively on the cognitive area. To help teachers meet and solve concerns on the affective level, he suggests that supervision should also include role playing of critical situations along with group discussions of anxieties and emotional problems encountered in the classroom.

In line with the goals of democratic supervision, I have advocated that beginning teachers of foreign language should develop

17. Gilles Dussault, *A Theory of Supervision in Teacher Education* (New York: Teachers College Press, 1970).

18. Wolfe, "Student Teaching: Toward a Confluent Approach," p. 114.

self-critiquing skills.[19] Teachers can record their classes on tape
and themselves analyze the records, using an agreed upon analytical
or evaluative instrument, such as a checklist of teaching strategies
or a scheme for interaction analysis. In this way, the threat of
criticism at a conference is sharply reduced. The teachers will
have made their own analysis and critique ahead of time and,
thus, can interact with the supervisor on a more collegial level,
with the supervisor providing support and guidance. The teachers
are more likely to have a positive self-concept from being able to
analyze classes on their own. Their self-images are protected by
raising suggestions for improvement, rather than receiving such
suggestions or other criticisms from the supervisor.

Supervision as ego-counseling. In another form of democratic
supervision, the ego-counseling approach, Mosher and Purpel focus
on teachers and their professional problems. Unlike Dussault, they
exclude any probing of the supervisee's personal needs or concerns,
and limit the discussion to difficulties encountered in classroom
teaching.[20] Thus, the supervisor plans a short-term association during which the teachers try to clarify professional role expectations
and then attempt to carry out realistic solutions to any role conflicts. Discussion is always related to teaching responsibilities and
tasks.

CLINICAL SUPERVISION

Goldhammer and Cogan have each developed a clinical form
of supervision that uses elements of both the scientific and the
democratic approach.[21] In clinical supervision, the supervisor and
teacher meet in a preobservation session to determine the goals
and sequence of activities for the class to be observed. The discussion includes exchange of factual information (for example, the
lesson plan or the goals) as well as clarification of the teacher's
feelings regarding that specific class or teaching in general. During
the observation, the supervisor gathers verbatim data on all that

19. Knop, "Developing a Model for Student Teacher Supervision," p. 638.

20. Mosher and Purpel, *Supervision: The Reluctant Profession.*

21. Robert Goldhammer, *Clinical Supervision* (New York: Holt, Rinehart
and Winston, 1969); Maurice Cogan, *Clinical Supervision* (Boston: Houghton
Mifflin Co., 1973).

is said and done during the class hour. These data are analyzed separately by the teacher and supervisor to discover any recurring patterns and to determine whether the patterns need change.

In the postobservation conference, the classroom activities and interactions are analyzed to provide a basis for continuing or for changing teaching behavior. This conference may include personal as well as professional concerns but, as in ego-counseling, clinical supervision will deal with personal problems only if they are affecting teaching performance. While students' learning is a subject to be discussed, the teacher's strategies and behaviors are given equal importance since change in teaching behavior and growth in the teacher's creativity are central goals. Thus, clinical supervision encompasses both the scientific approach (evaluating learning and analyzing teaching) as well as the democratic approach (discussing teacher's needs and feelings in order to encourage a positive self-concept, creativity, and change).

Given the variety of personalities and problems encountered in supervision, it is unlikely that any one approach will be effective or appropriate at all times. Instead, supervisors might acquaint themselves with the various theories and techniques presented here in an attempt to be ready to meet the needs and problems of any given situation or teacher.

Areas of Concern Encountered in Supervision

We turn now to areas of concern to teachers during their early professional development. In the process of supervising teachers, three basic areas of teachers' concern consistently emerge: concern about mastery of basic instructional techniques, concern for developing sensitivity to pupil-teacher interactions, and concern about the overall analysis and evaluation of teaching effectiveness. Each area requires different kinds of training, help, and guidance from the supervisor.

MASTERY OF BASIC INSTRUCTIONAL TECHNIQUES

During student teaching and again during the first few weeks of full-time teaching, novices express uncertainty and apprehension about the mechanics of planning and presenting different kinds of lessons, such as pattern practices or dialogue drills. Such expressions of concern are shown in a study that identified the twenty-six most common fears and apprehensions experienced by beginning teachers.[22] An analysis of these twenty-six items shows that over half of them deal with the teachers' uncertainties about their ability to prepare and teach a lesson. Several studies have indicated that such fears can be reduced if the teacher is told ahead of time, through performance criteria or checklists, what specific teaching skills or techniques the supervisor will be looking for in the presentation.[23]

Using microteaching and performance criteria. In some methods classes, a teacher's uncertainty is at least partly overcome by practice in microteaching[24] or peer-group teaching.[25] However, if student teachers or beginning teachers arrive in the school without such training, they will undoubtedly be experiencing the anxieties noted above with respect to their teaching skills. To help minimize the effect of such anxieties, the cooperating teacher or supervisor may try to use microteaching during the first few weeks of teaching. The beginning teacher is observed teaching just one kind of lesson several times in a row. At the outset, the teacher and supervisor work out mutually understood performance criteria for a specific learning activity. (See table 1 for samples of such performance criteria for a lesson in pattern practice and for a reading lesson.) The teacher then observes an experienced teacher or the supervisor presenting that type of lesson in several different classes and looks for specific examples of behavior consistent with each of the criteria. As an alternative, videotapes of sample lessons may be studied to find examples for the performance criteria. After the observations, the teacher and the supervisor meet to discuss the activity, analyzing and evaluating examples noted under each of the performance criteria.

22. Michael L. Thompson, "Identifying Anxieties Experienced by Student Teachers," *Journal of Teacher Education* 14 (December 1963): 436.

23. Dussault, *A Theory of Supervision in Teacher Education*, p. 85.

24. William E. DeLorenzo, "Microteaching as a Transitional Technique to Student Teaching," *Foreign Language Annals* 8 (October 1975): 239-48.

25. Ray T. Clifford, Helen L. Jorstad, and Dale L. Lange, "Student Evaluation of Peer-Group Microteaching as Preparation for Student Teaching," *Modern Language Journal* 61 (September-October 1977): 229-36.

TABLE 1

Suggested Performance Criteria for Teaching a Specific Lesson

A LESSON IN PATTERN PRACTICE	A READING LESSON
1. Establish understanding of the basic sentence taken from the text and reinforce meaning throughout the 8-10 variations (by key words such as "yesterday" or "tomorrow," acting out use of visuals such as time line or props, teaching in realistic personalized situations, and the like).	1. Choose 8-10 important words from a passage, including words crucial to understanding the meaning of the passage and words useful for building guessing ability (words with which one can do word-family work, prefix/suffix work, or context clue guessing).
2. Keep one part of the sentence constant and introduce minimal steps in the variations/categories.	2. For each word, employ at least two explicating devices (for example, synonym, antonym, circumlocution) appropriate to the goal for that word and a checking device (true-false question, either/or question, visual aids, acting out).
3. Employ a variety of drilling techniques (for example, mixture of choral, group, and individual practice, multiple repetition, speedup) to maintain a quick tempo and to insure that students are practicing.	3. Have students practice aloud the new words after the explanation by asking for straight repetition of the new word or by cueing with the explicating device (for example, ask for one synonym or antonym of one word).
4. Begin with a full cue (repetition/question-answer) to help students master saying sentences and then fade the cue (word cue, tag question, visual) to check whether students can produce sentences on their own.	4. After explicating a word, put it back into context of sentence in the text. After explicating all new words, have students read aloud or answer questions based on entire sentence.
5. Provide a final general question to elicit the variations presented from the students.	5. At end of the entire passage, oral work will be done on the passage, with students reading after teacher or answering questions.

Next, the teacher plans that kind of lesson and teaches it to a class, with the supervisor now recording examples of how the performance criteria were or were not met. Immediately after the presentation, the two meet to critique the activity and to decide on ways in which it might be improved. Following the critiquing session, the teacher teaches basically the same lesson to another class, trying to implement the suggestions for improvement. The supervisor again observes the lesson and gathers data about the presentation, focusing on the agreed upon areas for change. After a few days of working on this one kind of lesson, the teacher can then follow the same format in working on another type of lesson, such as a reading lesson for which suggested performance criteria are shown in table 1. In this way, the teacher's anxiety about supervision is reduced by knowing ahead of time the performance criteria to be met and by gradually but systematically mastering different kinds of lessons.

Analyzing strategies in error correction. Beginning language teachers also often feel inadequate about correcting errors made by students. Joiner has suggested that this is an area that should be covered in teacher preparation programs.[26] She has developed a useful set of exercises in French that could be readily translated into other languages. After studying such exercises, the teacher might observe several live or videotaped classes, noting the errors made and later analyzing why they were made, deciding how they might have been avoided, and planning alternate ways of correcting them. Such training was one of the most highly rated elements of a foreign language methods course in a study conducted at the University of Wisconsin-Madison.[27] In this way, beginning teachers gain insights into why students make errors in the given language and they start to acquire a repertoire of techniques for avoiding and correcting errors.

DEVELOPING SENSITIVITY TO PUPIL-TEACHER INTERACTIONS

Another concern of teachers relates to how students are responding to their teaching, to the teacher's interaction with the class (for example, rapport, rewards, overall discipline and control), and to what the students think of their teaching.

Studying students' behaviors. One activity that has been found useful in the study of students' behaviors is to have the teacher observe a videotape of a class taught by an experienced teacher or by the supervisor. This requires watching an entire class session and analyzing the sequence of activities as well as carefully noting students' behaviors. The guide sheet shown in figure 1 has been

26. Elizabeth G. Joiner, "Training Prospective Teachers in the Correction of Student Errors," *French Review* 49 (December 1975): 193-97.

27. Constance K. Knop, "An Investigation into Student Teacher Opinion Regarding a 'Methods of Teaching French' Course" (Ph.D. diss., University of Wisconsin-Madison, 1969).

successfully used by teachers and supervisors when observing other teachers as well as in planning for their own classes.

ACTIVITY	LENGTH	GOALS (IN EXPECTED BEHAVIOR/ PROGRESS)	CHECKS (DID LEARNING OCCUR?)	TEACHER'S CUES (VARIED? FADED?)	STUDENTS' BEHAVIOR (WHAT WERE STUDENTS DO-ING DURING EACH ACTIVITY?)

Fig. 1. Guidesheet for observing classes

As Jorstad has noted, such an analysis may reveal that, while the teacher's activities or behaviors might be quite varied, the students' behavior is exactly the same throughout each activity.[28] For example, the teacher might show pictures, teach a dialogue, do a pattern practice, and teach a song, while the students' behavior consists only of rote repetition. Subsequent planning of lessons and self-critiquing may then move to focusing on what the students are doing during each activity and how their learning and progress are demonstrated. Among the ways that may be suggested for checking on various types of learning are the following:

On a dialogue: individual repetition to check progress in accuracy, fluency, and intonation; question and answers to check on rote learning and factual information; recitation of sentences in response to visual cues; making up original dialogue.

On pattern practices and grammar: answering a final general question with one of the variations; answering questions that elicit statements of rules; applying rules to new sentences.

On reading passages: answering factual questions on the passage; making up a resume first with teacher's cues and then independently;

28. Helen L. Jorstad, "Developing Skills in Supervision" (Paper presented at the convention of the American Council of Teachers of Foreign Language, New Orleans, 1976).

creating visuals for the passage; checking vocabulary using synonyms and antonyms, definitions, word-family work.

On culture: showing recognitional knowledge by answering yes/no or either/or questions; answering questions on factual information; acting out the cultural situation.

Analyzing classroom interactions. Teachers may become aware of the interactions in their classes by recording a session either on audiotape or videotape and then analyzing the record to determine, for example, the proportions of time devoted to teacher's talk as compared with students' talk; to the use of English as compared with the use of the foreign language; to choral, group, and individual practice; the length of time devoted to each activity; the number of times each student speaks. The teacher could also look for the number of rewards made and the manner in which they were expressed.[29] These items incorporate some of the major areas of focus in the FLint system, to which reference has already been made, but the use of this short list of items does not require the memorization of the longer list of categories or the kind of on-the-spot decision making required in using the FLint system. As an alternative, Bailey's time-interval recording system may also be considered.[30] Using such instruments, the teacher can analyze a taped or observed lesson in the class of another teacher and plan with the supervisor the changes that might be made in that lesson. The teacher's own class could then be recorded and the record analyzed with a view to making suggestions for change to be discussed with the supervisor. Finally, the supervisor could use the same instruments for gathering data during an observation of the teacher's class. Since the instruments are familiar to the teacher and the data are gathered in a relatively objective and nonjudgmental fashion, the teacher's defensiveness regarding supervision is likely to be reduced. Defensiveness could also be reduced if the supervisor were to leave the data with the teacher for analysis, thus providing the teacher with an opportunity to make suggestions for changes in strategies, in interactions, or in activities planned for students. In the ensuing conference with the supervisor, these suggestions could be discussed.

29. Knop, "Developing a Model for Student Teacher Supervision," p. 634.
30. Bailey, "Observing Foreign Language Teaching."

Soliciting students' evaluations. Students seldom voluntarily give teachers much positive day-to-day feedback. When teachers solicit evaluations, however, they often find that students can make useful suggestions that the teachers can take into account before being observed again by the supervisor. Teachers can use this kind of evaluation regularly on their own as a base and guide for changing their instructional practices.

The evaluation form might be prefaced with a self-evaluation, asking the students in the course about their own effort and participation in the course.[31] Students are often fairer and more objective in evaluating the teacher if they consider their own performance first. A form that contains specific points to be evaluated will garner the specific information the teacher is seeking. For example, consider the advantages of an item such as, "The teacher's explanations are (always clear; usually clear; sometimes clear; rarely clear)." This type of item will obtain a rating on a specific point as opposed to a general question such as, "What do you think of the teacher's explanation?" Leaving space after each item encourages students to offer comments on that point. Overall suggestions for improvement can be solicited by including an open-ended question at the end of the evaluation such as, "The best things about the teacher's instruction are ———" or "A few things that teacher might change are ———." A discussion with the students after analyzing the evaluations can lead to joint planning for changes in the teaching, either in techniques, activities, or topics to be covered. In this way, teachers receive feedback about their teaching and directions for improvement from those most involved and most affected by their work.

OVERALL ANALYSIS OF THE EFFECTIVENESS OF LANGUAGE TEACHING

Teachers of language, are also concerned about their overall effectiveness, including such matters as clarity of directions or explanations, variety in appropriate drilling techniques, and the use of English as opposed to the foreign language by both teacher and students during the lesson. One procedure helpful to teachers

---

31. For ideas on involving students more in self-evaluation, see Karen Mathis, "Evaluating Students' Oral Work," *Wisconsin French Teacher* 4 (1976): 9-10.

in analyzing their classes is suggested by those involved in clinical supervision. An observer might gather data in the form of a complete written record of what is said or done by the teacher and by the students. These notes are given to the teacher, who analyzes them for positive or negative signs of learning and for recurring patterns in the teacher's or the students' behavior.

Gathering data on one problem area. The focus in gathering data could be initially on just one point of concern to the teacher, such as clarity in giving directions. The observer could provide a verbatim account of every direction the teacher gives. This procedure has the advantage of responding to the teacher's request for help in improving one general aspect of teaching. It is less threatening because it is teacher-initiated and because it focuses on only one area to change. It is also less exhausting for the observer than is the gathering of data during an entire class.

Gathering data on a given type of activity. Another option is to gather data on just one type of activity. Perhaps the teacher is concerned about presentations of lessons on grammar, as most of them are throughout their first few years of teaching. The observer would then take extensive notes on that one aspect of the class. The examination of such data from several lessons on grammar might lead the teacher to discover, for instance, that the practice of giving just two or three examples of a particular point in grammar results in students being unsuccessful in generating other examples or in producing a rule on their own with so few samples. Or one might find that whenever the teacher uses terminology such as "direct object" or "relative pronoun," either in English or in the foreign language, students ask questions in English about those words and can not produce the forms in the second language when cued by the teacher's terminology. By examining what was actually said or done in class, teachers can discover such recurring patterns in their teaching and can work with the supervisor to devise ways of making desired changes.

Eventually, the observer may gather data on several segments of the class. Analysis of those data may call the teacher's attention to teaching behaviors that might otherwise have been overlooked completely, including those that are effective as well as those that do not lead to students' progress in learning. The following record of a lesson illustrates the kinds of data that could be collected. The supervisor might look at the record with several questions in mind, such as: What are some recurring patterns the teacher might be able to identify and analyze as effective or ineffective? What are the examples of students' behavior showing that learning did (or did not) occur? What are the examples of the teacher's behavior that did (or did not) aid students' learning? What questions could be raised by the supervisor to guide teachers in analyzing the data and in looking for ways to improve their teaching?

Data Gathered on a Reading Lesson

10:10-10:31. *Et maintenant, ouvrez votre livre*. Reading lesson begins.

Teacher reads whole sentence. Calls for students' repetition. About one-half of the class repeats, petering out toward end of the utterance.

Teacher rereads sentence. Some students begin to repeat but she stops them. *Attention au mot, "près de."* *Regardez-moi. Je suis près de Pierre*. Students watch her but do not repeat expression. No comprehension check.

Teacher then rereads sentence and calls for choral repetition. About three or four students repeat. One student looks out the window. Another writes out of another book.

Teacher exhorts students to pay attention and speak up: *Plus fort. Tout le monde*. After three efforts like this, she gets most of students to say the sentence. Only choral work is done.

Teacher reads the second sentence twice, then calls for choral repetition. Only three of four students near her repeat. She moves down the row, repeating the sentence. Now about one-third of the class repeats, but some repeat with her and others after her.

Teacher shows a picture of a room with a bed in it and with red curtains. She isolates the vocabulary, *"des rideaux rouges,"* and shows picture. She does not point to curtains. Students look at picture and repeat phrase.

Teacher hears error on "r" and calls for following repetition: *Raymond, Rosalie, Richard, rouge, rayons*. Students repeat each word but look puzzled, exchanging glances with each other and shrugging shoulders.

One students says, "I don't get it. What does that sentence mean?" Teacher again points to picture, says sentence, calls for choral repetition. Then asks student, *"Comprenez-vous?"* Student says, "I guess so."

Overall, this does not appear to be a very successful lesson because of lack of students' attention, participation, or progress in using the language. Yet, the teacher has used some effective techniques and behaviors that might be reinforced, along with suggestions for making them more successful. The following questions might be raised with reference to successful elements of the lesson:

Comment on your use of French during the class hour. Did you use French consistently? Why or why not?
How much of the work was done chorally? Why did you use this technique?
At one point, you moved down the row of students. Why was this done? Comment specifically on hearing students' errors and getting their attention by being near them physically. What can be done about students who are not near you?

Questions could also be raised about procedures that did not appear to be successful. For example,

How can a teacher establish and reinforce meaning of separate vocabulary items in a sentence? Should vocabulary be isolated and drilled before beginning the passage?
How can you check whether or not students understand your explanation? Is "*Comprenez-vous*" a check?
How long should an activity last? What different techniques might you use to keep students' attention? Comment specifically on alternatives to choral repetition.
During rote drill, students used French. When communicating with you, they used English. What does this imply about the cummunicative value of French in your class? How can you encourage students to use French when talking to you?
When drilling a difficult sound in isolation and in minimal pairs, how can you help students focus on the purpose of the drill? Is it enough to have them hear and say the sound, or can you offer other help to them?

Gathering data on items in a checklist. Some teachers and supervisors prefer to gather data in a more structured way, using an outline of specific points to look for when observing a lesson. The following outline, developed by student teachers, cooperating teachers, and supervisors in French at the University of Wisconsin-Madison, identifies points viewed as important criteria for successful teaching:

Ways of Analyzing Different Learning Activities

I. Introduction to each activity: topic, purpose, and mechanics of activity clearly stated? clear directions given concerning teacher's cue and students' response? one or two examples practiced chorally?

II. Oral activities

A. Model: set often and correctly?
B. Repetition: sufficient for progress of group? varied (for example, choral groups, multiple repetition, chain drill)? individuals called on to check group learning?
C. Correction of errors: immediately after grammatical phrase, except in free conversation? teacher cue to encourage students' self-correction (for example, *Où est le verbe? Je n'ai pas—?*)? correct model reset? choral repetition to correct error? whole sentence practiced? individual called on again?
D. Pause in presentation of new material to review items just worked on?

III. Reading

A. Conducted in foreign language?
B. Comprehension of material provided by teacher (for example, objects, gestures, word explanation)?
C. Comprehension of material checked by teacher (for example, factual questions, personalized questions, resume elicited)?
D. Student practice on new items (for example, repetition, reading aloud individually or in small groups)?
E. Vocabulary development (for example, work on synonyms, antonyms, definitions, word families)?

IV. Grammar

A. Item taken from lesson studied or from familiar material?
B. Many examples of phenomenon provided? Oral practice of them?
C. Inductive or deductive formation of rule?
D. Rule clearly and correctly stated? In which language?
E. Application of rule to new sentences and exercises? Oral or written practice?

V. Homework

A. Day's assignment checked in class?
B. Next assignment: clearly given? assigned before bell? examples practiced? related to work being done in class?

VI. Rewards: varied? appropriate? verbal? physical (for example, smile, nod)?
VII. Tempo?
VIII. Variation in activities and in techniques for repetition?
IX. Opportunities for students' self-expression and interaction?

X. Teacher's motivation, discipline, and control of the class?
XI. Thoroughness in preparation and planning the lesson?

Specific examples and data drawn from the class being observed are recorded under the various categories in the outline and questions noted. The teacher and supervisor then study the record to see if recurring patterns emerge or if, in fact, no data were gathered at all on some points. This procedure avoids having the supervisor merely give intuitive impressions of the class. For example, instead of saying "I thought a lot of English was used in the class," the supervisor can cite specific examples of reading and grammar work done in English by the teacher and/or students. Or the teacher may insist that students understood all of the reading explanations; but when no examples of comprehension appear in III, C, it becomes clear that one does not know if the students understood or not.

Analyzing the data leads to a discussion of what needs changing in the teaching and then how to effect those changes. Giving the data to teachers prior to the postobservation conference may encourage them to analyze and plan for change on their own. Then the conference becomes truly interactive, with supervisor and teacher sharing their ideas and insights.

Conclusion

Foreign language teachers have called for more in-service training to improve their skills and expand their repertoire of teaching strategies.[32] Supervision is potentially one means of responding to that expressed need. The supervisor can help classroom teachers become more aware of their teaching by providing a detailed description of events and interactions occurring during a class session from an objective viewpoint that the involved teacher probably cannot attain alone. After studying the data together, the teacher and supervisor can work on identifying successful elements of the teaching and thus the teacher's skills of analysis and evaluation are developed. They also discuss ways of

32. William E. DeLorenzo, "New Teachers: Developing Flexible Foreign Language Teachers," in *New Contents, New Teachers, New Publics,* ed. Warren C. Born, in *Reports of the Working Committees* (Middlebury, Vt.: Northeast Conference on the Teaching of Foreign Languages 1978), p. 85.

improving areas of weakness and encourage the teacher to change less successful teaching patterns. In addition, the supervisor may share ideas for a variety of techniques and activities gathered from observing many other teachers. In these ways, the supervisor tries to improve the quality of instruction and attempts to motivate the teacher to work out alternate approaches to teaching. To gain the confidence of the teachers and make supervision effective as in-service training, the supervisor must be able to exhibit skill in the second-language area and successful teaching performance.

Ideally, the supervisor is also training teachers to act on their own in changing and improving their teaching. That is, the supervisor may be teaching the supervisee various techniques for examining and analyzing the effectiveness of the teaching in a given class. To achieve this goal, the supervisor could acquaint the teachers with observation instruments or checklists by which one can independently analyze teaching and then could encourage the teachers to use these items while replaying audio or video tapes of their classes. The supervisor could also organize collegial supervisory visits and suggest evaluations from students as alternate means of helping teachers look at their own teaching. Ultimately, it is the classroom teacher who must plan change and improvement in instruction. The supervisor is a key figure, however, in giving the teacher motivation, direction, techniques, and training in self-analysis and in strategies for change.

Improving instruction and giving teachers training in self-evaluation are, indeed, possible and valuable results of supervision. But before supervision can reach these goals, the supervisor must recognize and try to reduce the threat and insecurity that supervision seems to present to many teachers. Explaining the purposes and procedures to be used in supervision will perhaps help teachers better understand and value the supervisory act. Involving teachers in planning the supervision will also reduce its threatening aspect. This involvement may be developed by having a preobservation conference in which teachers explain their goals and decide on areas of focus for gathering data; by asking teachers to analyze the data or a recording of the class on their own and to formulate suggestions to share with the supervisor; and by conducting the postobservation conference in an interactive manner and in a supportive climate. The supervisor is thus treating the teacher as a partner and a colleague with whom ideas and insights are to be shared, not as an inferior to be judged or chastised. Supervision will only be effective when teachers begin to believe that the supervisor's role is not limited to evaluating and assessing their teaching performance but rather extends to helping them improve the quality of instruction.

CHAPTER XI

Changing Times and Changing Needs in Second-Language Learning

FRANK M. GRITTNER

Over the past ten years, the systematic study of the future has become a new, highly visible phenomenon. As Shane has noted, research on the future aims "to help policy makers clarify their goals and values and choose wisely from among the alternative courses of action available to them."[1] Cornish defines the new discipline of "futuristics" as "a field of activity that seeks to identify, analyze, and evaluate possible future changes in human life and the world. The word implies a rational rather than mystical approach to the future, but also accepts artistic, imaginative, and experiential approaches as offering contributions that can be useful and valid."[2] Where teachers and other educators are concerned, futures studies can be described as a methodical process of making educators aware of possible alternative futures and their consequences, in order to reach policy decisions regarding the development of curriculum, the improvement of educational administration, and various other factors involved in schooling.[3]

In this final chapter certain approaches to dealing with the future are examined with the intent of relating those approaches to the study of foreign languages in a society that is projected to be, and to the needs of students, most of whom will be spending the rest of their lives in the twenty-first century.

1. Harold G. Shane, "Education in and for the Future," in *Alternative Educational Systems,* ed. Edward Ignas (Chicago: Peacock Publishing Co., 1979), p. 1.
2. Edward Cornish and Associates, *The Study of the Future* (Washington, D.C.: World Future Society, 1977), p. 258.
3. Shane, "Education in and for the Future," p. 2.

Futurism and Society

It is often said that education reflects rather than shapes society and that it is, therefore, past-oriented rather than future-oriented. According to futurists, this backward focus is no problem so long as society remains stable from generation to generation, for the past, if replicated in the future, can be a good guide for determining the education of each successive generation of young people. But when rapid change is occurring, or if it is planned by those who control the social order, then a new basis for determining the content and process of education is required if society is to continue to function smoothly. The young must be educated to live in the society that *will* be rather than in the society that *used* to be.

Futuristic perceptions involve a series of stated or implicit value judgments. For example, when the Hitler government assumed power in Germany in the early 1930s, certain assumptions about the proposed society were rapidly impressed upon the public consciousness and were systematically imposed upon educators at all levels of schooling. Teachers who did not agree with the new futuristic image were replaced by others who did. This was totally consistent with the basic value system of Nazism, which called for adherence to the *Führerprincip* (leadership principle) in in which all authority resided in the leader. Once the conquest of the schools and universities was complete, education became a vehicle for reconstructing society rather than merely reflecting its existing structure.

In America during the same period, Counts was also advocating a form of social reconstruction by means of the educational system. He raised the question, "Dare the schools build a new social order?" and he answered it affirmatively by stating the need to indoctrinate students into the social values of democracy.[4] Much of what Counts wrote was a reaction to the totalitarian trends in Germany and in other societies around the world. It is not sufficient, he felt, merely to oppose fascistic governments; in addition, educators must use their skills to build a democratic society so as to secure the values of freedom for future generations; education

4. George S. Counts, *Dare the Schools Build a New Social Order?* (New York: John Day, 1932).

must shape the future, not merely reflect the social order of the past.

FUTURISM AND THE PAST

This view introduces one of the paradoxes of education. Because it is the vehicle for passing on the nonmaterial resources of the culture, education is to some degree necessarily rooted in the past. Yet those resources must be used in such a way as to enable coming generations to deal productively with a technologically oriented and rapidly changing society, as Toffler has stated in his book *Future Shock*.[5] The metaphorical language of the term "future shock" can be somewhat misleading, for it implies that the future is something definite, fixed, and immutable, and that dealing with it is similar to coping with the "culture shock" often experienced when individuals must contend with a foreign culture that differs markedly from their own. Many futurists, however, believe that the future is not fixed and predetermined. They suggest that, with the help of education, alternative and preferable courses of action can be identified and acted upon. Thus, the futurist movement holds the optimistic view that the future is amenable to change if people will only consider the options and make wise choices. At the same time, futurists tend to reject the dogmatic views of the social reconstructionists of the past and to be skeptical of the process of "human engineering" in which future citizens would be educationally "programmed" for the good of themselves and of society.

FUTURISM AND HUMAN ENGINEERING

Perhaps the leading proponent of human engineering is B. F. Skinner. Unlike Counts or the totalitarian rulers of the 1930s, Skinner does not state with any precision the final "output performance" toward which humans are to be engineered. Skinnerian behaviorists tend to shy away from value judgments of this kind. Yet it would seem to be more than a minor consideration in projecting future human behaviors to determine in advance whether the behavioral specifications are to be written by a person like

5. Alvin Toffler, *Future Shock* (New York: Random House, 1970), p. 410.

Joseph Goebbels or one like Counts. These somewhat extreme examples help to illustrate the following points:

1. Conditioning techniques for engineering human behavior may indeed be extrapolated from empirical laboratory evidence; however, the purposes toward which these techniques are used upon human beings are necessarily based upon futuristic value judgments; and

2. In the past, "output behaviors" as defined by educators have tended to be focused on highly specific lower-level psychomotor and cognitive skills. Yet students appear to be moving toward a fluid future society in which specific training may be of little value.

Futurism and the Individual

TRAINING VERSUS FREE INTELLIGENCE

There are enormous problems associated with trying to reconstruct an entire society through the process of training all of its citizens to fit a predetermined role. As Cornish has noted, specific solutions often create a chain of problems at least as troublesome as those that the solutions attempted to correct.[6] For example, increasing the gross national product to improve the standard of living has led to more rapid depletion of irreplaceable natural resources. Improving health care has contributed to overpopulation and, ultimately, to increased pollution of the environment. And rapidly developing technologies have provided jobs but have also given many people the feeling of being depersonalized and dehumanized. Thus, many futurists, like the progressive educators earlier in the century, have moved away from the concept of massive social reform. Instead, they have sought to focus on the individual and to cut through the formalism, compartmentalization, and rigidity of existing modes of schooling. As one progressivist said in 1938, "Conditions in industry are changing so rapidly that the problem of enabling the individual to readjust himself as circumstances may require becomes a matter of primary importance. The demand is for 'free intelligence' rather than for skills in con-

6. Cornish and Associates, *The Study of the Future.*

nection with established patterns." [7] The progressivists favor a more widely applicable kind of mental flexibility as opposed to narrow social and career training. The futurists, looking to the 1980s and beyond, also see the need for this mental flexibility as urgent. Not only are occupations and life-styles coming, going, and changing with increased rapidity, but human beings are more mobile than ever before both within and beyond the boundaries of their homeland. Moreover, the world is becoming economically, politically, and perhaps even psychologically interdependent to a degree unknown in the past. According to some futurists, the emerging situation will require that individuals develop a new system of skills in such areas as learning how to learn, relating to other people, and making intelligent choices. [8]

EDUCATION AND INTERNATIONALISM

Shane and Silvernail project a broader range of needs for future citizens based on the observation that "powerful contemporary stirrings have burst many of society's old structures and have caused a new and interrelated world to emerge from the isolated national cocoons of the early twentieth century." [9] According to these authors, a number of economic, political, and social factors have contributed to the emerging and growing necessity for international cooperation. We are living in an interdependent, planetary culture in which humans everywhere must break with their parochial pasts and become world citizens. [10] To create this important "global sense of community" students of the future should be able to (a) gain knowledge, understanding, and appreciation of the different cultures and races of the world; (b) value cultural pluralism and diversity in ways of thinking, acting, and feeling; (c) ac-

7. Boyd H. Bode, *Progressive Education at the Crossroads* (New York: Newsom and Co., 1938), p. 92.

8. Benjamin D. Singer, "The Future-focused Role-image," in *Learning for Tomorrow: The Role of the Future in Education*, ed. Alvin Toffler (New York: Vintage Books, 1974), pp. 19-32.

9. Harold G. Shane and David L. Silvernail, "Foreign Language Study for a World in Transition," in *The Language Connection: From the Classroom to the World*, ed. June K. Phillips (Skokie, Ill.: National Textbook Co. 1977), pp. 8-9.

10. Ibid., p. 14.

quire values and moral standards of conduct that reflect membership in a global community and enhance the well-being of all
humankind; (d) perceive alternative futures and the consequences
of these alternatives; (e) bring their knowledge and skills to bear
on the social, political, and economic problems confronting humankind; and (f) become self-directed, lifelong learners and students
of the global community.[11]

The proper realization of such goals can contribute to perpetuating democratic processes at the international level, minimiz-
ing the danger of world-wide conflicts, dealing more effectively
with environmental pollution, stabilizing economic conditions
throughout the world, and making more equitable and reasonable
use of the world's natural resources. The ideal student of the future
would be one who accepts cultural and linguistic diversity at home
and abroad. Leestma has a similar list of goals and potential benefits to be derived from properly designed school programs that
emphasize cultural pluralism, cross-cultural understanding, and
respect for the ecological system upon which all people depend for
survival. And he states that, "Citizenship education must be resized
to include world-mindedness, a sense of the future, and the dynamics of change in an interdependent world." [12]

EDUCATION AND VALUE JUDGMENTS

Another consideration for education in the future involves
learning to make value judgments. According to the humanistic
view, scientific knowledge and technological know-how are of
little use in making such judgments.

It is pointless to know how to get things done without having any idea
of what is worth doing, so that informed study in applied science demands reflection in the humanities. Otherwise, we are reduced to the
absurd prospect of doing what we are able to do for the inane but
popular reason that we are able to do it—whatever it is.[13]

11. Ibid.

12. Robert Leestma, "Global Education," *American Education* 14 (June
1978): 13.

13. Edwin J. Delattre, "The Humanities Can Irrigate Deserts," *Chronicle
of Higher Education*, 11 October 1977, p. 32.

Thus, humanistic educators are urged to stop aping the hard sciences under the guise of being scientifically neutral. Instead, it is suggested that they must take a personal stand on critical, value-laden issues and must learn to relate humanistic content to the burning issues that face their students in the present and are likely to persist in the future.[14]

Foreign Language Education and the Future

NEGATIVE ATTITUDES TOWARD LEARNING OTHER LANGUAGES

One of the basic tenets of futurism is that the *nature* of one's futuristic view will tend to shape the nature of the future that subsequently emerges. In the case of foreign-language study in America, a unique series of problems is presented. Historical events have produced a particular climate in American society that is generally inhospitable to second-language learning.[15] As a result, it is difficult for many young Americans to see themselves in future situations where they would be using the skills and knowledge gained from learning a second language. According to Turner, the pressures to conform to the values of our anglicized mass society, coupled with the deep-seated rejection of the immigrant heritage, have thwarted all recent attempts to teach foreign languages effectively to any substantial portion of the school and college population.[16] The answer to this long-term dilemma, according to Turner, is for educators to put forth an enormous effort to educate the general public concerning the inherent values of learning a foreign language for virtually all children. Turner cautions, however, that the effort can succeed only if it "is accompanied by massive and long-term governmental support to make foreign language study useful for Americans at home as teachers, and as businessmen, administrators, and missionaries over-

14. Nell Eurich, "The Humanities Face Tomorrow" in *Learning for Tomorrow*, ed. Toffler, pp. 146-50.

15. Frank Grittner, *Teaching Foreign Languages* (New York: Harper and Row, 1977), pp. 9-12.

16. Paul Turner, "Why Johnny Doesn't Want to Learn a Foreign Language," *Modern Language Journal* 58 (April 1974): pp. 191-96.

seas." [17] Fishman states that second and even third languages are indispensable for the Americans of the future. He notes the irony of the fact that the international success of English as a second language has tended to deprive Anglos of the benefits of being multilingual.[18] Initial steps were taken toward the realization of the goals outlined by Turner and Fishman in the late 1970s. Under the leadership of the Modern Language Association, language educators established a series of task forces that made recommendations for improving second-language teaching and for communicating the value of such education to the widest possible audiences.[19] The work of the task forces led to the following resolutions, which expressed priorities for future action with regard to language study:

Resolutions on Language in American Education

Believing that all Americans should have the opportunity, either in school or college, or as adult learners, to acquire competence in a foreign language and understanding of a foreign culture, we urge support for the following resolutions:

1. The high schools of the United States must offer every student the opportunity to learn a widely-used world language, in addition to English, by providing a full sequence of foreign language study. To develop existing language resources, students from non-English-speaking backgrounds should be offered the opportunity to study their home language.

2. Students wishing to acquire full proficiency in languages and international studies should have access to district-wide or regional "magnet" schools which provide such instruction. These international schools would be supported primarily by local funds, but federal funds should be made available for planning and development.

3. Institutions of higher education have a special responsibility to provide instruction in less commonly taught languages and in area studies. Existing federal programs must be expanded to provide effective support to institutions committed to offering instruction in languages important to the national interests of the United States.

17. Ibid., p. 196.

18. Joshua A. Fishman, "Will Foreign Languages Still Be Taught in the Year 2000?" in *Materiale en Marcha* (San Diego, Calif.: San Diego City Schools, December 1973), p. 15.

19. Richard I. Brod, ed., *ADFL Bulletin* 10 (September 1978): 1-11.

4. Institutions of higher education must assure a supply of competent foreign language teachers to meet needs at all levels of education, and must assist in the creation of programs for upgrading the competencies of experienced teachers. Federal funds should be made available to support this effort.

5. International exchange and study abroad programs should be strengthened and made more accessible in order to provide the experience of foreign study and residence to qualified students and researchers.

6. National data on the acquisition of competence in foreign languages must be collected each year and made available to educators and the general public. The cost of developing appropriate measures of proficiency and of monitoring competence should be borne by the federal government.[20]

THE PRESIDENTIAL COMMISSION

The move toward governmental support that Turner had identified as essential also began in the late 1970s, spurred by Representative Paul Simon of Illinois. Simon had noted that the deterioration in international education and in language study in the United States was in violation of the Helsinki Accords in which the United States and the other signators had agreed to increase and promote such learning. In October 1978, President Carter announced the appointment of a Presidential Commission on Foreign Language and International Studies, the purposes of which are to:

1. Recommend means for directing public attention to the importance of foreign language and international studies for the improvement of communications and understanding with other nations in an increasingly interdependent world.

2. Assess the need in the United States for foreign language and area specialists, ways in which foreign language and international studies contribute to meeting these needs, and the job market for individuals with these skills.

3. Recommend what foreign language area studies programs are appropriate at all academic levels and recommend desirable levels and kinds of support for each that should be provided by the public and private sectors.

4. Review existing legislative authorities and make recommendations for changes needed to carry out most effectively the Commission's recommendations.[21]

20. Richard I. Brod, ed., "Resolutions Published by the Modern Language Association" (New York: Modern Language Association, November 6, 1978).

21. *Federal Register*, 25 April 1978, pp. 7-8.

Presumably, the activities of the Modern Language Association Task Forces and of the Presidential Commission will produce a vision of a "preferable future" for second-language education in America. As Strasheim has noted, it cannot be assumed that any program involving a second language will automatically enable students to break out of their Anglo-American cultural cocoons and to transcend "the inherent insularity of the monolingual's world."[22] If it is true that foreign languages, like the rest of the humanities, "have retreated from the front lines of creative and original thought and become priests of the past," then the goal of promoting global education and the other future oriented goals discussed at the beginning of this chapter are unlikely to be realized.[23] Similarly, if classroom instruction in foreign languages is devoted predominantly to mimicry and memorization, linguistic analysis, and the dissection of literary works of the past, then its validity as a contributor to a future global society will come increasingly under critical scrutiny.

LANGUAGE, CULTURE, AND MEANING

There are many positive signs that the foreign language profession is breaking away from the more sterile practices of the past and is moving toward instructional strategies that are designed to promote both cultural pluralism and cross-cultural understanding.[24] The communicative competence movement of the late 1970s within the foreign language profession places heavy emphasis upon the creative use of language structures for genuine, real-life communication in contrast both to the traditional method of grammatical analysis and to the audio-lingual approach, which often involves students in the memorization of nonmeaningful language utterances. In addition, there are many in the profession who are beginning to involve students in communicating feelings and values as well as communicating on a purely cognitive level. These move-

22. Lorraine A. Strasheim, "The Role of Foreign Languages in Global Education" (Paper given at the meeting of the American Council on Teaching of Foreign Languages, New York, June 1978), p. 10.

23. Eurich, "The Humanities Face Tomorrow," pp. 148-49.

24. See *The Challenge of Communication*, ed. Gilbert A. Jarvis (Skokie, Ill.: National Textbook Co., 1974).

ments relate to the goals of helping students to learn how to learn, to relate to other people, and to make intelligent choices.

With regard to the goal of gaining better understanding and appreciation of different cultures and races of the world, foreign language and bilingual programs have given increasing attention to cultural material both foreign and indigenous. The emphasis upon culture is evidenced by the content of recent textbooks, the topics discussed at the various national conferences on foreign language, the articles appearing in professional journals, and the items available from the Materials Center of the American Council on the Teaching of Foreign Languages (ACTFL). The interdisciplinary nature of much of the newer curricular material tends to involve students not only in the acquisition of knowledge but also in the application of that knowledge to social, political, and economic problems confronting all of humankind. The newer language curricula deal increasingly with such topics as world-wide environmental concerns, political understanding, cross-cultural comparisons, and the like.[25] If properly structured, foreign-language study can also equip young people with insights and attitudes about a symbolic system of a culture other than their own and thus help them to resist the linguistic manipulations of propagandists and others who use the powerful instruments of the media to manipulate human minds.[26]

STUDENTS' NEEDS AND SECOND-LANGUAGE LEARNING

It has also been suggested that second-language learning could contribute to the fulfillment of some basic human needs.[27] Maslow has identified human needs, in order of priority, as follows: physiological needs, safety needs, social needs, ego needs, and the need

25. See *The Language Connection: From the Classroom to the World*, ed. Phillips.

26. Frank Grittner, "Futurism in Foreign Language Learning" in *Foreign Language Learning Today and Tomorrow: Essays in Honor of Emma M. Birkmaier*, ed. Jermaine Arendt, Dale L. Lange, and Pamela Myers (New York: Pergamon Press, forthcoming).

27. Frank Grittner, "Futurism, Basic Education, and the Foreign Language Curriculum," *Teaching the Basics in the Foreign Language Classroom*, ed. David P. Benseler (Skokie, Ill.: National Textbook Co., 1979), pp. 1-14.

for self-actualization.[28] The physiological needs include everything required to stay alive, such as food, clothing, shelter, and rest. When individuals have moved beyond survival, they then try to stabilize the environment, to make it more secure for the future, to get a feeling of ability to protect what they have. After survival and safety have been assured, people next seek something larger than themselves; they want to belong, to share, to give and receive friendship and love. Once people feel socially accepted, they still want to feel good about themselves, to be self-confident, independent, and respected by peers. People can be healthy, safe, socially useful, and self-assured and still feel a strong lack of something in their lives. This need, even beyond that for ego satisfaction, is what Maslow calls the need for "self-actualization." When all the more basic needs are satisfied, people still have a compelling desire to move toward realizing their full potential as human beings.

Curricular futurists would tend to give preference to language programs that involve students actively in social interactions and in cross-cultural communication as a way of meeting social needs.[29] Language programs that promote individual success and are based upon establishing an emotionally supportive environment have a good chance of contributing to the ego needs of the students involved.[30] Further research and program development are needed to refine this aspect of foreign-language instruction, for there has been a tendency in the past to look upon a positive self-concept as a prerequisite for language learning rather than as an outcome of it.[31] Many Americans seem to feel that their personal self-realization would be facilitated if they had studied a foreign language. For example, in 1978 a Gallup Poll showed that foreign language was listed fourth among those subjects mentioned in response to the question "Are there any subjects you wish you had studied (in

28. Abraham H. Maslow, *Motivation and Personality* (New York: Harper and Row, 1954), pp. 80-106.

29. Donald K. Jarvis, "Making Cross-cultural Connections" in *The Language Connection*, ed. Phillips, pp. 168-70.

30. Renee S. Disick and Laura Barbanel, "Affective Education and Foreign Language Learning" in *The Challenge of Communication*, ed. Jarvis, pp. 200-201.

31. Ibid., p. 202.

high school) and didn't that would be of special help to you now?" [32] This suggests that attention should be given in the future to an expansion of foreign-language programs in the schools. Encouragement could also be given in the future to the already apparent trend among adults to include the study of a foreign language in their plan for lifelong learning. Many futurists forecast large amounts of leisure time in the emerging postindustrial society. The study of foreign language as a leisure time activity and the use of foreign language in international travel for profit and pleasure would appear to fit logically into the forecasts of the future.

Summary

In projecting future trends, one futuristic technique is to create a series of scenarios and then to consider the possible future consequences of each scenario. With regard to foreign languages in the future, for example, it would be possible to project current circumstances in which mainstream America retains its present level of monolingualism and ethnocentrism with respect to Anglo-Saxon cultural patterns, language usages, and value systems. Possible consequences of perpetuating these national characteristics and the educational climate that supports them could also be projected, taking into consideration such factors as rising economic expectations in non-English-speaking undeveloped countries, the diminishing supply of fossil fuels, pollution of the ecological system, the value of the dollar against other currencies, political alliances, and the fact that for 80 percent of the world's people English is not the native language. An alternate future scenario could also be projected in which a majority of Americans would develop multilingual skills and improved knowledge of other cultures. If the alternate future of a multilingual and multicultural America is deemed desirable, then ways of creating that preferable future would be sought out. In this more positive context, many of the suggested changes and innovations currently under consideration would take on new meaning. Foreign language learning has been projected to have within it the potential to move young

32. George H. Gallup, "The Tenth Annual Gallup Poll of the Public's Attitudes toward the Public School," *Phi Delta Kappan* 60 (September 1978): 44.

people in the direction of what Shane calls "neoculturation," a curricular approach which involves students in exploring new ways of moving with confidence into the future.[33] Traditionally, education has been directed toward "enculturation," a process by means of which an individual learns the traditional content of the society or culture of which he is a part. In the well-designed foreign language program the student is required to function in a new language that is based upon a non-Anglo set of cultural realities. This need to cope with the new, the different, and the unexpected is parallel to the "neoculturation" needs of all young people in learning to deal with the ever changing global society of the future. It would appear, however, that these skills should be viewed as relevant to *all* young people within modern American society, not merely to the few who have the inclination and financial resources to attend a liberal arts college or university. For, if the proper study of a second language can contribute in a positive way to the intellectual, cultural, occupational, and recreational needs of children and youth, then it is incumbent upon leaders in American education to devise curricula and to prepare teachers who can make such instruction accessible to all. The rest of the developed world has accomplished this goal; it is a reasonable future scenario for the United States. George Bernard Shaw has stated that "Some people see things as they are and ask, 'Why?' I see things as they could be and should be and ask, 'Why not?'" With regard to a preferable future in which every American has the opportunity to benefit from the study of a second language, perhaps it is time for American educators to look toward the future and ask, "Why not?"

33. Shane, "Education in and for the Future," p. 33.

Name Index

223

Subject Index

Academies, as replacement for Latin grammar schools, 6

Achievement, measurement of: use of criterion and norm-referenced tests in, 157; use of tests of skill-getting and skill-using in, 156, 158-60; commercial tests for, 160-61; reliability and validity as problems in, 157-58

Additive principle in second-language learning, 93, 96, 125-26

Affective factors in language learning, 63-65

Aims of Education (Alfred N. Whitehead), 149

American Association of Community and Junior Colleges, 137

American Association of Teachers of Spanish and Portuguese, 10

American Association of University Professors, 132

American Council of Learned Societies, 170

American Council on the Teaching of Foreign Languages, 25, 78, 86, 114, 175, 218

American Institutes of Research, 120

Army Language Schools, 151

Army Specialized Training Program, 14

Aspira of New York, Inc. v. Board of Education of the City of New York (1974), 118

Association of Departments of Foreign Language, 131, 135, 137

ADFL Bulletin, 135, 141

Attitude toward foreign-language study: need for change of, 214-15; questionnaire for determination of, 153-54; relationship of, to motivation, 153

Audiolingual methods in language teaching: criticisms of, 49; description of, 47-48; modifications of, 49-50

Back to basics movement, 29

Bidialectalism, 96, 97

Bilingual education: background of, in U.S., 104; decision in *Lau v. Nichols* pertaining to, 18, 21; different views on, 23; early supporters of, 110-12; relationship of, to TESOL, 93-94; selected quotations on, from Epstein report, 119-20; state legislation on, 104, 115-16; studies of, 23-24. *See also* Bilingual education programs, Bilingualism

Bilingual Education Acts (1968, 1974, 1978): emphasis on transitional programs in, 113; projects approved under, 106; provisions of, 92, 112-13, 114, 121; purpose of, 112-14

Bilingual education programs: evaluations of, 23-24, 120; federal funding for, 106; future of, 126-27; introduction of, 105-6; models for, 123-24; need for, 107-110; suggestions for planning and development of, 122-23; types of, 22

Bilingualism, 2, 10, 21-22, **92, 93**

Black English, **95**

Center for Applied Linguistics, **91, 114**

Central States Conference on the Teaching of Foreign Language, 83

Civil Rights Act (1964), 18, 115, 116

Classical tradition in language study, 4, 7-8

Classroom behaviors, uses of analysis of, in supervision, 189-90, 191-92, 197, 199

Cognitive-code learning, 51, 52

Cognitive processes in language learning, 33-34, 51-52, 62-63

Coleman (Algernon) report (1929), 13, 168

Coleman (James S.) report (1966), 109

Communicative competence as feature of foreign language teaching, 58-59

Competency-based education, 191

Council of Europe, 61

Court decisions affecting foreign-language study, 10

Creativity in language use, 52-53

TESOL professionals: beginnings of, in U.S., 105; lack of cohesiveness among professional organizations of, 102; need for new concept of, 103

Teaching load in foreign-language classes, 72

Teaching schedules, samples of, for foreign-language classes (tables), 73-74

Teaching style, 163

Tests in foreign languages, 156-60, 162-63, 167

Textbooks: instrument for evaluation of, 86-87; need for improvement of, 146-48; selected list of, containing provisions for individualized instruction, 84-85

Typical second-language programs (table), 75

Two-year colleges, foreign-language study in, 130, 137

U.S. Commission on Civil Rights, 109

U.S. Information Agency, 91

U.S. Office of Education, 106

INFORMATION ABOUT MEMBERSHIP IN THE SOCIETY

From its small beginnings in the early 1900s, the National Society for the Study of Education has grown to a major educational organization with more than 4,000 members in the United States, Canada, and overseas. Members include professors, researchers, graduate students, and administrators in colleges and universities; teachers, supervisors, curriculum specialists, and administrators in elementary and secondary schools; and a considerable number of persons who are not formally connected with an educational institution. Membership in the Society is open to all persons who desire to receive its publications.

Since its establishment the Society has sought to promote its central purpose—the stimulation of investigations and discussions of important educational issues—through regular publication of a two-volume yearbook that is sent to all members. Many of these volumes have been so well received throughout the profession that they have gone into several printings. A recently inaugurated series of substantial paperbacks on Contemporary Educational Issues supplements the series of yearbooks and allows for treatment of a wider range of educational topics than can be addressed each year through the yearbooks alone.

Through membership in the Society one can add regularly to one's professional library at a very reasonable cost. Members also help to sustain a publication program that is widely recognized for its unique contributions to the literature of education.

The categories of membership, and the dues in each category for 1980, are as follows:

> *Regular.* The member receives a clothbound copy of each part of the two-volume yearbook (approximately 300 pages per volume). Annual dues, $15.

> *Comprehensive.* The member receives clothbound copies of the two-volume yearbook and the two volumes in the current paperback series. Annual dues. $28.

> *Retirees and Graduate Students.* Reduced dues—Regular, $12; Comprehensive $24.
> The above reduced dues are available to (a) those who have retired or are over sixty-five years of age and who have been members of the Society for at least ten years, and (b) graduate students in their first year of membership.

Life Membership. Persons sixty years of age or over may hold a Regular Membership for life upon payment of a lump sum based upon the life expectancy for their age group. Consult the Secretary-Treasurer for further details.

New members are required to pay an entrance fee of $1, in addition to the dues, in their first year of membership.

Membership is for the calendar year and dues are payable on or before January 1. A reinstatement fee of $.50 must be added to dues payments made after January 1.

In addition to receiving the publications of the Society as described above, members participate in the nomination and election of the six-member Board of Directors, which is responsible for managing the business and affairs of the Society, including the authorization of volumes to appear in the yearbook series. Two members of the Board are elected each year for three-year terms. Members of the Society who have contributed to its publications and who indicate a willingness to serve are eligible for election to the Board.

Members are urged to attend the one or more meetings of the Society that are arranged each year in conjunction with the annual meetings of major educational organizations. The purpose of such meetings is to present, discuss, and critique volumes in the current yearbook series. Announcements of meetings for the ensuing year are sent to members in December.

Upon written request from a member, the Secretary-Treasurer will send the current directory of members, synopses of meetings of the Board of Directors, and the annual financial report.

Persons desiring further information about membership may write to

KENNETH J. REHAGE, Secretary-Treasurer
National Society for the Study of Education

5835 Kimbark Ave.
Chicago, Ill. 60637

PUBLICATIONS OF THE NATIONAL SOCIETY FOR THE STUDY OF EDUCATION

1. The Yearbooks

NOTICE: Many of the early yearbooks of this series are now out of print. In the following list, those titles to which an asterisk is prefixed are not available for purchase.

*First Yearbook, 1902, Part I—*Some Principles in the Teaching of History.* Lucy M. Salmon.

*First Yearbook, 1902, Part II—*The Progress of Geography in the Schools.* W. M. Davis and H. M. Wilson.

*Second Yearbook, 1903, Part I—*The Course of Study in History in the Common School.* Isabel Lawrence, C. A. McMurray, Frank McMurry, E. C. Page, and E. J. Rice.

*Second Yearbook, 1903, Part II—*The Relation of Theory to Practice in Education.* M. J. Holmes, J. A. Keith, and Levi Seeley.

*Third Yearbook, 1904, Part I—*The Relation of Theory to Practice in the Education of Teachers.* John Dewey, Sarah C. Brooks, F. M. McMurry, et al.

*Third Yearbook, 1904, Part II—*Nature Study.* W. S. Jackman.

*Fourth Yearbook, 1905, Part I—*The Education and Training of Secondary Teachers.* E. C. Elliott, E. G. Dexter, M. J. Holmes, et al.

*Fourth Yearbook, 1905, Part II—*The Place of Vocational Subjects in the High-School Curriculum.* J. S. Brown, G. B. Morrison, and Ellen Richards.

*Fifth Yearbook, 1906, Part I—*On the Teaching of English in Elementary and High Schools.* G. P. Brown and Emerson Davis.

*Fifth Yearbook, 1906, Part II—*The Certification of Teachers.* E. P. Cubberley.

*Sixth Yearbook, 1907, Part I—*Vocational Studies for College Entrance.* C. A. Herrick, H. W. Holmes, T. deLaguna, V. Prettyman, and W. J. S. Bryan.

*Sixth Yearbook, 1907, Part II—*The Kindergarten and Its Relation to Elementary Education.* Ada Van Stone Harris, E. A. Kirkpatrick, Marie Kraus-Boelté, Patty S. Hill, Harriette M. Mills, and Nina Vandewalker.

*Seventh Yearbook, 1908, Part I—*The Relation of Superintendents and Principals to the Training and Professional Improvement of Their Teachers.* Charles D. Lowry.

*Seventh Yearbook, 1908, Part II—*The Co-ordination of the Kindergarten and the Elementary School.* B. J. Gregory, Jennie B. Merrill, Bertha Payne, and Margaret Giddings.

*Eighth Yearbook, 1909, Part I—*Education with Reference to Sex: Pathological, Economic, and Social Aspects.* C. R. Henderson.

*Eighth Yearbook, 1909, Part II—*Education with Reference to Sex: Agencies and Methods.* C. R. Henderson and Helen C. Putnam.

*Ninth Yearbook, 1910, Part I—*Health and Education.* T. D. Wood.

*Ninth Yearbook, 1910, Part II—*The Nurses in Education.* T. D. Wood, et al.

*Tenth Yearbook, 1911, Part I—*The City School as a Community Center.* H. C. Leipziger, Sarah E. Hyre, R. D. Warden, C. Ward Crampton, E. W. Stitt, E. J. Ward, Mrs. T. C. Grice, and C. A. Perry.

*Tenth Yearbook, 1911, Part II—*The Rural School as a Community Center.* B. H. Crocheron, Jessie Field, F. W. Howe, E. C. Bishop, A. B. Graham, O. J. Kern, M. T. Scudder, and B. M. Davis.

*Eleventh Yearbook, 1912, Part I—*Industrial Education: Typical Experiments Described and Interpreted.* J. F. Barker, M. Bloomfield, B. W. Johnson, P. Johnson, L. M. Leavitt, G. A. Mirick, M. W. Murray, C. F. Perry, A. L. Stafford, and H. B. Wilson.

*Eleventh Yearbook, 1912, Part II—*Agricultural Education in Secondary Schools.* A. C. Monahan, R. W. Stimson, D. J. Crosby, W. H. French, H. F. Button, F. R. Crane, W. R. Hart, and G. F. Warren.

*Twelfth Yearbook, 1913, Part I—*The Supervision of City Schools.* Franklin Bobbitt, J. W. Hall, and J. D. Wolcott.

*Twelfth Yearbook, 1913, Part II—*The Supervision of Rural Schools.* A. C. Monahan, L. J. Hanifan, J. E. Warren, Wallace Lund, U. J. Hoffman, A. S. Cook, E. M. Rapp, Jackson Davis, J. D. Wolcott.

*Thirteenth Yearbook, 1914, Part I—*Some Aspects of High-School Instruction and Administration.* H. C. Morrison, E. R. Breslich, W. A. Jessup, and L. D. Coffman.

*Thirteenth Yearbook, 1914, Part II—*Plans for Organizing School Surveys, with a Summary of Typical School Surveys.* Charles H. Judd and Henry L. Smith.

*Fourteenth Yearbook, 1915, Part I—*Minimum Essentials in Elementary School Subjects—Standards and Current Practices.* H. B. Wilson, H. W. Holmes, F. E. Thompson, R. G. Jones, S. A. Courtis, W. S. Gray, F. N. Freeman, H. C. Pryor, J. F. Hosic, W. A. Jessup, and W. C. Bagley.

*Fourteenth Yearbook, 1915, Part II—*Methods for Measuring Teachers' Efficiency.* Arthur C. Boyce.

*Fifteenth Yearbook, 1916, Part I—*Standards and Tests for the Measurement of the Efficiency of Schools and School Systems.* G. D. Strayer, Bird T. Baldwin, B. R. Buckingham, F. W. Ballou, D. C. Bliss, H. G. Childs, S. A. Courtis, E. P. Cubberley, C. H. Judd, George Melcher, E. E. Oberholtzer, J. B. Sears, Daniel Starch, M. R. Trabue, and G. M. Whipple.

*Fifteenth Yearbook, 1916, Part II—*The Relationship between Persistence in School and Home Conditions.* Charles E. Holley.

*Fifteenth Yearbook, 1916, Part III—*The Junior High School.* Aubrey A. Douglass.

*Sixteenth Yearbook, 1917, Part I—*Second Report of the Committee on Minimum Essentials in Elementary-School Subjects.* W. C. Bagley, W. W. Charters, F. N. Freeman, W. S. Gray, Ernest Horn, J. H. Hoskinson, W. S. Monroe, C. F. Munson, H. C. Pryor, L. W. Rapeer, G. M. Wilson, and H. B. Wilson.

*Sixteenth Yearbook, 1917, Part II—*The Efficiency of College Students as Conditioned by Age at Entrance and Size of High School.* B. F. Pittenger.

*Seventeenth Yearbook, 1918, Part I—*Third Report of the Committee on Economy of Time in Education.* W. C. Bagley, B. B. Bassett, M. E. Branom, Alice Camerer, J. E. Dealey, C. A. Ellwood, E. B. Greene, A. B. Hart, J. F. Hosic, E. T. Housh, W. H. Mace, L. R. Marston, H. C. McKown, H. E. Mitchell, W. V. Reavis, D. Snedden, and H. B. Wilson.

*Seventeenth Yearbook, 1918, Part II—*The Measurement of Educational Products.* E. J. Ashbaugh, W. A. Averill, L. P. Ayers, F. W. Ballou, Edna Bryner, B. R. Buckingham, S. A. Courtis, M. E. Haggerty, C. H. Judd, George Melcher, W. S. Monroe, E. A. Nifenecker, and E. L. Thorndike.

*Eighteenth Yearbook, 1919, Part I—*The Professional Preparation of High-School Teachers.* G. N. Cade, S. S. Colvin, Charles Fordyce, H. H. Foster, T. S. Gosling, W. S. Gray, L. V. Koos, A. R. Mead, H. L. Miller, F. C. Whitcomb, and Clifford Woody.

*Eighteenth Yearbook, 1919, Part II—*Fourth Report of Committee on Economy of Time in Education.* F. C. Ayer, F. N. Freeman, W. S. Gray, Ernest Horn, W. S. Monroe, and C. E. Seashore.

*Nineteenth Yearbook, 1920, Part I—*New Materials of Instruction.* Prepared by the Society's Committee on Materials of Instruction.

*Nineteenth Yearbook, 1920, Part II—*Classroom Problems in the Education of Gifted Children.* T. S. Henry.

*Twentieth Yearbook, 1921, Part I—*New Materials of Instruction.* Second Report by Society's Committee.

*Twentieth Yearbook, 1921, Part II—*Report of the Society's Committee on Silent Reading.* M. A. Burgess, S. A. Courtis, C. E. Germane, W. S. Gray, H. A. Greene, Regina R. Heller, J. H. Hoover, J. A. O'Brien, J. L. Packer, Daniel Starch, W. W. Theisen, G. A. Yoakam, and representatives of other school systems.

*Twenty-first Yearbook, 1922, Parts I and II—*Intelligence Tests and Their Use.* Part I—*The Nature, History, and General Principles of Intelligence Testing.* E. L. Thorndike, S. S. Colvin, Harold Rugg, G. M. Whipple, Part II—*The Administrative Use of Intelligence Tests.* H. W. Holmes, W. K. Layton, Helen Davis, Agnes L. Rogers, Rudolf Pintner, M. R. Trabue, W. S. Miller, Bessie L. Gambrill, and others. The two parts are bound together.

*Twenty-second Yearbook, 1923, Part I—*English Composition: Its Aims, Methods and Measurements.* Earl Hudelson.

*Twenty-second Yearbook, 1923, Part II—*The Social Studies in the Elementary and Secondary School.* A. S. Barr, J. J. Coss, Henry Harap, R. W. Hatch, H. C. Hill, Ernest Horn, C. H. Judd, L. C. Marshall, F. M. McMurry, Earle Rugg, H. O. Rugg, Emma Schweppe, Mabel Snedaker, and C. W. Washburne.

*Twenty-third Yearbook, 1924, Part I—*The Education of Gifted Children.* Report of the Society's Committee. Guy M. Whipple, Chairman.

*Twenty-third Yearbook, 1924, Part II—*Vocational Guidance and Vocational Education for Industries.* A. H. Edgerton and others.

*Twenty-fourth Yearbook, 1925, Part I—*Report of the National Committee on Reading.* W. S. Gray, Chairman, F. W. Ballou, Rose L. Hardy, Ernest Horn, Francis Jenkins, S. A. Leonard, Estaline Wilson, and Laura Zirbes.

*Twenty-fourth Yearbook, 1925, Part II—*Adapting the Schools to Individual Differences.* Report of the Society's Committee. Carleton W. Washburne, Chairman.

*Twenty-fifth Yearbook, 1926, Part I—*The Present Status of Safety Education.* Report of the Society's Committee. Guy M. Whipple, Chairman.

*Twenty-fifth Yearbook, 1926, Part II—*Extra-Curricular Activities.* Report of the Society's Committee. Leonard V. Koos, Chairman.

*Twenty-sixth Yearbook, 1927, Part I—*Curriculum-making: Past and Present.* Report of the Society's Committee. Harold O. Rugg, Chairman.

*Twenty-sixth Yearbook, 1927, Part II—*The Foundations of Curriculum-making.* Prepared by individual members of the Society's Committee. Harold O. Rugg, Chairman.

*Twenty-seventh Yearbook, 1928, Part I—*Nature and Nurture: Their Influence upon Intelligence.* Prepared by the Society's Committee. Lewis M. Terman, Chairman.

*Twenty-seventh Yearbook, 1928, Part II—*Nature and Nurture: Their Influence upon Achievement.* Prepared by the Society's Committee. Lewis M. Terman, Chairman.

Twenty-eighth Yearbook, 1929, Parts I and II—*Preschool and Parental Education.* Part I—*Organization and Development.* Part II—*Research and Method.* Prepared by the Society's Committee. Lois H. Meek, Chairman. Bound in one volume. Cloth.

*Twenty-ninth Yearbook, 1930, Parts I and II—*Report of the Society's Committee on Arithmetic.* Part I—*Some Aspects of Modern Thought on Arithmetic.* Part II—*Research in Arithmetic.* Prepared by the Society's Committee. F. B. Knight, Chairman. Bound in one volume.

*Thirtieth Yearbook, 1931— Part I—*The Status of Rural Education.* First Report of the Society's Committee on Rural Education. Orville G. Brim, Chairman.

Thirtieth Yearbook, 1931, Part II—*The Textbook in American Education.* Report of the Society's Committee on the Textbook, J. B. Edmonson, Chairman. Cloth, Paper.

*Thirty-first Yearbook, 1932, Part I—*A Program for Teaching Science.* Prepared by the Society's Committee on the Teaching of Science. S. Ralph Powers, Chairman.
*Thirty-first Yearbook, 1932, Part II—*Changes and Experiments in Liberal-Arts Education.* Prepared by Kathryn McHale, with numerous collaborators.
*Thirty-second Yearbook, 1933—*The Teaching of Geography.* Prepared by the Society's Committee on the Teaching of Geography. A. E. Parkins, Chairman.
*Thirty-third Yearbook, 1934, Part I—*The Planning and Construction of School Buildings.* Prepared by the Society's Committee on School Buildings. N. L. Engelhardt, Chairman.
*Thirty-third Yearbook, 1934, Part II—*The Activity Movement.* Prepared by the Society's Committee on the Activity Movement. Lois Coffey Mossman, Chairman.
Thirty-fourth Yearbook, 1935—*Educational Diagnosis.* Prepared by the Society's Committee on Educational Diagnosis. L. J. Brueckner, Chairman. Paper.
*Thirty-fifth Yearbook, 1936, Part I—*The Grouping of Pupils.* Prepared by the Society's Committee. W. W. Coxe, Chairman.
*Thirty-fifth Yearbook, 1936, Part II—*Music Education.* Prepared by the Society's Committee. W. L. Uhl, Chairman.
*Thirty-sixth Yearbook, 1937, Part I—*The Teaching of Reading.* Prepared by the Society's Committee. W. S. Gray, Chairman.
*Thirty-sixth Yearbook, 1937, Part II—*International Understanding through the Public-School Curriculum.* Prepared by the Society's Committee. I. L. Kandel, Chairman.
*Thirty-seventh Yearbook, 1938, Part I—*Guidance in Educational Institutions.* Prepared by the Society's Committee. G. N. Kefauver, Chairman.
*Thirty-seventh Yearbook, 1938, Part II—*The Scientific Movement in Education.* Prepared by the Society's Committee. F. N. Freeman, Chairman.
*Thirty-eighth Yearbook, 1939, Part I—*Child Development and the Curriculum.* Prepared by the Society's Committee. Carleton Washburne, Chairman.
*Thirty-eighth Yearbook, 1939, Part II—*General Education in the American College.* Prepared by the Society's Committee. Alvin Eurich, Chairman. Cloth.
*Thirty-ninth Yearbook, 1940, Part I—*Intelligence: Its Nature and Nurture. Comparative and Critical Exposition.* Prepared by the Society's Committee. G. D. Stoddard, Chairman.
*Thirty-ninth Yearbook, 1940, Part II—*Intelligence: Its Nature and Nurture. Original Studies and Experiments.* Prepared by the Society's Committee. G. D. Stoddard, Chairman.
*Fortieth Yearbook, 1941—*Art in American Life and Education.* Prepared by the Society's Committee. Thomas Munro, Chairman.
Forty-first Yearbook, 1942, Part I—*Philosophies of Education.* Prepared by the Society's Committee. John S. Brubacher, Chairman. Cloth, Paper.
Forty-first Yearbook, 1942, Part II—*The Psychology of Learning.* Prepared by the Society's Committee. T. R. McConnell, Chairman. Cloth.
*Forty-second Yearbook, 1943, Part I—*Vocational Education.* Prepared by the Society's Committee. F. J. Keller, Chairman.
*Forty-second Yearbook, 1943, Part II—*The Library in General Education.* Prepared by the Society's Committee. L. R. Wilson, Chairman.
Forty-third Yearbook, 1944, Part I—*Adolescence.* Prepared by the Society's Committee. Harold E. Jones, Chairman. Paper.
*Forty-third Yearbook, 1944, Part II—*Teaching Language in the Elementary School.* Prepared by the Society's Committee. M. R. Trabue, Chairman.
*Forty-fourth Yearbook, 1945, Part I—*American Education in the Postwar Period: Curriculum Reconstruction.* Prepared by the Society's Committee. Ralph W. Tyler, Chairman.
Forty-fourth Yearbook, 1945, Part II—*American Education in the Postwar Period: Structural Reorganization.* Prepared by the Society's Committee. Bess Goodykoontz, Chairman. Paper.
*Forty-fifth Yearbook, 1946, Part I—*The Measurement of Understanding.* Prepared by the Society's Committee. William A. Brownell, Chairman.
*Forty-fifth Yearbook, 1946, Part II—*Changing Conceptions in Educational Administration.* Prepared by the Society's Committee. Alonzo G. Grace, Chairman.
*Forty-sixth Yearbook, 1947, Part I—*Science Education in American Schools.* Prepared by the Society's Committee. Victor H. Noll, Chairman.
*Forty-sixth Yearbook, 1947, Part II—*Early Childhood Education.* Prepared by the Society's Committee. N. Searle Light, Chairman. Paper.
Forty-seventh Yearbook, 1948, Part I—*Juvenile Delinquency and the Schools.* Prepared by the Society's Committee. Ruth Strang, Chairman. Cloth.
Forty-seventh Yearbook, 1948, Part II—*Reading in the High School and College.* Prepared by the Society's Committee. William S. Gray, Chairman. Cloth, Paper.
Forty-eighth Yearbook, 1949, Part I—*Audio-visual Materials of Instruction.* Prepared by the Society's Committee. Stephen M. Corey, Chairman. Cloth.
*Forty-eighth Yearbook, 1949, Part II—*Reading in the Elementary School.* Prepared by the Society's Committee. Arthur I. Gates, Chairman.
*Forty-ninth Yearbook, 1950, Part I—*Learning and Instruction.* Prepared by the Society's Committee. G. Lester Anderson, Chairman.
Forty-ninth Yearbook, 1950, Part II—*The Education of Exceptional Children.* Prepared by the Society's Committee. Samuel A. Kirk, Chairman. Paper.
Fiftieth Yearbook, 1951, Part I—*Graduate Study in Education.* Prepared by the Society's Board of Directors. Ralph W. Tyler, Chairman. Paper.
Fiftieth Yearbook, 1951, Part II—*The Teaching of Arithmetic.* Prepared by the Society's Committee. G. T. Buswell, Chairman. Cloth, Paper.
Fifty-first Yearbook, 1952, Part I—*General Education.* Prepared by the Society's Committee. T. R. McConnell, Chairman. Cloth, Paper.

Fifty-first Yearbook, 1952, Part II—*Education in Rural Communities.* Prepared by the Society's Committee. Ruth Strang, Chairman. Cloth, Paper.
*Fifty-second Yearbook, 1953, Part I—*Adapting the Secondary-School Program to the Needs of Youth.* Prepared by the Society's Committee: William G. Brink, Chairman.
Fifty-second Yearbook, 1953, Part II—*The Community School.* Prepared by the Society's Committee. Maurice F. Seay, Chairman. Cloth.
*Fifty-third Yearbook, 1954, Part II—*Mass Media and Education.* Prepared by the Prepared by the Society's Committee. Edgar L. Morphet, Chairman. Cloth, Paper.
Fifty-third Yearbook, 1954, Part II—*Mass Media and Education.* Prepared by the Society's Committee. Edgar Dale, Chairman. Paper.
*Fifty-fourth Yearbook, 1955, Part I—*Modern Philosophies and Education.* Prepared by the Society's Committee. John S. Brubacher, Chairman.
Fifty-fourth Yearbook, 1955, Part II—*Mental Health in Modern Education.* Prepared by the Society's Committee. Paul A. Witty, Chairman. Paper.
*Fifty-fifth Yearbook, 1956, Part I—*The Public Junior College.* Prepared by the Society's Committee. B. Lamar Johnson, Chairman.
Fifty-fifth Yearbook, 1956, Part I—*Adult Reading.* Prepared by the Society's Committee. David H. Clift, Chairman. Paper.
Fifty-sixth Yearbook, 1957, Part I—*In-service Education of Teachers, Supervisors, and Administrators.* Prepared by the Society's Committee. Stephen M. Corey, Chairman. Cloth.
Fifty-sixth Yearbook, 1957, Part II—*Social Studies in the Elementary School.* Prepared by the Society's Committee. Ralph C. Preston, Chairman. Cloth, Paper.
Fifty-seventh Yearbook, 1958, Part I—*Basic Concepts in Music Education.* Prepared by the Society's Committee. Thurber H. Madison, Chairman. Cloth.
Fifty-seventh Yearbook, 1958, Part II—*Education for the Gifted.* Prepared by the Society's Committee. Robert J. Havighurst, Chairman. Paper.
*Fifty-seventh Yearbook, 1958, Part III—*The Integration of Educational Experiences.* Prepared by the Society's Committee. Paul L. Dressel, Chairman. Cloth.
Fifty-eighth Yearbook, 1959, Part I—*Community Education: Principles and Practices from World-wide Experience.* Prepared by the Society's Committee. C. O. Arndt, Chairman. Cloth, Paper.
*Fifty-eighth Yearbook, 1959, Part II—*Personal Services in Education.* Prepared by the Society's Committee. Melvene D. Hardee, Chairman. Paper.
*Fifty-ninth Yearbook, 1960, Part I—*Rethinking Science Education.* Prepared by the Society's Committee. J. Darrell Barnard, Chairman.
Fifty-ninth Yearbook, 1960, Part II—*The Dynamics of Instructional Groups.* Prepared by the Society's Committee. Gale E. Jensen, Chairman. Cloth, Paper.
Sixtieth Yearbook, 1961, Part I—*Development in and through Reading.* Prepared by the Society's Committee. Paul A. Witty, Chairman. Cloth, Paper.
Sixtieth Yearbook, 1961, Part II—*Social Forces Influencing American Education.* Prepared by the Society's Committee. Ralph W. Tyler, Chairman. Cloth.
Sixty-first Yearbook, 1962, Part I—*Individualizing Instruction.* Prepared by the Society's Committee. Fred T. Tyler, Chairman. Cloth.
Sixty-first Yearbook, 1962, Part II—*Education for the Professions.* Prepared by the Society's Committee. G. Lester Anderson, Chairman. Cloth.
Sixty-second Yearbook, 1963, Part I—*Child Psychology.* Prepared by the Society's Committee. Harold W. Stevenson, Editor. Cloth.
Sixty-second Yearbook, 1963, Part II—*The Impact and Improvement of School Testing Programs.* Prepared by the Society's Committee. Warren G. Findley, Editor. Cloth.
Sixty-third Yearbook, 1964, Part I—*Theories of Learning and Instruction.* Prepared by the Society's Committee. Ernest R. Hilgard, Editor. Paper, Cloth.
Sixty-third Yearbook, 1964, Part II—*Behavioral Science and Educational Administration.* Prepared by the Society' Committee. Daniel E. Griffiths, Editor. Paper.
Sixty-fourth Yearbook, 1965, Part I—*Vocational Education.* Prepared by the Society's Committee. Melvin L. Barlow, Editor. Cloth.
Sixty-fourth Yearbook, 1965, Part II—*Art Education.* Prepared by the Society's Committee. W. Reid Hastie, Editor. Cloth.
Sixty-fifth Yearbook, 1966, Part I—*Social Deviancy among Youth.* Prepared by the Society's Committee. William W. Wattenberg, Editor. Cloth.
Sixty-fifth Yearbook, 1966, Part II—*The Changing American School.* Prepared by the Society's Committee. John I. Goodlad, Editor. Cloth.
Sixty-sixth Yearbook, 1967, Part I—*The Educationally Retarded and Disadvantaged.* Prepared by the Society's Committee. Paul A. Witty, Editor. Cloth.
Sixty-sixth Yearbook, 1967, Part II—*Programed Instruction.* Prepared by the Society's Committee. Phil C. Lange, Editor. Cloth.
Sixty-seventh Yearbook, 1968, Part I—*Metropolitanism: Its Challenge to Education.* Prepared by the Society's Committee. Robert J. Havighurst, Editor. Cloth.
Sixty-seventh Yearbook, 1968, Part II—*Innovation and Change in Reading Instruction.* Prepared by the Society's Committee. Helen M. Robinson, Editor. Cloth.
Sixty-eighth Yearbook, 1969, Part I—*The United States and International Education.* Prepared by the Society's Committee. Harold G. Shane, Editor. Cloth.
Sixty-eighth Yearbook, 1969, Part II—*Educational Evaluation: New Roles, New Means.* Prepared by the Society's Committee. Ralph W. Tyler, Editor. Paper.
Sixty-ninth Yearbook, 1970, Part I—*Mathematics Education.* Prepared by the Society's Committee. Edward G. Begle, Editor. Cloth.
Sixty-ninth Yearbook, 1970, Part II—*Linguistics in School Programs.* Prepared by the Society's Committee. Albert H. Marckwardt, Editor. Cloth.
Seventieth Yearbook, 1971, Part I—*The Curriculum: Retrospect and Prospect.* Prepared by the Society's Committee. Robert M. McClure, Editor. Paper.

Seventieth Yearbook, 1971, Part II—*Leaders in American Education.* Prepared by the Society's Committee. Robert J. Havighurst, Editor. Cloth.

Seventy-first Yearbook, 1972, Part I—*Philosophical Redirection of Educational Research.* Prepared by the Society's Committee. Lawrence G. Thomas, Editor. Cloth.

Seventy-first Yearbook, 1972, Part II—*Early Childhood Education.* Prepared by the Society's Committee. Ira J. Gordon, Editor. Cloth, Paper.

Seventy-second Yearbook, 1973, Part I—*Behavior Modification in Education.* Prepared by the Society's Committee. Carl E. Thoresen, Editor. Cloth.

Seventy-second Yearbook, 1973, Part II—*The Elementary School in the United States.* Prepared by the Society's Committee. John I. Goodlad and Harold G. Shane, Editors. Cloth.

Seventy-third Yearbook, 1974, Part I—*Media and Symbols: The Forms of Expression, Communication, and Education.* Prepared by the Society's Committee. David R. Olson, Editor. Cloth.

Seventy-third Yearbook, 1974, Part II—*Uses of the Sociology of Education.* Prepared by the Society's Committee. C. Wayne Gordon, Editor. Cloth.

Seventy-fourth Yearbook, 1975, Part I—*Youth.* Prepared by the Society's Committee. Robert J. Havighurst and Philip H. Dreyer, Editors. Cloth.

Seventy-fourth Yearbook, 1975, Part II—*Teacher Education.* Prepared by the Society's Committee. Kevin Ryan, Editor. Cloth.

Seventy-fifth Yearbook, 1976, Part I—*Psychology of Teaching Methods.* Prepared by the Society's Committee. N. L. Gage, Editor. Cloth.

Seventy-fifth Yearbook, 1976, Part II—*Issues in Secondary Education.* Prepared by the Society's Committee. William Van Til, Editor. Cloth.

Seventy-sixth Yearbook, 1977, Part I—*The Teaching of English.* Prepared by the Society's Committee. James R. Squire, Editor. Cloth.

Seventy-sixth Yearbook, 1977, Part II—*The Politics of Education.* Prepared by the Society's Committee. Jay D. Scribner, Editor. Cloth.

Seventy-seventh Yearbook, 1978, Part I—*The Courts and Education,* Clifford P. Hooker, Editor. Cloth.

Seventy-seventh Yearbook, 1978, Part II—*Education and the Brain,* Jeanne Chall and Allan F. Mirsky, Editors. Cloth.

Seventy-eighth Yearbook, 1979, Part I—*The Gifted and the Talented: Their Education and Development,* A. Harry Passow, Editor. Cloth.

Seventy-eighth Yearbook, 1979, Part II—*Classroom Management,* Daniel L. Duke, Editor. Cloth.

Yearbooks of the National Society are distributed by

UNIVERSITY OF CHICAGO PRESS, 5801 ELLIS AVE., CHICAGO, ILLINOIS 60637

Please direct inquiries regarding prices of volumes still available to the University of Chicago Press. Orders for these volumes should be sent to the University of Chicago Press, not to the offices of the National Society.

2. The Series on Contemporary Educational Issues

In addition to its Yearbooks the Society now publishes volumes in a series on Contemporary Educational Issues. These volumes are prepared under the supervision of the Society's Commission on an Expanded Publication Program.

The 1980 Titles

Minimum Competency Achievement Testing: Motives, Models, Measures, and Consequences (Richard M. Jaeger and Carol K. Tittle, eds.)

Collective Bargaining in Public Education (Anthony M. Cresswell, Michael J. Murphy, with Charles T. Kerchner)

The 1979 Titles

Educational Environments and Effects: Evaluation, Policy, and Productivity (Herbert J. Walberg, ed.)

Research on Teaching: Concepts, Findings, and Implications (Penelope L. Peterson and Herbert J. Walberg, eds.)

The Principal in Metropolitan Schools (Donald A. Erickson and Theodore L. Reller, eds.)

The 1978 Titles

   Aspects of Reading Education (Susanna Pflaum-Connor, ed.)

   History, Education, and Public Policy: Recovering the American Educational Past (Donald R. Warren, ed.)

   From Youth to Constructive Adult Life: The Role of the Public School (Ralph W. Tyler, ed.)

The 1977 Titles

   Early Childhood Education: Issues and Insights (Bernard Spodek and Herbert J. Walberg, eds.)

   The Future of Big City Schools: Desegregation Policies and Magnet Alternatives (Daniel U. Levine and Robert J. Havighurst, eds.)

   Educational Administration: The Developing Decades (Luvern L. Cunningham, Walter G. Hack, and Raphael O. Nystrand, eds.)

The 1976 Titles

   Prospects for Research and Development in Education (Ralph W. Tyler, ed.)

   Public Testimony on Public Schools (Commission on Educational Governance)

   Counseling Children and Adolescents (William M. Walsh, ed.)

The 1975 Titles

   Schooling and the Rights of Children (Vernon Haubrich and Michael Apple, eds.)

   Systems of Individualized Education (Harriet Talmage, ed.)

   Educational Policy and International Assessment: Implications of the IEA Assessment of Achievement (Alan Purves and Daniel U. Levine, eds.)

The 1974 Titles

   Crucial Issues in Testing (Ralph W. Tyler and Richard M. Wolf, eds.)

   Conflicting Conceptions of Curriculum (Elliott Eisner and Elizabeth Vallance, eds.)

   Cultural Pluralism (Edgar G. Epps, ed.)

   Rethinking Educational Equality (Andrew T. Kopan and Herbert J. Walberg, eds.)

All of the above volumes may be ordered from

McCutchan Publishing Corporation
2526 Grove Street
Berkeley, California 94704

The 1972 Titles

Black Students in White Schools (Edgar G. Epps, ed.)

Flexibility in School Programs (W. J. Congreve and G. L. Rinehart, eds.)

Performance Contracting—1969–1971 (J. A. Mecklenburger)

The Potential of Educational Futures (Michael Marien and W. L. Ziegler, eds.)

Sex Differences and Discrimination in Education (Scarvia Anderson, ed.)

The 1971 Titles

Accountability in Education (Leon M. Lessinger and Ralph W. Tyler, eds.)

Farewell to Schools??? (D. U. Levine and R. J. Havighurst, eds.)

Models for Integrated Education (D. U. Levine, ed.)

PYGMALION *Reconsidered* (J. D. Elashoff and R. E. Snow)

Reactions to Silberman's CRISIS IN THE CLASSROOM (A. Harry Passow, ed.)

The 1971 and 1972 titles in this series are now out of print and are no longer available.